*The Green Thumb Book of
Indoor Gardening*

Also by George Abraham

THE GREEN THUMB GARDEN HANDBOOK

THE GREEN THUMB

PRENTICE-HALL, INC., ENGLEWOOD CLIFFS, NEW JERSEY

Book of Indoor Gardening

A COMPLETE GUIDE

by

George Abraham

10 9 8 7

To Katy, Leanna and Darry
who worked with me for nearly
a quarter of a century in our
greenhouse and florist business

hy this book was written:

It is said that Mohammed once declared, "If I had but two loaves of bread, I would sell one and buy hyacinths to feed my soul." Likewise, Nebuchadnezzar is known to have built the hanging gardens of Babylon to satisfy the insistent craving for beauty that haunted his wife.

For modern man, living near his industries in crowded cities, houseplants can satisfy that same craving.

Statistics show that three out of every four of America's 20 million men and women over 65 years of age grow houseplants, and it is reasonable to assume that indoor gardening has perhaps the same proportion of adherents among younger age groups. The purpose of this book is to offer our know-how and to kindle and guide a homeowner's imagination so that he can enjoy indoor flowers and plants to the best advantage in his home.

Raising and arranging flowers to beautify a home need involve no greater effort and expense than any particular homemaker is willing and able to devote to it. The cost in terms of effort and money can be very small compared to expenditures for other decorative items, such as draperies, slip covers, rugs, wall paper or inanimate centerpieces.

In contrast to all of these, houseplants and flowers are living things and through their life they make a unique contribution. Imagination is more important than dollars, know-how more valuable than musclepower, in the selection, nurturing and arranging of plants and flowers in the home.

Most of the ingredients that turn a house into a home cannot be readily measured or taught. But at least one of them does lend itself to easy explanation. That is the raising and arranging of plants and flowers indoors to inspire those who live and visit there.

Imaginatively arranged, well-tended houseplants and flowers add a decorative touch and create a friendly, even festive, atmosphere on any day. Thus, they enhance any residence, be it a modest room, a flat or apartment, a house or a mansion.

In the preparation of this book, we were largely influenced by the nearly 100,000 questions we receive yearly from readers of our "The Green Thumb" column appearing in nearly 100 daily and weekly newspapers, and from listeners to our weekly radio program over Station WHAM, Rochester, New York.

Thus, in any list of credits, first mention of our appreciation must go to these readers and listeners. Their tips, suggestions and questions about gardening form as much the basis for this book as they did our first book, *The Green Thumb Garden Handbook* published in 1961.

These ideas and questions, which we answer either in our columns, radio program, or directly by mail in the senders' stamped return envelopes, have kept us abreast, more than anything else, of the needs, wants and interests of indoor and outdoor gardening hobbyists.

In the foreword to our first book, prominent mention for assistance was given to my wife Katy, who, as did I, studied horticulture at Cornell University. Since our marriage shortly after graduation, she has been my loyal partner in all the Green Thumb ventures, including close collaboration with this book—which is the reason for the use of the pronouns "we" and "ours" throughout this foreword.

Our daughter Leanna and son Darryl, who were 14 and 12 years old respectively at the time of publication of our first book, provided much help and encouragement. Our home is adjacent to our greenhouse and small-town florist business and the experimental farm on which we frequently test products and techniques before recommending them to readers, and so our children grew up very much a part of all our Green Thumb ventures.

I am grateful to the publishing firm of Prentice-Hall, Inc., which also published our first book, and especially to Dan Moses, trade book editor, for his numerous helpful suggestions, criticisms and friendly cooperation.

Special thanks go to a long-time personal friend, Walter Froehlich, Science Editor, of the U. S. Information Agency in Washington. Nearly a quarter of a century ago he offered valuable guidance for our then newly started "Green Thumb" column which made its initial appearance in a small upstate New York weekly of which he was then editor. His comments, born of seasoned editorial judgment, brought improvements to parts of our first book and even to a portion of this one.

We are particularly grateful for valuable information and help received from several state colleges including Cornell University, University of Illinois, University of California; Conard Pyle, Rose Co.;

Merry Gardens; Missouri Botanical Gardens.

The list of all others who richly deserve personal thanks is too long for inclusion here, but mention for direct assistance goes to: Hazel Potter, who has done such a magnificent job processing our mail and helping us select items for the book; Russell Mott, in charge of the Cornell University Conservatories, for checking our manuscript and allowing us to use the study of his collection of greenhouse plants; American Mushroom Institute; Mrs. Carole Jerome, for helping check the manuscript and coordinating the material; U.S.D.A. and Missouri Botanical Garden Bulletin for recipes, *Horticulture* Magazine for letting me use our chart on bulbs which appeared in it; Robert Wood in charge of the George B. Hart Conservatories; Louise Warren; Peg Pridmore and Elaine Canning for their magnificent help with the art work; Gulf Oil Company; Carol Fleischman for typing the manuscript; and to our many gardening friends, and radio and newspaper followers who have sent us their ideas and recipes over the years.

George "Doc" Abraham
The Green Thumb
Naples Valley Greenhouse

CONTENTS

CHAPTER I

Houseplant

Culture

FLOWERING HOUSEPLANTS

Houseplants are divided into two groups: the flowering types and the foliage types. There's a strong trend toward foliage plants for planters. The selection is so large it's possible to use the foliage to brighten drab corners and add distinction to the modern interior. Flowers on foliage plants are usually inconspicuous, and the main interest is the foliage itself.

To get more fun and enjoyment from your houseplants you should be able to answer this commonly asked question: "Why do my houseplants fail?" There are three main reasons for poor plant growth indoors: (1) wrong selection, (2) neglect and (3) injurious gases. Once you understand the cultural tips on houseplants, you should get more mileage from them. I'm going to mention the care of flowering houseplants first because they are the most popular plants grown indoors.

LIGHT

To some plantsmen, no other factor is more important in governing the growth of plants than light. Indoors, most plants do best in a southwest window. Sunlight is needed to produce flowering buds on nearly all flowering plants, some needing less light than others. Most foliage plants, such as philodendron, are of tropical origin and thus need less light. Some plants need a shorter day to produce blooms;

they are called short-day plants. Others need a longer day before they'll bloom. By influencing the length of day, greenhouse owners can produce chrysanthemums the year around, even though the plants are traditionally and strictly a fall-blooming flower. Mums will set flower buds, and bloom only when the day length is short; hence their profusion in fall months. And that's why your mums do not bloom in June when the day is longer. The recent discovery known as "photoperiodism," or ability of plants to be affected by length of day, is one of the most important recent developments of the plant world. As we learn more about it, we'll be able to tell you why some plants don't bloom or produce seeds or bulbs in some areas, but do in others.

TEMPERATURE

Plants are like people. Some like it hot, some like it cold. Probably the best temperature for most plants in winter is 70° during the day and 55° at night, with a few exceptions such as African violets. A high night temperature causes food in plants to be used up, followed by yellowing of foliage. You can have a day fluctuation between 45° and 80° with no serious results, if your plants have a low night temperature. One reason why our grandmothers grew better houseplants than we do now is because the room temperatures then were lower, especially at night. In those days, bedrooms were seldom heated. If your houseplants have soft spindly growth, pale foliage, and the buds blast or drop prematurely, you can often look to the temperature as being hot. At night put your plants in a cool room, 60° or lower, and see how much difference it makes in prolonging their life.

HUMIDITY

Although most of our modern homes are too hot and dry, it's still possible to raise good flowering plants by resorting to some green thumb tricks. While the proper humidity in the home is from 35 to 40 percent, the air indoors often goes as low as 12. This is 8 to 11 percent lower than the average relative humidity in the Sahara Desert in the summertime, and while it may be fine for camels, it's much too dry for human or plant comfort. Plants grow best when the humidity is from 80 to 90 percent, although we cannot obtain this in our homes. In a greenhouse the relative humidity is 60 percent or more. This explains why plants start to turn brown around the edges, flowers drop and buds shed soon after being moved from the moist atmosphere of the greenhouse or even from the garden in the fall.

You can increase the moisture in the house by putting a pan of water on the radiator or register. Also place a galvanized or zinc tray in the window for your plants and fill with pebbles. Syringing foliage increases humidity if done once or twice a week. And don't forget the old kitchen teakettle. It used to sing songs and make plants happy because they enjoyed the extra humidity. Plants themselves help release moisture into the room and, thus, are healthy for humans. For example, the leaves of an average-sized cineraria give off as much as three times more water as would be evaporated from the surface of a 4-inch pan of water. Really it isn't as bad as it sounds. Your house gets a lot more moisture than meets the eye—and nose. For example, some whimsical researcher found that whenever you mop and rinse an 8 × 10 kitchen floor you release about 2½ pounds of water (or 2½ pints) vapor into the air. Whenever your wife cooks dinner for you and two children, she adds another 2½ pints of water, and when you help her wash dishes afterward, the chore adds at least another half pint. A family of four puts another 12 pints of water a day into the air simply by breathing and sweating. And how about your houseplants? They are constantly giving off moisture.

Yet, in spite of all this, some plants do suffer from browned leaves due to dry air. Take the palm, for example. Its worst enemy is dry air; but if you keep the soil uniformly moistened, it will live and grow and be nice and green, in spite of the dry air.

VENTILATION

All plants need fresh air. Coal gas or cooking gas is harmful; one part gas in 1,000,000 parts of air is harmful to some flowers. Traces of gas cause flower buds to drop, droop or fail to open. Give plants plenty of air, but do not subject them to sudden drafts or chilling, as this causes foliage to wilt or buds to shed.

WATERING

Watering is an art. A greenhouse operator will tell you that the man with the hose determines the profits and losses.

During my 25 years as a greenhouse operator and florist, I became convinced that more houseplants are killed by improper watering than any other cause.

Young seedlings moved into pots should be watered immediately; give them a good soaking. Young plants just potted should be watered once, then again soon after. The first application may not wet the soil completely, but if followed immediately with another watering the entire soil will be wet. Plants just repotted should be watered well. Water them once, then give another application. Double watering after repotting insures thorough wetting of the soil.

Well-established houseplants received for holidays should be given good soakings whenever necessary to prevent wilting. Don't tease them with a cup of water. Plants in small pots dry out fast because of a limited soil volume and need watering several times a day. When soil dries in a pot, the earth shrinks away from the sides of the pot. When water is applied, much of it runs down the inside, and is lost before it can be absorbed. So actually, the plant doesn't get all the water, even though "I gave it lots of water!"

Plants which have drooped and withered from lack of water should be put in a pan of warm water and allowed to soak for one hour. You'll be surprised to see how badly wilted plants can snap back.

One reason homeowners have so much trouble watering plants is due to the pots themselves. Plastic and glazed pots are trickier to use than the good old-fashioned florist's clay pot. Plastic or glazed pots are not porous and do not "breathe" or allow air to enter. For that reason the soil does not dry as fast, and when plants are watered with the same frequency as those in clay pots, the result is overwatering. This shuts off oxygen to the roots; water accumulates and causes stunting, yellowing of foliage and shedding of buds. You can help such plants along by knocking them out of the pots and setting them back in. This step provides a column of air around the edge of the ball of soil and helps formation of new roots.

Some plants can take dry or wet soil; others can take one and not the other. For example, kalanchoes will take a dry soil, while hydrangeas or gloxinias will wilt quickly if the soil becomes dry. Severe wilting is bad for foliage and blooms, as it sometimes brings on dried or scorching edges.

WATERING PLANTS WHILE YOU VACATION

Your plants need not go dry while you take a vacation from home. One helpful trick is to set a few building bricks in the bathtub with about 1½ inches of water. Pots placed on the bricks are automatically watered for at least two weeks. Another trick is to place several thicknesses of newspapers in a pan, saturate them well and place the pots on these. Other gardeners sink their pots in vermiculite, wet sand or sawdust. Saturate these materials and water the plants first before packing the pots to their rims. Plants will keep three or four weeks in this manner. Another trick worth trying: Place a plastic bag over the plants and tie securely around the pot. This forms a vapor-tight greenhouse which makes a fine "plant-sitter" for you for three or four weeks. Some plants do not tolerate the excess humidity inside the plastic sheet, but it's worth a try.

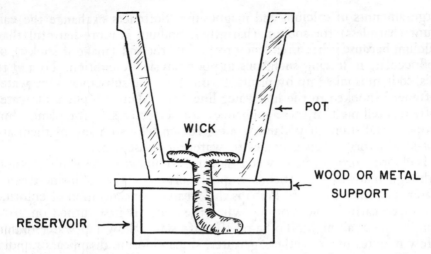

WICK

POT

WOOD OR METAL
SUPPORT

RESERVOIR →

You can easily convert a clay pot into a self-watering flower pot. Place a piece of glass wick in bottom and let it extend through hole, into a pan (reservoir) of water.

Another trick is to wrap the clay pot with a sheet of plastic to conserve moisture while you're away.

Hard Water vs. Soft Water

Some gardeners depend on rain or melted snow for watering their plants. African violets, azaleas and other "acid loving" plants do not like hard water and nearly all water coming from wells in limestone areas will have some degree of hardness. Hardness is caused when water containing dissolved carbon dioxide comes in contact with limestone. How to tell if water is hard: If your soap curdles or doesn't mix well, chances are it's hard. Another simple test is to look for scale inside the teakettle. If you don't own a teakettle, test water with litmus paper. If the litmus paper turns blue, the water is alkali or hard, and if it turns red, the water is acid and not likely to be hard. Litmus, available in drugstores, is a purplish coloring matter made from lichens. These lichens are ground to a pulp with water and mixed with lime.

Is a Water Softener Harmful to Plants?

In most cases water passing through mechanical softeners does have a harmful effect on plant growth. Hard water is hard because it contains large amounts of calcium and magnesium. Softeners exchange the calcium (harmless) for sodium (harmful). Sodium is more harmful than calcium because it has a tendency to puddle the soil (make it sticky) or deflocculate it, leaving such soils in poor physical condition. To add to this, sodium is taken up by plants, forming a toxic substance. Our water softener is hooked to the hot-water line only. Many suppliers of water softeners tell me that these appliances are perfectly safe for plants. Improper installation, they claim, is a big reason why so many of them are not satisfactory when it comes to watering houseplants.

Is chlorine or fluorine in water harmful to houseplants? Probably not, although many of my friends emphatically state that chlorine-treated water is harmful to plants. Perhaps the greatest concentration of chlorine is noticed early in the morning when the water is first turned on after lying in pipes all night. To be on the safe side, allow tap water to run a few minutes before gathering water, since chlorine disappears rapidly upon aeration. Allow tap water to remain in a pail before applying to plants.

INSTANT SOIL FOR PLANTS

For years, sand and peat moss have been the standard rooting mediums for starting new plants. These materials are still very good. However, recently new materials, used for insulating homes, have been found satisfactory. One of these is vermiculite, which has caused considerable interest among gardeners. Vermiculite is mica ore that has been exposed to high heat until it pops. This results in layers of mica being separated to make the material spongy, water retentive and free from disease, making it ideal for rooting cuttings. Root hairs penetrate the particles and enable cuttings to root fast. We mix it with peat, and some use it with sand. Vermiculite is sold under many trade names and can be purchased in any hardware store. Perlite, a volcanic-ash material, is also ideal for rooting. It can be used alone or with sand and peat.

Vermiculite: A micaceous material that has been heated to 1400° F. and weighs approximately 6–8 pounds per cubic foot. The horticulture grade of vermiculite (Terralite, etc.) should be used. Vermiculite has a relatively high "cation exchange capacity," which means it can hold nutrients in reserve and release them. The nutrients and water are held within the plate-like structure of the particles. This exchange capacity also enables the grower to use higher fertility levels with no plant damage than he could with soil. Vermiculite also has good "buffering" characteristics that resist rapid changes in pH, a term used to measure soil reaction—is it "sweet" or "sour?" Most houseplants like a sweet or partly alkaline soil. A few acid-loving plants are azaleas, gardenias, and hydrangeas. For information on culture on any specific plant, refer to index. Vermiculite contains small amounts of potassium, calcium and magnesium that are available for the growth of plants.

Perlite: A form of volcanic rock that has been expanded by heating to 1800° F. It weighs 6–9 pounds per cubic foot. This material contains no mineral nutrients and, unlike vermiculite, has no cation exchange capacity or buffering capacity. It does not decay or deteriorate, but the particles can be broken into smaller pieces. Perlite holds water on its irregular surfaces. The particle size perlite that has been used is approximately $\frac{1}{16}$ to $\frac{1}{8}$ inch in diameter. Some growers have preferred the finer material since it has less tendency to wash out than the coarser material.

Peat and Sand: Many gardeners are substituting peat moss for garden loam and use it in equal parts with Canadian peat moss and sand. One operator, I know, still uses the time-honored formula of equal parts loam, peat moss and sand, but adds into each bushel a pound of steamed bone meal, a favorite of many old-timers.

Because pastuerizing the soil for houseplants is messy, many gardeners are using the so-called "peat-lite" mix recommended by Cornell University. Here is their recipe for mixing one peck:

Vermiculite (Terralite)	4 quarts
Shredded peat moss	4 quarts
20% superphosphate (powdered)	1 teaspoon
Ground dolomitic limestone	1 tablespoon

Plus either of the following (not both):

33% ammonium nitrate	1 tablespoon
5-10-5 commercial fertilizer	4 tablespoons

Moisten this mixture well before using for houseplants or starting seeds. Five to six weeks after potting plants in it, start biweekly feedings, with a house plant fertilizer such as Ra-pid-gro (23-19-17).

POTS FOR PLANTS

Home gardeners ask me if it makes any difference what kind of pots they use for growing plants. It makes no difference if you understand the nature of the pot. You can grow plants in any type of container but the frequency of watering must be adjusted to the type of pot. Red clay (florist's pot) has long been the standard in pot-plant culture and is still hard to beat. They have drainage holes in the base and also are porous so that water can evaporate through the walls of the pot. By contrast, other pots are made of ceramics, metals or plastics and have no provision for drainage. Little or no water is lost through the walls. That means you must be more careful in watering. They do not dry out as fast as clay pots. You may overwater, and leaves will turn yellow and roots start to rot. Yellowing of foliage is often due to excess watering, which shuts off oxygen to the roots. On the other hand, if you forget to water, the soil in a non-porous container will stay moist longer than soil in a clay or porous pot.

If you water plants according to the "feel" of the soil rather than on a set schedule, you'll have luck growing plants in any kind of a container. Plants grown in glazed or non-porous containers need to be fed less frequently than those in porous containers, since less frequent watering means less loss of nutrients.

Greenhouse men will tell you that the frequent waterings needed by plants in clay pots probably result in the loss of one half or more of the plant foods applied. Those white salts you see on top of soil and sides of pots are fertilizer residues. They can be stirred into the soil and washed back in.

Sterilizing Pots: Home gardeners who want to sterilize flower pots and seed boxes (called "flats" by florists) can mix up some household bleach, one part of bleach to 10 parts of water. Let soak for 20 minutes and this will kill off most surface organisms. If you want to bake soils, try it at 180° for ½ hour; this will kill all harmful organisms. If soil is used for sowing seed or for potting up houseplants, we recommend you bake it first and treat old pots.

Jiffy-Pots (made of peat) are the original root penetration transplanting pots and are widely known for their rapid root penetration qualities.

George J. Ball, Inc.

Peat Pots: Many home gardeners are resorting to peat pots, the kind florists use for raising foliages and other houseplants. Peat pots can be an answer to transplanting troubles. Some gardeners start difficult-to-root cuttings, which grow well until potting time; then the rooted cuttings wither and rot away. The new concept of peat pots prevents root disturbance. The pots are made of compressed peat or manure. The moist walls of the pots permit roots to penetrate freely. Seeds and cuttings can be started right in the pots; then the pots are planted, lock, stock and barrel, into your larger decorative containers or into the garden. This prevents transplanting shock for the roots are never disturbed.

If you want to sow seed from your favorite houseplant, perennials or annuals, start them directly in the pot. Use a good soil mixture, something that's loose and provides good drainage, such as ⅓ loam, ⅓ sand and ⅓ peat. Or you can use the so-called "peat-lite" mixture, recommended by Cornell. Even some cuttings can be rooted in these "quick pots," but you must be sure to water frequently, maintain high humidity and keep out direct sun.

I've noticed some special points of culture to watch for in my experience with peat pots. One of them is watering. A Jiffy-Pot is a reservoir of water. All those peat fibers will soak up lots of water and help keep soil moisture on an even keel by gradually supplying more as it is needed. When first planted, though, the pot-reservoir is empty, and it must be filled. This is done by thorough watering the first day and again the second day.

After it's thoroughly soaked, that moisture-filled pot will keep the soil watered for some time, so don't be anxious to re-water. When the soil is quite dry is time enough, and, then again a good soaking is best.

The fertilizer in the pot walls will help produce an ideal growth for the first few weeks; you won't want to fertilize plants for some time. After this first "feeding" has been used up, you can go back to your normal fertilizing schedule.

HOMEMADE LABELS FOR HOUSEPLANTS AND SEEDLINGS

Labeling perennials, shrubs and bulbs, or even houseplants can be perplexing, especially when you cannot readily purchase labels. One gardener passes along a good tip for making your own labels out of aluminum from leftover TV dinner trays. Cut strips about 1 inch by 4 inches. Take a sharp nail and write the plant name on the aluminum and affix it to the plant or to a piece of redwood stick. Don't use copper tacks as these will corrode aluminum. The aluminum strip can also be tied onto a plant, using aluminum wire. The label will last for years, costs very little and is not easily seen by those who like to pull up white plastic labels.

Some gardeners cut plastic bleach bottles into strips. These can be written on easily with a soft pencil or marking pencil. Writing lasts for months. Perhaps your local florist will sell you some wooden labels, if you think they'd work out better for you

SOIL MIXTURES

Good soils mean good drainage, an important factor for husky growth. Plants in a heavy soil will turn yellow due to poor drainage and a lack of air. Some authorities recommend dozens of complicated soil mixes. Frankly, there is no need for these because plants just aren't that fussy. Greenhouse operators use just one mix for a wide variety of plants. A good soil mixture for all houseplants is made up of 1 part peat moss (or compost), one part sand and one part garden loam. The only plants to benefit from a larger amount of peat are gardenias, azaleas and other acid-loving items.

Organic matter in some form is important, as it provides drainage, helps hold nutrients. You cannot go out to your garden and scoop up soil for houseplants. Good soils are made, not born. The earth from rotted stumps is a fine source of humus. You may note that some florists also add vermiculite or perlite to a soil mixture along with peat. Peat holds the moisture, whereas vermiculite and perlite add porosity, resist decay and aid in root growth. Charcoal, while it contributes very little plant food nutrients, is a valuable soil conditioner and purifier. Florists use small pieces of charcoal in the soil for drainage and for its ability to absorb impurities from the soil solution.

"Musty" or moldy soils mean poor drainage and, usually, additions of charcoal or sand will prevent this. If you're interested in sterilizing soil for houseplants, see section under Plant Propagation, "Starting Plants from Seeds."

Are you starving your houseplants? You may be giving them more than enough fertilizer, but you could still be starving them.

Houseplants, like all plants, must have light to manufacture food from fertilizer. Therefore light is the limiting factor to most indoor plants, not fertilizer.

During winter months houseplants are actually light-starved; there just isn't enough daylight for them to be at their best. However, it *is* possible to help the plant make the most of the light it does get.

The surest way to do this is to keep leaves clean. Wash them with soap and water if necessary, but make certain they're as clean as possible. Not only will this make the plant look better, but the leaves will be able to absorb more light, to manufacture more food, and, so, to become stronger and healthier.

FEEDING HOUSEPLANTS

Nearly all plants respond to regular applications of plant food, applied preferably in liquid form and in light doses. Such items as coffee grounds, tea leaves, eggshell water, castor oil, etc. offer very little encouragement to starved plants. Liquid plant foods are increasingly popular for all types of houseplants because they are safe and easy to use. All of my house and greenhouse plants are fed with liquid food (23%N-19%P-17%K), at the rate of 1 level teaspoon to 2 quarts of water, applied every three or four weeks.

If you use a dry chemical fertilizer, such as 5-10-5, do not apply it dry. Dissolve a teaspoon in a quart of water and feed it in liquid form. While many plants are dormant in winter, it's still a good idea to feed them lightly to maintain color.

Liquid Feeding for Houseplants: Indoor gardeners who add dry fertilizers to houseplants are often asking for trouble. Use a specially prepared liquid plant food for your houseplants and you'll avoid the danger of burning them. Pour the solution into the soil, or, if the plants are hard leaved, you can even foliage-feed them. Do not use liquid plant foods more than once every two weeks on small plants in small containers. In many cases poor or weak plants can be revived by dipping them (roots and all) in a liquid plant food solution such as Ra-pid-gro (23-19-17).

For starting seedlings, as a rooting medium, or for hanging baskets, try soaking the sphagnum moss with a liquid plant food; squeeze out lightly and you will have a reservoir full of nutrients. If you own a small greenhouse, liquid feeding may be applied with any sprinkling can, sprayer or hose feeder.

In my greenhouse I use a liquid plant food with a 23%N-19%P-17%K formula mixed with pesticides on all crops; it never burns even the tenderest plants. I prepare a stock solution of 1 cup of the concentrated plant food to 2 gallons of water. A Hozon applicator is inserted into this and attached to the water faucet. As I water the crops, it automatically feeds them. To foliage-feed, always buy a plant food made especially for spraying on the leaves.

Starter Solutions: Liquid plant foods make ideal "starter" or "booster" solutions, helping young transplants get off to a better start. You simply place a teaspoon of concentrated fertilizer in 2 quarts of water and dip the roots and plant. A word of caution: If you make a homemade booster solution, try it first on a few plants because it may burn. You can make one from a common grade of fertilizer, such as 5-10-5 (any garden store has it), by dissolving 1 pound in 5 gallons of water. This liquid can also be applied to the garden row at the rate of 1 gallon to

20 feet of row, before planting or later.

Liquid plant foods have many extra uses. (1) Soak bulbs in them one hour prior to planting. (2) Hasten decay of compost. (3) Color up evergreens. (4) Feed fruits and flowers. (5) In greenhouse, feed both benched and potted crops; apply with sprinkler or Hozon applicator. (6) Feed starting seeds in non-organic materials such as perlite, vermiculite or similar items. (7) Apply to soil-less culture (hobby) to replace lost solution. There is no known plant which does not respond to liquid plant food.

SHIFTING OR POTTING HOUSEPLANTS

Some houseplants become "potbound" (the roots fill the pot). A little "potboundness" is desirable in that it encourages blooming, too much is followed by stunted growth, falling leaves and a generally unsightly plant. No hard and fast rule can be made for repotting, since plants vary greatly in their habits. Probably the best time for repotting is in spring when new growth is starting. The pot size is determined by the growth habit. For example, slow-growing items, such as cacti, do not need large pots nor frequent potting. Rapid-growing plants, such as begonias, can be shifted from a 4-inch pot to a 6-inch size if potbound. After you take the ball of soil and roots from the pot, remove a portion of the old soil and the matted roots. This stimulates development of new roots. You should also replenish the old soil with a new mixture.

Potting soils should be moist but not wet; very wet soils often pack too hard. And keep in mind that finely sifted soils are fine for seedlings, but not acceptable for houseplants. Fine soils bake, crack and often become hard.

TRICKS FOR STARTING HOUSEPLANTS

One of the greatest joys to come from home gardening is plant propagation, the science of increasing plants from existing ones. Plant propagation falls into two main groups: (1) Those raised from seed. Such plants involve sexual union, and the process is referred to as sexual propagation. (2) Those raised "vegetatively" or without benefit of sexual union. This method is known as asexual propagation, or vegetative reproduction. It includes division, cuttings, grafting and budding, which are described later. Sexual propagation by seed gives rise to many new strains which are of value to horticulture. Without it we would not get most of our new varieties. Asexual increasing does not produce new strains, but is of importance to the home gardener because it maintains the identical characteristics of the parent plant. For example, a white rose started from cuttings (described below) will produce plants with white flowers. However, seed from a white rose may not produce white flowers.

Asexual or Vegetative Propagation of Plants

Division: The simplest form of increasing plants asexually is known as division. All you do is take an axe, a large knife or spade and cut the clump or rootstock into convenient sizes for planting. The other vegetative means for multiplying plants are cuttings, layering, budding and grafting.

Cuttings: Most of our common shrubs can be propagated from cuttings. Some root best from hardwood cuttings, others respond to the

Home Plant Propagator
(Left) A large flower pot filled with sand with a small pot plunged into the center is ideal for rooting all kind of plants. The drainage hole of the small pot is plugged with a cork and then the pot is kept filled with water. Uniform moisture is maintained in the sand by water seeping from the small pot's porous sides. (Right) A small bottle with tap water is useful for starting cuttings of plants such as coleus, geraniums, ivies and African violets.
Purdue University Cooperative Extension Service

softwood cutting, while some can be started by both methods. Softwood cuttings should be taken from shrubs during the summer months. Select only the tips (3 to 8 inches in length). Cut the stem at a node. About half the leaves should be removed from the lower end and the cutting then planted firmly in sand to a depth equal to about one-half its length. You can propagate roses, hydrangeas, dogwood and many other plants this way.

We want to mention the semi-hardwood cutting method. This is similar to softwood cuttings (such as you use in starting geraniums, mums, begonias, to name a few), except that the wood is somewhat hardened.

Most semi-hardwood cuttings are made between June 1st and the middle of July from shrubs growing outdoors. These include roses, blueberries, boxwood, oleander, weigela, dogwood, forsythia, privet, viburnum and deutzia.

Take 4- to 6-inch cuttings from the end or side shoots that are still growing or that have only recently stopped growing. These are stuck in clean moist sand and kept shaded for several days. After that, give them stronger light and keep the humidity high. Always protect them from strong sun and drying out. An inverted glass jar makes a fine miniature greenhouse.

Perennial flowers may also be started by cuttings. Take cuttings in early spring when young shoots are about 3 inches above ground. Cuttings should be planted in semi-shade and covered with an inverted fruit jar.

Start hardwood cuttings by gathering cuttings in the fall (anytime after frosts have matured the wood) or during winter dormancy. The cuttings can be from 6 to 10 inches long. With most plants it's best to cut about $\frac{1}{2}$ inch below the lowest bud and $\frac{1}{2}$ or more above the uppermost bud. Tie the cuttings in a bundle (anywhere from 10 to 25, if you wish), with the basal ends (butt end) all in the same direction. Bury them horizontally in moist sand or sawdust in the cellar.

In the spring, set the cuttings in rows about 18 inches apart, with the cuttings 2 to 4 inches from each other. The top bud should be about even with or slightly above ground level. Make sure the earth is packed firmly about the lower end so the cuttings will not dry out. Water the cuttings regularly to hasten rooting. Some cuttings which are hard to root in sand will often do better in a mixture of sand and granulated peat, equal parts by volume. Usually at the beginning of the second year, the cuttings should be transplanted and at the end of the second year they can be moved to a permanent position in a garden.

Rooting Powders: Gardeners who want to use plant hormone powders to stimulate rooting can do so, but you don't gain anything on cuttings easy to root. The best way to apply the plant hormones is in a powder form.

You can buy small packets or pound cans, but for the home garden a packet is plenty since a pound can will treat over 40,000 cuttings. Just dip the base end in the powder before inserting it in the rooting material. In the spring, hardwood cuttings have a callus on the lower end and that is the time to dip them in plant hormone powder.

Stem Cuttings: You don't need a greenhouse to root plants from stem cuttings. Simply fill a 5-inch clay pot with coarse sand and let stand in a tray of water. This makes a neat propagating "bench" for starting geraniums, ivy and other subjects. You will be surprised to see how quickly these take root in sand. The sand should be free from dirt and trash. There are very few cuttings that will not start in sand.

Leaf Cuttings: Any plant that has fleshy leaves or leaf stalks (petioles) can be propagated by leaf cuttings. This is commonly used with begonias, lifeplant (bryophyllum), African violets, gloxinia, peperomia and others. You need coarse sand, perlite or vermiculite (some have good luck with plain water but we prefer sand).

Cut the stem short. Insert the stem and a small portion of the leaf base into the sand. With begonia, all of the leaf may be used, or it may be cut into wedge-shaped pieces, each having a large vein through the center. Several new plants may be obtained from a single begonia leaf laid flat on the sand and pinned in with a hairpin. Puncture each main vein and cover lightly with moist sand. A new plant will form at each point of injury. Almost all houseplants can be slipped any time of the year.

Grafting and budding are other means of propagating plants. These methods are recommended for the indoor gardener who wants to experiment. Most state colleges have booklets illustrating the techniques of budding and grafting as practiced by nurserymen.

PLANTS FROM SEED

Seed is one of the cheapest methods for starting home plants. Start with good seed.

Light: Light is not necessary for germinating the seed, so you can put the seed box in a dark place, but once they have started to sprout, move them to full light. Attic windows are fine, if the temperature does not drop too low at night.

Temperature: A temperature of around 68° during germination period is good, and after the seedlings appear, about 60° is ideal. Too high a temperature causes "spindly" soft growth.

Soil Mixture: Seeds do not need a rich soil for germination. The lighter the soil, the better. If you have access to muck soil, use it for starting

seeds. It's light and seeds push up thru it easily. If not available, use
1 part garden loam, 1 part peat moss or leaf mold and 1 part coarse sand.
Be sure to sow seed very lightly for husky plants. If seeds are sown too
thickly you get spindly plants. Plan to sow about 7 to 10 small seeds or
4 to 7 large seeds per inch of row, and don't cover too heavily. Using a
flour sifter, shake a very light coat of peat moss or muck on the seed.

One reason why gardeners have bad luck growing plants and starting
seeds is the soil or starting mixture. Potting soil can be loaded with harmful organisms which pounce on the tiny seedlings and young plants.
Also, if the soil contains clay, drainage will be poor and growth will be
spotty.

STERILIZING SOILS FOR HOUSEPLANTS AND SEEDS

Growing plants indoors can be easier if you take the time to sterilize
your soil mixture either by heat or chemicals. Here are the accepted
methods for sterilizing your soils: (1) Bake in oven at 190° for ½ hour.
(2) Pressure cooker. Use a home-canning type. Put several cups of
water in the bottom of the cooker, scoop the moistened soil into shallow
pans (no more than 3 inches deep), level, but don't tamp. Stack the pans
on the rack inside the cooker, separating each pan with lath strips for
free circulation of steam. When pressure reaches 10 pounds, run at this
level for 15 minutes, then cut off heat. To me, pressure cooking is
the poorest way to sterilize it. (3) Hot water. Pour boiling hot
water on the flat of soil. Insert a bulb thermometer into the bottom and
continue adding until temperature reaches 180° to 200° F. Allow to cool
slowly. The disadvantage is that it takes a lot of water and soil is badly
puddled. (4) Steam. Not practicable for the home gardener. (5) Boiling. Boiling is not practical for soil, but is one good way to sterilize pots.
First wash them and then boil for 30 minutes in water. Don't put plastic
pots into hot water unless you're sure they won't soften. (6) Formaldehyde (poisonous) can be purchased in drug store as formalin, which is
37 to 40 percent formaldehyde in water. Add about 2½ to 3 tablespoons
of formaldehyde, diluted with four times that much water, to each
bushel of soil (32 quarts). For heavy or mucky soils, use heavier dosages.
Sprinkle the soil with the mixture, put your garden tools on top and
cover tightly with piece of plastic to hold all fumes for at least 24 hours.
Fumes are toxic and will sterilize tools as well as soil. Keep temperature
around 65°–75°. Remove the cover. Be sure that all fumes have left
before you use the soil mixture for seeding or planting. You can also
use one tablespoon of carbon tetrachloride to one peck of soil. The soil
is placed in a tight tin container, then the fluid is added and the top is
placed on it. This seems to do a good job killing any soil organisms.

If you want to treat soil in a cold frame, seed flat or unplanted flower bed outdoors, use the formaldehyde drench. Work soil loosely and sprinkle it lightly. Add 1 gallon of formaldehyde to 50 gallons of water or 1 cup to 3 gallons, and apply ½ to 1 gallon to each square foot of soil. Place a plastic sheet over the area and leave it on for two days. This works best when the soil is warm. Uncover and allow to air for a week or two before planting. Garden tools can also be sterilized with formaldehyde, 1 pint of formalin to 10 quarts of water. Immerse tools for about 5 minutes (pots, twice as long).

You can buy other volatile or gas-forming soil fumigants, such as chloropicrin, methyl bromide, carbon disulfide, ethylene dibromide and calcium cyanide. These fumigants are sold in various forms and under various trade names, such as DD, Dowfume, Iscobrome, Larvacide, MC_2, Vapam, etc. For the home gardener, they are a bit tricky and we suggest you follow directions on the label.

Instant Soils: If you don't want to bother with this type of soil sterilization, then try a method developed at Cornell University and used by commercial growers. Use the "peat-lite" mix.

One of the advantages of the so-called "peat-lite" soil-less mixtures is that disease organisms are at a minimum. Florists use the soil-less mixtures for growing pot plants and germinating seed. Home gardeners have not accepted them as much as they should and continue to use the old standby containing garden loam, organic matter and sand. These ingredients are excellent and will produce good growth. However, they are not sterile and contain disease organisms (bacteria and fungi), plus weed seeds and pests such as insects and nematodes.

Sowing Seed: Do not sow seeds, especially fine seeds, too thickly. They should be at least ⅛ inch apart. DO NOT COVER SEED TOO DEEPLY. Fine seed, such as petunias, snapdragons, etc., has little "pushing up" power and will rot before it can germinate if covered too deeply. Sow thinly, either broadcast or in rows, and omit covering if seed is fine. Just press it into the soil. Coarse seeds can be covered with vermiculite, sifted muck, pulverized peat moss, or "rubbed" sphagnum moss. After the seed has been sown and watered from below, cover the seed flats or boxes with a pane of glass or newspapers to save moisture. Check them every day to see if any mold has formed or if the soil is dry. If a mold has formed, there is not enough air circulation or there is too much moisture. In such cases, place the seed box in a light, airy place until mold disappears. Dust with Fermate.

Seedling Care: Just as soon as seedlings pop up, remove the glass or paper and place the seeds in full light. Seedling plants are 90 to 95 percent water. Seeds need air as well as water. Soak your seed flats in a pan of water (called subirrigation) until the soil is automatically watered by capillary action from beneath. DO NOT WATER FROM THE TOP.

Transplanting Seedlings: As soon as the seedlings are about 1½ inches high move them to other boxes or pots. Space them 2 inches apart each way. This is done after the first true leaves have appeared and root systems are well branched. Cut out blocks of seedlings and transplant each young plant separately without breaking off roots. A slightly richer soil mixture of compost, sand, loam is good. Nearly all seedlings can be grown in these flats or boxes for 3 or 4 weeks, after which they can be set outdoors.

If seedlings get a bit tall, pinch them back to make them stocky. Pinching simply means nipping out the growing tip with your thumb and forefinger. This make plants bushier and you get more blooms per plant. If you don't pinch your plants they'll be spindly and weak. Pinching is necessary.

Use of Cold Frames and Hotbeds: If you don't have good indoor facilities for starting seed you can do the job by sowing directly in the hotbed, or a little later in cold frames. These structures are handy because they can be used to "toughen" up or "harden" plants before planting outdoors.

Starting your own plants from seed is a great experience. As a final word, dust your seed with a good fungicide, such as Captan, Fermate, Semesan, etc., before sowing.

IT PAYS TO PINCH OR PRUNE PLANTS

One reason most houseplants are tall, spindly and lopsided is that they are never pinched back. Most greenhouse operators would go out of business if they never pinched their snapdragons, mums and other crops. Pinching merely consists of removing the tip of a plant after it has developed anywhere from four to six leaves. To pinch, you simply take your thumb and forefinger and pinch out the tip. This makes your plants nice and bushy, so they branch out instead of growing straight up. Clipping a hedge amounts to "pinching" the plants. In most instances, the pinched tips of your house plants may be rooted in just plain sand or tap water to make new plants.

SUMMER CARE OF HOUSEPLANTS

Summer's a fine time to give your plants a vacation outdoors, as it helps build up vigor for winter growth. Sink the potted plants directly into the ground up to the rim of the pot in shade or semi-shade and water them once or twice a week. If you have a shady back porch or terrace, try moving house ferns, gardenias, begonias, and your other plants there. Hosing these items will give them a new lease on life.

WINTER CARE OF HOUSEPLANTS

In winter, days grow shorter, our light supply is of lower intensity and will get still lower. Our homes are tightly closed, making a drier atmosphere in the home. All of these conditions are not ideal for the growth of houseplants. Therefore, everything possible should be done to compensate for this less than ideal environment. Repot houseplants in fall in a mixture of 50 percent good garden soil and 50 percent peat moss. Mix in a complete fertilizer at the time of soil preparation. A level 4-inch flower potful of 5-10-5 fertilizer per 4 to 5 bushels of soil is sufficient. If plants are heavily potbound, shift them to the next larger sized pot. Be certain to place sufficient drainage material, (a 1-inch layer of gravel or crushed stone) in the bottom of each pot. Feed plants periodically, using one of the readily soluble houseplant fertilizers available from your florist or garden supply store. Mix and apply at the rates and intervals recommended on the package.

To insure that your plants have a uniform, constant moisture supply, put them in clay pots and plunge the pot in a container of peat moss. Keep the peat moss moist at all times and the plants will remain constantly moist. Surface watering will not be necessary.

Poinsettia and Christmas cactus are two flowering houseplants which require special care if they are to bloom in the home. Both plants set flower buds under short-day conditions; that is, when they are exposed to long, continuous dark night periods such as occur naturally from mid-October on. If the dark period is interrupted by light for only a short time, the plants will not set buds. Therefore if you wish poinsettia and Christmas cactus to flower in the home, you must place the plants where they will have absolute darkness from 5:00 P.M. to 8:00 A.M. daily, starting around October 20 and continuing for a minimum of 40 days. This may be accomplished by moving the plants into a dark closet each night or by completely covering them with black cloth for the night. Remember, reading lamps, street lights and other outside light sources are sufficient to interrupt the dark period and prevent flowering. (See section on POINSETTIA)

BE YOUR OWN PLANT DOCTOR

Houseplants fall heir to physiological troubles, as well as to insect and disease pests. Armed with a few green thumb facts you can track down most houseplant ailments and correct them. I'm listing a few of the common physiological problems you're apt to come across with your flowering plants.

Blindness: This is failure of plants to produce flower buds. Environment is likely to be the cause. Look for poor light, improper nutrition, low or high temperature. Flower buds form on hydrangeas at temperatures below 60° and azaleas form their buds at a temperature above 65°, so you can see that many plants have "hidden" requirements which must be met before buds set.

Chlorosis: A sickly, yellowed condition of plants, often due to a lack of nitrogen or a lack of iron. Balanced feeding or iron chelates corrects this. (See chapter on "soils and fertilizers")

Leaf Scorching: Found among ferns, begonias, and hundreds of other items. This can be a sign of little water, excess fertilizer, sun-burning or not enough humidity.

Stunted Growth: Poor growth accompanied by dark undersized leaves is often a sign of lack of phosphorus. Balanced feeding corrects this. A lack of moisture will also cause the same type of growth. Soft growth during winter is generally due to a combination of high heat and insufficient light.

Effect of Gas Fumes on Plants: Artificial or manufactured gas and coal gas have a bad effect on many houseplants. Natural gas isn't as hard on plants. Quite often a concentration so small as to be undetected by the human nose will cause carnations to "go to sleep". Many plants will lose their foliage from leaking gas or gas fumes, especially in winter when rooms are poorly ventilated.

Bottled gas is not bad and many say it doesn't bother plants one bit. Bottled gas is also called L-P (liquified petroleum) gas. Other names given it are propane, butane, tank gas, rural gas, country gas, although L-P gas is now considered the correct name.

L-P gas is usually either butane or propane or a mixture of the two. When confined in a tank, it's liquid, but released for use as a fuel it is a gas.

How about the effects? If the L-P gas is allowed to leak in a room, without burning, yes, it can be harmful to plant growth and humans alike. However, if the gas is burned as a fuel in a range, heater, water heater, or other appliances, the products of combustion are not harmful to plant growth, but actually helpful.

Greenhouse growers are taking advantage of this fact and are burning propane for release of carbon dioxide into the atmosphere. Lettuce, cucumbers, tomatoes, spinach, chrysanthemums and snapdragons have increased in size when propane was burned in the greenhouse.

One grower found that the carbon dioxide from burned propane cut down growing time by a third and gave him a third more yield.

The reason behind this is simple: Plants take on carbon dioxide, and the more CO_2 you pump into the greenhouse atmosphere, during daylight hours, the faster they'll mature. So don't worry about your gas appliances releasing harmful products of combustion. The reverse is true for your houseplants.

Drainage: Next to light, drainage is the most important factor. Plants will turn yellow in a heavy clay soil because of poor drainage. They also wilt if roots do not have proper air circulation. Sandy soils provide too much drainage and sometimes leaves wilt or flag due to lack of moisture.

Hunger Signs to Look for in Houseplants: You can detect and remedy nutritional ailments in plants, indoors or outdoors. If the top leaves of your plants first become yellow, the trouble may be due to too much fertilizer or lack of iron. Yellowing between the leaf veins is another good indication of either of these troubles. If foliage has uniform yellowish-green color (mottled) while roots appear healthy, it's a sure sign that nitrogen is lacking. With many plants, this causes the underside of the leaves to appear purple.

Foliage dying from the base upwards: Due to lack of light, dry soil, high room temperature or leaking gas.

Yellowing of foliage: Too much fertilizer, too wet a soil, poor light. If roots are injured by plant food or any other way, yellowing starts. Lack of nitrogen can be corrected by feeding a liquid plant food. If soil is too alkaline, you get yellowing or chlorosis.

Rotting at the base: Due to fungi, bacteria; aggravated by too much water. Dead areas on the edges of leaves result from injury to roots by insects, too much plant food or improper watering.

Dark undersized leaves accompanied by stunted growth are often good signs of lack of phosphorus. Superphosphate corrects this. Lack of moisture will cause same type of growth. Soft growth during winter months is generally due to a combination of too much heat and insufficient light.

Dwarfism or yellowed foliage can be due to insects, such as symphilids, feeding on the roots. Dusting soil with Chlordane or DDT and watering it in, will banish these.

Poorly drained soils will cause yellowing of foliage, shedding of leaves and poor growth. Sterilize your houseplant soil (and soils used for starting seed) with 2½ tablespoons of formaldehyde (obtainable as "formalin") to one cup of water. Sprinkle this on a bushel of soil. Mix it well. Cover with blanket and wait 2 or 3 days before sowing. Or you can bake your soil in moderate oven (190° F.) for 30 minutes or so. Allow soil to cool before sowing. Or you can pressure cook your soil at 10 pounds pressure for 20 minutes.

INSECTS AND DISEASES OF HOUSEPLANTS

Houseplants are subject to attack from insects and diseases 365 days of the year, but, fortunately, we have chemicals to combat them. Probably the safest effective insecticides are Malathion, Rotenone, Pyrethrum and DDT. These come in three forms: dust, liquids and in the handy aerosol containers. Whichever you use, follow the manufacturer's instructions. Malathion is just about the best all-purpose bug killer for houseplants. Mix a teaspoon of the liquid to a quart of soapy water and spray the plants. Some gardeners dip their houseplants into a bucket of the solution. Cover the pot with wax paper or aluminum foil to keep soil from falling into the bucket. Two treatments a week apart should control your pests. The new aerosol pushbutton cans are handy. The only precaution necessary here is to make sure the material is for use on plants; the kerosene-base formulations made to kill flies and mosquitoes will burn plants. Hold the spray about 10 inches from the surface of the leaves and cover both top and undersides.

COMMON HOUSEPLANT PESTS
(Insects)

Pests	What to Look For	Control Measure
Aphids (Plant Lice)	Small plump insects (black, brown, green) on tips and undersides of leaves. Secrete a messy honeydew.	Nicotine sulfate or Malathion, 1 tsp. to 2 qts. of soapy water.
Fungus-Gnats	Young are slender, legless white maggots. Hatch from eggs laid in soil by black flies you see buzzing around plants.	Dust 1 tsp. of DDT, Chlordane or Lindane on surface and water it into the soil.
Leaf-Chewing Pests	Chewed or ragged foliage.	Spray with DDT.
Mealybugs	Oval, white, waxy-coated sapsucking insect in leaf axils and on stems. Secrete sticky honeydew.	Swab a matchstick with rubbing alcohol and apply to the cottony masses. Try Malathion also, at rate of ½ tsp. per qt. water.
Nematodes (soil)	Poor growth, stunted, knotty roots. Affects over 500 different kinds of plants.	Bury sodium selenate capsules in soil. If unsuccessful, discard plant, pot and all.

Pests	What to Look For	Control Measure
Nematodes (foliage)	Cause brown areas in leaves.	Discard plant.
Scale Insects	Oval or hemispherical spots on leaves and stems. Secrete honey-dew. Do not confuse scale with black dots on back of fern leaves. (They are the "seed" or spore-bearing structures.)	Same as for Mealybugs. Malathion 50%, ½ tsp. per qt. water.
Spidermites (Red Spider & Cyclamen Mites)	Nearly microscopic; needle-like mouthparts cause speckled or stippled foliage, bleaching, curling and webbing of leaves.	Malathion; or try Dimite or Kelthane 25% EC, 1 tsp. per qt. water, or treat soil with sodium selenate capsules. Syringing foliage weekly is helpful.
Slugs	"Shell-less" snails which leave a slimy trail.	Dust soil with 15% metaldehyde bait.
Sowbugs (Pillbugs)	Segmented, shell-like bodies. They roll up in a ball. Eat decaying organic matter.	Lindane 25% W.P., ½ tsp. per pot, watered into soil. Also controls Millipedes.
Springtails	Tiny slender-bodied pest which jumps when plant is watered. Not serious unless severe infestation.	Dust 1 tsp. of DDT, Chlordane or Lindane on surface and water it into the soil.
Symphylids	Small swift-moving pest, ¼" long, feeding on roots of plants, causes stunting and yellowing. Often brought in with manure.	Same as for Springtails.
Thrips	Slim pests which cause gray speckled foliage; flower buds fail to open.	Malathion or aerosol sprays. DDT 25%, ¾ tsp. per qt. of water.
White flies	Small white-winged insect which flies out when plant is touched. Secretes honeydew.	Same as for thrips.

ADDITIONAL HELPFUL HINTS

1. Dilute Kelthane (mite killer) in water. Then add ¼ teaspoon of mild household detergent.
2. Sodium selenate is very toxic. It controls mites and nematodes and should be used with great care.
3. Malathion is the best all-round bug killer. You can increase its wetting power and efficiency by adding ⅛ teaspoon of mild household detergent per quart of spray. Avoid Malathion on anthurium, ferns, cacti, crassula and kalanchoe.
4. Those spots you see on back of fern leaves are not insects, but spore ("seed") bearers.
5. EC on a package stands for emulsifiable concentrate which means it can be diluted in water. WP means wettable powder which means it can be added to water.

COMMON HOUSEPLANT DISEASES

Crown Rot or Stem Rot	Due to fungi or bacteria which cause foliage to yellow or rot at soil level.	Dust with Ferbam or Captan.
Damping-Off	Young plants rot at base and topple over.	Dust soil with Captan, Ferbam or Terrachlor.
Powdery Mildew	White, fuzzy spots on leaves.	Dust weekly with Mildex, sulfur, Karathane, or Actidione.
Rust	Rusty spots on leaves or stems.	Keep foliage dry. Spray or dust with Zineb.
Virus (mosaic, ring spot, etc.)	Mottled foliage, stunted growth.	Destroy plant.

HOW TO CONTROL INSECTS IN THE ATTIC OR BASEMENT

More and more gardeners have converted attics or basements into a "poorman's greenhouse." Usually in the fall, when the weather starts to get cool, insects begin to invade these attics and cellars, making it unpleasant. Here are a few pests you might encounter and the control methods you can use. If none of them works get out the vacuum cleaner and sweep up these pests periodically.

Cluster Flies: These flies are dark gray and slightly larger than a house fly. They are sometimes called fall flies or buckwheat flies, etc., You see them congregating in fall on the outside walls and eaves by the thousands, looking for a way to get into the house. During warm periods in winter, cluster flies will leave attics, vacant bedrooms or other winter hideouts and migrate to various parts of the house. You see them on the sunny side of the house, around window sills, floors. You can easily tell them from house flies by the fact that they are bigger, and they crawl very slowly with half-spread wings. Cluster flies cause no damage to the house, except for spotting the walls, windows and furniture. They are a nuisance as they buzz about a light at night when you try to read.

The adult fly can squeeze itself thru the smallest of cracks. Since the fly is commonly seen between screens and windows, it is believed they gain entrance thru the grooves in which sash cords travel. Control: Chink the sash cord grooves with cotton. Spray the outside walls and eaves with a strong solution of DDT, Lindane or Chlordane in early fall. Screen off any large openings and use a caulking compound on smaller openings. Inside the building, use a 5 percent DDT solution, Lindane, or Chlordane. These concentrates will not give satisfactory control unless a heavy deposit is built up by two doses made three weeks apart. THE MAIN OBJECT IS TO APPLY A RESIDUE OR DEPOSIT THAT WILL KILL THE INSECTS AS THEY TRY TO CRAWL OVER IT. You can also use a good household aerosol bomb. In spite of all you can do, some bugs will still get into the house. When this happens, all that can be done is to kill them several times a day. A spray around the foundation of the house in early fall will kill large numbers by the spray residue. Also use a vacuum cleaner to banish June flies.

Box Elder Bugs: This pest is about ½ inch long, and brightly marked with red and black. They feed on box elder trees and other plants. In fall, after frost, they move indoors. They don't bite or harm the home itself, but are a nuisance in large numbers. Control: A tough pest, since just as soon as one bug is killed there are a dozen more to take its place. Spray the foundation with 5% DDT, or 2% Chlordane, or 0.5% Dieldrin. Spray indoors same as for cluster flies above.

Elm Leaf Beetles: These develop from larvae that feed on foliage of elm trees. Beetles are black, enter homes thru chimney. It's often helpful if a 14-mesh screenwire is pushed into all chimneys to keep out beetles. Control: Same as for above. Apply DDT to cracks using a rag mop or paint brush.

Spiders: These gain entrance by cracks in foundations, around doors, windows and, once inside, they usually seek dark, undisturbed corners. Their webs catch flies, dust and dirt. Control: Sweeping down the webs

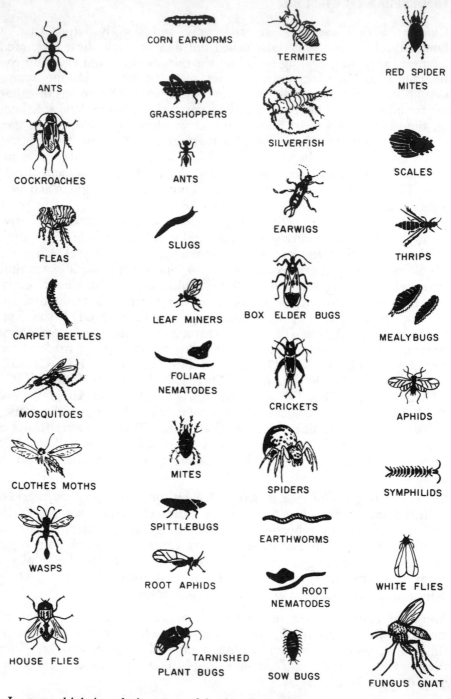

ANTS

CORN EARWORMS

TERMITES

RED SPIDER MITES

COCKROACHES

GRASSHOPPERS

SILVERFISH

SCALES

FLEAS

ANTS

EARWIGS

THRIPS

CARPET BEETLES

SLUGS

BOX ELDER BUGS

MEALYBUGS

MOSQUITOES

LEAF MINERS

CRICKETS

APHIDS

CLOTHES MOTHS

FOLIAR NEMATODES

SPIDERS

SYMPHILIDS

WASPS

MITES

EARTHWORMS

WHITE FLIES

HOUSE FLIES

SPITTLEBUGS

ROOT APHIDS

ROOT NEMATODES

TARNISHED PLANT BUGS

SOW BUGS

FUNGUS GNAT

Insects which invade homes and bother houseplants. Some do not attack houseplants but are a nuisance.

(See chart on Control Measures)

is a temporary measure, new webs pop up overnight. Spray the area with Lindane, either wettable powder or emulsion in water. One spray will do the trick.

Wasps & Hornets: Break up their nests, inside or outside. Spray the area with DDT or Chlordane and you won't have any trouble. Their paper-like comb nests should be treated with care or you'll get stung. Move them on a cold day. You can squirt some pesticide into the nest opening and other places where wasps will crawl.

House Flies: The common house fly represents about 98 percent of the fly population around the home. Control: Malathion, an all-purpose insecticide, does a fine job, also any of the aerosol bombs on the market.

Ants: Chlordane will lick this pest. Spray or dust where ants are seen to enter. Ant hills outside should be treated also.

Crickets: A cricket in the thicket is pleasant. In the home it eats holes in paper, woolens, furs and cotton. Chlordane or DDT dusted or sprayed into dark places, crevices, closets, etc. will kill them.

Other Insect Pests: You might find ticks, carpet beetles, centipedes, cockroaches, clothes moths, crickets, mosquitoes, scorpions, silverfish, termites, waterbugs and other pests in the attic. Try using Chlordane, spray or dust, for these pests. Make sure you apply enough. Most insects are killed by contact, by eating or simply touching the chemical. No matter how careful you are, some insect pests will still slip in. When they do, get rid of them fast. Your local supply store will have most of the above chemicals. Perhaps the best all-purpose insect killer is Malathion, but the others we've mentioned will do a good job in most cases.

AEROSOL SPRAYS ("PUSH BUTTON" CONTROLS)

If you're using aerosol spray cans for fighting insects, the U.S. Department of Agriculture recommends the following method: Take a cardboard box of about 4 cubic feet, lay it on its side and place your plants in it. Point the aerosol at the plants and with a sweeping motion spray them from a distance of 18 inches for 4 seconds, or 1 second per cubic foot. Close the box for two minutes.

CHAPTER II

Flowering

Houseplants

AFRICAN VIOLETS (*Saintpaulia*)

The African violet has remained the Number 1 houseplant for years. Even men get pleasure raising this sometimes fussy item. Books have been written about violets, and fanciers who want more information on the plant should resort to them. Here are some facts I've gleaned through the years from good and bad violet fanciers.

Green Thumb Tips: African violets, unlike many plants, do not have a dormant period. If cultural conditions are satisfactory, they continue to grow twelve months of the year. Actively growing plants bloom.

Soil: Pot the plants in a 3- or 4-inch pot, with a soil mixture of ⅓ peat and leaf mold, ⅓ clean sand, ⅓ garden loam. Add about one-half cup of superphosphate to each half bushel of this soil mixture. Sterilize the soil by baking in moderate oven (190 degrees F. for ½ hour). Or use formaldehyde, 2½ tablespoons to one cup of water. Sprinkle this on a bushel of soil. Work it in well, then wait 2 or 3 days before sowing seed.

Feeding the Plants: More violets are overfed than underfed. Every 3 to 4 months, ½ teaspoon of complete fertilizer (such as 5-10-5) may be applied to the surface of the soil. Once each year, remove most of the old soil and repot the plant in new soil. Violets should never be fed unless they are growing and need the food.

Watering: Water from below until the soil is moist. Never allow the soil to become dry, nor should the pot stand in water for a long time. Yellowing leaves is usually due to cold water splashed on the leaf. When surface-watering the plant, use lukewarm water. White salts on surface are fertilizer salts which have worked upward. Scratch these with nail, and water plants from top to wash them back. Give your violets a bath every now and then. Put them in the bath tub and syringe the foliage with warm water. If you plan to go on vacation, put some bricks in a bathtub. Place wet papers on top of bricks and fill tub with water to a depth of 2 or 3 inches. Set potted plants on top of paper and they will be automatically watered for days.

Light: African violets are sensitive to light. With too little light, plants will grow vigorously but will produce few, if any, flowers. Grow the plants in a bright north window, or just out of the sun in other windows. These plants prefer a temperature of 60° to 62° at night, and 70° to 72° in the daytime. Lack of light will prevent flowering. Too much light will cause yellowing of leaves. Hold your hand about 6 inches above the plant. If it casts a shadow just barely visible, the light is right. If a distinct shadow is cast, the plant should be moved to a place where the light is less intense, or the window should be shaded with light drapery.

Some other indications of too much light are: Plants turn gray, similar to an infestation of spider mites. It will also cause the variegated types to revert to solid green. The petioles or stems of the new leaves growing from the center become shortened. The whole aspect of the plant becomes droopy. The leaves turn down as if they are growing away from the light. Spoon-leafed varieties of violets flatten out. In extreme cases, flowering will stop completely.

Too little light will cause the following conditions: Petioles or stems of the leaves become long and leggy. Leaves become more soft and succulent. Foliage becomes a lighter color, on the gray side, and not a healthy dark green. Bloom is sparse or non-existent. Lack of light is the most frequent cause of non-blooming.

Sex Life of Violets: "Is it true that you must have several African violet plants around for cross pollination?" No! Nearly all African violets have perfect flowers on the same plant. That means the flowers contain both stamen (male) and pistil (female) floral parts and thus can pollinate themselves without benefit of a nearby plant. The term "boy" and "girl" as related to violets has nothing to do with sex, but rather with different leaf types.

One African violet named "Blue Boy" sported or mutated and gave rise to a different leaf, more rounded and with an irregular green, yellow to white area on the leaf base. This sport was called "Blue Girl." Ever since this time, violets with a rounded leaf and color markings of yellow-white have been called girl-type violets. Sex has had nothing to do with the naming of the plants.

Variegated Violets: Cause of variegation is not known. Sometimes variegated plants bloom, sometimes they don't. If you have a variegated plant and like the colors, keep the buds picked off, as they tend to weaken the plant. When some all-green leaves show up on a variegated plant, leave them on, as they will give vigor. Sometimes suckers or side branches may cause the varigated parts to dwindle away, so it's a good idea to pick them off immediately. You can propagate variegated plants by nipping the center out of your best one, forcing it to grow side shoots. Albino plants, those having no clear, green color in leaves, are delicate and hard to grow. For us, they have a tendency to die young or turn green. Spray yours with the following sugar solution: 1 pint of distilled water, 1½ ounces of granulated sugar and two grams of sulfanilamide. Add a tablespoonful of soapy water for a spreader. Your druggist will mix this for you.

Pruning Violets: One reader tells us she prunes her violets with an ordinary pencil. Using a pencil point, she snips off the new little crowns which grow on the sides of the plants. She does this just as soon as they are noticeable. Prune the stems of each violet as soon as the blooms have fallen. This makes remaining blooms last longer. Always prune faded blooms to prevent seed pods. Seed deters further bud development. If blooms drop off while still fresh, don't worry. This is natural. These flowers pollinate easily and after pollination, they slide off quickly. If the plants drop their blooms before they open, the cause is usually low humidity or low temperature.

Propagation: African violets are best started by leaf and stem cuttings. Just cut a leaf with one or two inches of its stem attached. Then stick the stem in moist sand or a mixture of sand and peat moss. Or use plain water in a bottle or a glass. If you split the stem about ¾ inch at tip end, it will grow a bigger cluster of roots. Allow the cut end to dry for 3 hours prior to putting it in sand or water. Vermiculite or similar material makes a good rooting medium. Place cutting in it, but do not pack the vermiculite tightly around the base. Remove and pot when roots are ½ inch long.

Roots will form at base of stem in 3 to 4 weeks, and soon a small rosette of leaves will appear. When well rooted, the cuttings should be potted in clean pots. It takes about 6 to 8 months to produce a good flowering plant from a cutting. Some folks boil the clay flower pots in a solution of 1 oz. vinegar to a gallon of water. Seal the rim with paraffin, or wrap a strip of aluminum foil about the edge. This stops or prevents rot by keeping the stems from rubbing on the rim of the pot.

Treating Leaves: If you have trouble with rotting leaves, try dipping them in a solution of Fermate. Put ½ teaspoonful of Fermate (Ferbam) into a pint jar, pour in a little water to form a paste, then fill with luke-warm water and mix thoroughly. With a razor, cut leaf off the plant, leaving a stem only about 1½ inches long. Dip the entire stem and leaf in the Fermate solution. Then place on absorbent paper to drain. Captan is OK too.

African Violets from Seed: Used for originating new varieties. If you've never tried this, you are missing a real experience. You may get new plants, and you may not. First, take a look at your blooms. Note the two little yellow sacs (anthers, male elements) in the center of the flower. They contain the pollen. Now, notice a tiny floral part resembling a feeler on a butterfly. Your job is to transfer pollen to the tip of this pistil (known as stigma). Take one of these yellow sacs (anthers, or male) open it up with a needle, and, with a brush of your finger, smear some pollen dust on the gummy stigma. Best time to pollinate is in middle of day, when the air is warm. Pollen will keep for at least three months in a dry, tightly corked bottle (you may wish to pollinate a plant at a later date). Now that you have pollinated the plant, wait and see what happens. Seed pod starts forming in a week.

When the stem and seed pod turn brown and start to shrivel, you know the seeds are ripe. It takes 7 to 9 months for the pod to ripen. Pollinated in spring, pods may ripen in a shorter time. When pod is ripe, pinch it off and place in a dish to dry. Takes a week to a month to dry the pods. Break pods open and sow the seeds in vermiculite. Do not cover seed, but press down lightly. Seedlings appear in 2 to 3 weeks. Transplant them an inch apart when they have 3 leaves. When plants have 5 or 6 leaves, transplant into 3-inch pots. Young plants from seed begin to bloom when 6 months old.

Troubles: Violets Get Plenty! !

Leaf Bleaching: Leaf bleaching may be due to excess light or lack of nitrogen in soil. Move plants to darker window. Too much light also causes mushy spots to develop. Grayish foliage is often indicative of lack of nitrogen. Lengthening of the stem is due to overwatering, espe-cially by subirrigation, or to inadequate light. When this is combined with brown edges on the leaves, the cause is usually overfeeding with nitrate or potassium. If the leaves bleach out and tend to curl down around the pot, plant is getting too much light.

Wilted or Curled Leaves: Usually associated with rotting of stem (petiole or stem rot) due to accumulation of fertilizer salts on the rim of the pots, causing damage to the underside of the leaf stalk and sub-sequent rotting. This happens when plants are watered from below. If troublesome, be sure to wrap aluminum foil on edge of pot or dip in wax.

Stunt: A virus trouble and outwardly looks like mite attack. Young leaves are thickened and brittle, become dwarfed and light colored. However, they tend to curve downward instead of up as in the case of mite injury. Hairs lie flat instead of upright, presenting an appearance of glassiness. There is no control. Burn your plants to prevent the virus from spreading to others.

Mildew: Grayish patches of fuzzy growth on leaves and flower stalks. If spores are present, high humidity followed by drop in temperature will start mildew. Control: Dust with sulfur or Fermate, or Karathane.

Thrips: Small insects which cause petals to drop, also leave silver streaks on underside of leaves. Spray with DDT or Malathion.

Crown Rot: Very common. First sign is wilting of lower row of leaves, as if plants are dry. If plant has crown rot, take it out of pot and you'll see it is rotted off at crown. Cut off the rotted portion, dust wound with Fermate or sulfur and repot it in clean sterile soil.

Plant Lice: Aphids or plant lice bother violets. They leave gray specks on the leaves. Control: Spray with nicotine sulfate, 1 teaspoon to two quarts water, plus 2 level tablespoons of soap flakes (or detergent). Spray on plants in warm room, dry plants off in a sunny window. Spray may cause loss of blooms, nothing serious.

Wilting: When the leaves droop, check the soil or roots to see if the crown is rotted. Crown rot sometimes sets in due to excess water. When this happens, cut out the diseased portion and re-root. If your plants look poor, show no growth or blooms, chances are they need repotting and change of soil. Repot, especially if the thick stem of an old plant stands up above the soil or hangs over the edge of the pot. Replant and sink the main stem deeper.

Wilting might also be due to poor soil, too much water, too little water, or too much direct sunlight. It may also be due to the acid soil, or the temperatures that are too hot and dry. Often wilted leaves can be revived by placing them in water overnight; then use them as new cuttings. Snow or sun glare is harmful. Anemic plants are often the result of poor soil. Many growers mix charcoal and pulverized sheep manure with soil to give plants a husky root system and luxuriant foliage and blossoms.

Failure to Bloom: May be due to insufficient light for flower bud formation. Move them to a brighter window. Some growers have good luck forcing stubborn plants into bloom by adding a solution of aluminum sulfate, one teaspoonful to a quart of water. Apply once a week until the buds appear.

Lazy Violets: A grower tells me she wakes up lazy African violets by using this homemade formula: 1 teaspoon each of baking powder, Epsom salts and saltpeter, ½ teaspoon of household ammonia, all poured into a gallon of tepid water. Water your stubborn violets only once a month with this solution. She says it works on all stubborn plants. Probably a simpler method would be to use a balanced plant food such as 23-19-17 (Ra-pid-gro). Mix a teaspoon to a quart of water and apply it once every 2 or 3 weeks.

Another trick for coaxing stubborn violets into flowering is to set the pot in a pan of hot water (115° F.). This "hotfoot" treatment shocks the plants into blossoming, if there is enough light.

If the leaf stems become elongated and leaves tend to reach upward it means that the plants are not getting enough light. Move them to a bright room. Giving your plants a half turn once a week helps to produce a better-shaped plant. Most people overfeed and overwater their plants. Keep plants away from cold drafts and cold window panes. Keep pots in shallow containers of moist sand or gravel to increase air moisture. Water when the surface soil seems dry. Keep soil well moistened but never soggy or wet. Dust plants with soft brush. Single-crown plants are usually best. Remove the side shoots when they are very small for best results. Long leaf stems mean not enough light, very short leaf stems, too much light. Water from water softeners is harmful to houseplants. Chlorinated water does not harm plants as many commonly believe. Rainwater is excellent. Hard water can be acidified by adding 1 ounce of vinegar to a gallon of water. Water with this once every 6 weeks.

Green Mold on Soil: This means the roots of your plants aren't getting enough air. Scratch the surface of the soil now and then with tines of an old fork. Too much water or poor soil drainage packs the soil and causes the moldy growth. Mildew and mold on leaves means poor sunlight, or poor ventilation, or both.

Nematode Troubles: Small microscopic worm which causes galls on roots and poor growth. No control once started, but you should use sterile soil and clean pots as a preventative. Bake soil and pots in oven (½ hour at 180° to 190°) or use a pressure cooker. Cyclamen mite is a worse pest. Causes stunted plants, curled leaves and flower buds that fail to open properly.

If Your Blooms Change Color or Fade, Here Is Why: First, it's normal for a violet bloom to fade as the blossom grows older. Light, heat and soil will all cause variations in color. Some pinks will be very deep in strong light, fairly pale in weaker light. High temperatures will lighten the blue colors and cause blooms with a variegated edge to lose their edge. For example, Lady Geneva may not show a white edge during the hot summer months, but will in cool weather. Alkaline soil may cause a blue to pale, and a small feeding of aluminum sulfate will splotched cream-white.

Green Thumb Tips: Does best in semi-shade, turns brown on edges in direct sunlight. Likes ample moisture and prefers humidity of glass gardens.

Propagation: Divide clumps any time of the year.

Troubles: Browning of foliage due to too much sun, dry soil.

APOSTLE PLANT (Walking Iris)

Neomarica gets its common name, apostle plant, from the twelve sword-shaped leaves growing fan-shaped. *N. gracilis* has white and blue flowers, *N. northiana* has yellow flowers, small and resembling blooms of iris. After flowering is over, baby plants develop where the flowers had been; these bend over and root in soil wherever they touch; hence, the other common name, walking iris.

Green Thumb Tips: Prefers a bright window, out of direct sun. Best temperature is around 70° or less. Use the standard soil mixture, equal parts sand, loam and peat. Make sure it's kept uniformly moistened.

Propagation: Simply pin the small plants to the soil in a pot. When they've rooted, you can cut them off from parent plant. Rhizomes can be divided just as irises are.

Troubles: None.

AZALEA

Florist's or greenhouse type. Few houseplants are more popular than the showy azalea. These will grow successfully in the home if you're willing to give them the care they need.

Green Thumb Tips: Azaleas like an acid soil. If you happen to live in a hard water area, keep in mind that hard water rapidly lessens the acidity each time you water the plants. To overcome this, you can use rain water or water that has been boiled for a few minutes and allowed to cool. If this is not possible, apply a pinch of alum or ¼ teaspoon of dusting sulfur to the surface of the soil every 3 weeks. Vinegar is good for azaleas, 1 teaspoon to a quart of water, applied 2 or 3 times a month.

Azaleas need lots of moisture and sunlight after they have flowered. After blooming, keep moist (NEVER DRIED OUT), then in May put in a sunny window. When shirt-sleeve weather comes, put the plant, pot and all, in a shady spot in garden. Prune back any leggy shoots until July, so you'll have a nice bushy plant. Repot if necessary.

bring the color back to normal. If one or several blooms have change color, it's either sporting or reverting to a strong characteristic of som ancestor.

Many varieties (such as Painted Girls) change from a white-and orchid-variegated bloom to a solid orchid one. This is called reverting to their strong orchid parent. The variety was not stabilized before it was placed on the market.

Dropping of Buds: Can be due to low humidity, hot and dry air. Even the smallest amounts of gaseous fumes, especially from artificial gas, will also cause buds to drop. A test for gas: Introduce a fresh-cut carnation bloom. If gas is present, blossom goes to "sleep" or petals curl. Dry soil or soil containing too much nitrogen will also cause buds to drop. Extremes of temperature may be responsible. Dropping of petals soon after opening may be due to attack of thrips which pollinate the flowers and start seed development. It's natural for violets to shed blooms once pollination has been effected. Also, the optimum chemical level for violets is quite low, hence, blossoms ripen too fast (and shed) when plant is overfertilized.

If the leaves sag or bend over, look for low temperature; a factor which also causes leaves to rot and drop and prevents the formation of buds. Plants making vigorous growth, with few, if any flowers, may often have too little light.

Violets are sensitive to sudden drafts and the lack of fresh air, which is important for good violet growth. They like a warm, moist atmosphere and ample water in summer, but less water in winter.

Diseases and Insects of African Violets: Mealybug is a common pest. Control by dipping the tip of a small brush in alcohol and touching each cottony mass. Sometimes plants rot off at soil surface. This may be due to too much water or too little fertilizer. Mites cause twisting and stunting of flowers and plants; also cause poor growth and few blooms. Young leaves appear more hairy than usual. Flower stalks curve and swell. Mite infected plants can be treated by immersing plant, pot and all in water, kept 110° F., for two minutes. Mites can be killed by using sodium selenate, 1 dose every 3 weeks, or you can use mite killers such as Dimite, Ovatran, Kelthane. The latter is the best miticide for violets. Mites cause small flowers, misshapened and often streaked. If your soil has small white maggots, they may kill your plant by feeding on the roots. We get 100% control by dusting the soil with Chlordane.

Ring spots on leaves are due to cold water. Water your plants with water that is room temperature.

ACORUS (Sweet Flag—*Acorus gramineus variegatus*)

This item is useful in dish gardens and terrariums. Has iris-like leaves,

As for the soil, you can use pure peat moss or a mixture of sand and peat. Florists use 100 percent peat. During the summer you can give the azalea 2 or 3 doses of ammonium sulfate, ¼ teaspoon per pot for each application. Keep the soil moist during summer months. Then during the early part of September, bring plant indoors before frost hits. Place in a cool location having a night temperature of 40° to 50°.

Outdoor Care: The florist's azalea is not hardy outdoors in the north and will winterkill. If you repot yours, use peat or a mixture of peat and sand. Outdoor or hardy azaleas like a mulch of oak leaves, pine needles, sawdust, or acid peat moss. Never use maple leaves as they are alkaline and azaleas need the opposite, acidity, for best growth. All outdoor azaleas should have a mulch around their roots to protect against dry weather, low temperatures and to keep the soil cool and moist in summer.

Propagation: Azaleas are easily started by cuttings taken from the plant in July. Cuttings are made of the present season's wood, about 4 inches long. Root the cuttings in a pot of half-sand and half-peat moss. This should be kept moist and it's a good idea to syringe the foliage on hot days if you use a cold frame. Leaves should be stripped from the lower half of the cutting. Stick cuttings in sand and peat about half their length and tap lightly around cuttings. They can be set close together in rows. Water regularly (DO NOT ALLOW TO DRY OUT). In about 8 weeks roots will develop, then you can pot them up in a peat-sand mix, or peat alone.

Seed: Many azaleas are propagated by seed. Hybrid forms or "sports" will not be reproduced by seeds. Collect seed pods in fall. Keep dry until February when you sow seeds out on sphagnum moss or peat moss. Keep moss wet. In a few months the seedlings will be ready to transplant in a peaty mixture. Peat moss is excellent for seed germination of both rhododendrons and azaleas.

Troubles: Drying up of leaves is due to lack of water. If the azalea is allowed to become dry at any time while it is being grown or forced indoors, leaves will drop, dry up, or plant will die. Peat should never be allowed to become so dry that it turns light brown in color, or that the pot becomes very light when lifted. Keep plants sprayed with Malathion, 1 teaspoon to quart of water (do job outdoors) to check red spider mites, thrips, aphids, azalea leaf miner and, perhaps, mealybugs. Light is important for retention of leaves. Dark rooms and extreme variation in moisture content should be avoided. Keep the temperature cool in fall, 55° to 60° until November, since this favors flower-bud development.

Yellowing of leaves (chlorosis) is due to lack of soil acidity, too much plant food, lack of nitrogen, or not enough light. If you live in a hard water area, this will bring about yellowing due to alkaline water. That's why you should increase acidity by adding iron sulfate, sulfur dust, or vinegar water to soil.

Failure to bloom is due to insufficient cool period in fall, not enough light, or not enough moisture. The greenhouse azalea won't live outdoors in the cold area, but must be placed outdoors for summer in cool, partially-shaded place. Keep it moist throughout summer and give an occasional feeding of an iron chelate (key-late) preparation, such as Sequestrene. Bring indoors in fall, place in a cool place (50° F.) and keep soil barely moist until December or January. Then bring to a sunny window, keep moist and cool. Indoors and outdoors, syringe the foliage from time to time.

BEGONIAS

This constitutes one of the largest and most handsome groups of houseplants grown. Begonias are classified according to the type of roots they have. For example, they may have fibrous, rhizomatous or tuberous roots. The homeowner is more interested in the culture of these types than he is in classification. To many, the begonia is queen of all the houseplants. Certainly, the group is one of the largest and most fascinating of all the plant kingdom; there are over 1,000 species. Here are a few green thumb notes on how to care for the most co-mon begonias.

Angel Wing is a fibrous-rooted type with lopsided leaves resembling an angel's wings. They are easy to grow and very showy. Sometimes angel wing grows out of bounds, but you can keep it in shape by pinching the tips back. Start new plants with the tips you cut off by rooting them in water or sand. Keep soil moist. Avoid overwatering as this causes shedding of the foliage. Avoid direct sunlight.

Rex Begonia

Rex begonia: This and all of the rhizomatous forms grow best in bright light, but not direct sun. Rex foliage is speckled, very showy and, to me, one of the best. Foliage is the main show with this variety.

Calla begonia is a real queen, but a stubborn one too! Often called youth and old age, the leaves are blotched, very interesting and shaped similarly to the calla-lily blossom. Some leaves are pure white (lack of chlorophyll), some contain a touch of pink. Sometimes there are too many white leaves; a lack of chlorophyll reducing the plant's ability to make food. You can bypass this shortage by purchasing chlorophyll tablets in a drugstore: dissolve one in a glass of water and root cuttings in the solution. Calla begonia likes a west window. NEVER direct sunlight. It's grown primarily for its foliage.

Christmas begonia or *begonia socotrana* is probably the showiest of them all. This is a plant sold by florists at Christmas time. Keep the plant in a bright window, with a room temperature of around 60°. Prefers a humusy soil and ample water. Too little light causes the plant to become spindly. After flowering you can cut the plant back to within 3 inches of the pot and let new growth come on. Store the mother plant in a basement or sun porch until spring. Do not allow the soil to become bone dry during summer. Give it a bright window until fall. Dropping of flowers is due to age of plant, poor light or high temperatures.

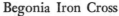

Begonia Iron Cross

Beefsteak begonia has blood red coloring on the back of smooth shiny foliage. This and the *Begonia heracleifolia*, as well as the palm begonia (*B. recinifolia*) are grown for their foliage effect.

Wax begonias (*Begonia semperflorens*), a fibrous-rooted type, is about the easiest of all to grow. This type is used in porch and window boxes and in shaded garden borders. One of the best varieties is the Indian Maid, a type with beautiful bronze leaves. The double rosebud begonia is a good example of an improved wax begonia.

TUBEROUS BEGONIAS

This is a popular plant raised by florists for Easter and Mother's Day sales. Culturally, there are few things easier to grow than tuberous begonias. The dry bulbs may be started in the house or in a frame any time from February to the first of June and set outside, after hardening off, any time after May 15th, or the tubers may be planted directly outside after the first of May.

Begonias delight in a rich soil. It is best to start the bulb in 4- or 5-inch pots. The soil should be composed of at least ⅓ peat, and ⅓ light loam. It is important for the mixture to be of light coarse character so that it will drain well. Finely sifted soil will pack down without permitting the circulation of air.

To provide perfect drainage, which is most important, place at least one inch of gravel on the bottom of the pot.

Place the bulbs, concave side up, with the surface of the bulb showing. Put in a warm dark place or cover with paper. Water sparingly until growth appears.

When the sprouts are an inch or two high, cover the bulbs with soil and increase the water gradually. Keep the surface barely moist until the growth is well developed. Then heavier watering is justified. If you overwater the soil in the beginning, it will become sour; the plants will make only a sickly growth; buds will fall off before blooming, and the plants may die out entirely. This is true especially of hanging basket types.

If very strong growth is desired, additional feeding can be given when the plants reach 4 or 5 inches in height. One teaspoon of bone meal should be worked into the soil, not too close to the stem.

Place outdoors after all danger of frost is past. Cool shaded locations are best.

In autumn when the foliage turns yellow, withhold water gradually. When all growth dies down entirely, take tuber out of soil, wash off (taking care not to bruise the tuber), thoroughly dry in sunlight for a day or two, then store in open flats in cool dry place.

See that all particles of the old stem are removed until healthy tissue shows; if left on, they will decay and destroy the tuber.

The most common failure in begonias is the falling off of buds before they develop. This is caused either by drying out or severe overwatering. Abundant growth with little or no flowers is the result of too heavy shade. Curly, shiny foliage is a sign of too strong an exposure to the sun.

Do not prune tuberous begonias. Any open wound will be immediately attacked by fungus, especially when crowded growth hampers air circulation. If you cut the flowers, cut only half the stem. The other half will mature and fall off without leaving a wound.

If well-balanced hanging baskets are desired, pick off all buds until the growth is advanced and branching develops. Some hanging types are strong growers and, if only one to three stems are on the tuber, the buds should be pinched off to induce the side shoots to develop.

After flowering, cut the plant back to within 3 inches of the pot and let new growth come on. Store the mother plant in a basement or sun porch until spring, then give it a bright window until fall. Do not allow the soil to become bone dry during summer. Dropping of flowers is due to age of plant, poor light or high temperature.

Green Thumb Tips for All Begonias

Soil: All begonias like a soil that is loose, well drained and full of humus. Waterlogged soil means rot and poor success. Mix up a soil of 2 parts coarse leaf mold, 1 part rotted cow manure, 1 part sandy loam, 1 part broken charcoal, and to this mixture add about a handful of 5-10-5 fertilizer for each bushel of soil. Mix in some Chlordane dust to kill any soil insects that may be present.

Whenever potting a begonia, be especially careful not to overwater for a few weeks, otherwise rot will set in. Soil should be given just enough water to keep from drying out. Pot should never be allowed to stand in water constantly.

Light: Most begonias like ample light, but seldom prefer direct sunlight. If the leaves turn yellowish and develop brown tips, it may mean too much light. Move to a shadier window; or use curtains that shut out more light. If your leafstalks are long or leggy, it may mean lack of light.

Dropping of Buds: May be due to lack of light, too dry a room, lack of sufficient moisture, or low temperature. Most begonias like a temperature of 55° to 65°. Gas fumes may also cause the buds to drop.

Failure to Bloom: This may be due to too much nitrogen in the soil or lack of light. If your begonias do not bloom in spite of good soil, move them to a bright window. Begonias must be shielded from direct sun, but good light is needed for flower-bud production, especially during the winter months.

Pruning Begonias: Just about all begonias need some pruning, except the tuberous types. The angel wing, for example, will make tall leggy growth if left unpruned. You can keep them in good shape by pruning the tips, which in turn can be rooted to make new plants. Any begonia which makes leggy, ungainly growth should be pinched back to induce bushiness.

Some begonias, such as the star begonia and rex, have a habit of growing over the side of the pot. You can correct this only at repotting time, simply by setting the plant in a different position so that the growing point is centered. Many of the rhizome-type plants have a rambling, sprawling growth habit.

Propagation: Nearly all varieties will start from seed except the calla, which should be started from cuttings. Stem cuttings can be used to grow all the branching types. To make a cutting, cut a stem at or below the joint; remove the lower leaves and root in sand, or a mixture of peat and sand. Dip the ends in Fermate to prevent rot. Keep the cuttings shaded by cloth and maintain a temperature of 60° or 70°. Begonia slips will root in 3 or 4 weeks, without difficulty.

Leaf cuttings: Take a leaf with about an inch of stalk attached. The leaf is cut across the main rib (or vein) on the underside. The leaf is pinned (hairpins are fine) so that it lies flat on surface of sand. Leaves form roots.

If begonia slips rot in water while rooting, try rooting them in sand, a preferable method. Some begonias are harder to root than others. If you plan to root the calla begonia, select the greenest slips for cuttings because the white ones lack food-making machinery (chlorophyll) and will not grow. Green slips of calla begonias will produce white tips later on. You might have better luck rooting this under a fruit jar.

When sowing begonia seed, make sure the soil is light, and finely sifted. Sow dustlike seed evenly, cover with glass plate instead of soil. Keep in dark room, temperature of 70°. When seed germinates, move to light window and water from below to prevent damping off. Tuberous begonias can be started from seed or tubers.

Troubles: If leaves are brittle and crinkly, look for mites. Keep plant dusted with fine sulfur. Also look for root-knot nematode, causing swellings on roots. If leaves have brown patches, it's nematode infestation; destroy entire plant.

Be on the lookout for aphids. They suck juices and secrete a honeydew material. Mix up a solution of nicotine sulfate, 1 teaspoon to a quart of water (soapy) and dip plants into solution, or spray it on.

Malathion is an excellent aphid-killer.

If your soil has tiny worms in it, sprinkle some Chlordane dust on it and water it in. Chlordane will take care of nearly all pests in the soil.

One of the worst diseases to plague begonias is mildew, causing a flour-like coating over the foliage. Severely affected leaves are killed outright. Avoid wetting the foliage, dust with Karathane, and avoid moist shaded conditions if possible. Badly infected plants should be discarded.

Brown spots on leaves are due to dry soil, changes in temperature and often fungus. Keep foliage free from water; give plant uniform supply of moisture at all times.

Nematodes cause yellowing, dwarfing of plants. Look for small lumps on roots. If present, discard the plants.

BELLFLOWER (*Campanula*)

The white and blue bellflowers are excellent for hanging baskets. *C. isophylla alba* has white flowers, and *C. isophylla mayii* has blue blossoms. Both have bright green foliage. *C. alba elatines plena* has double white flowers, and *C. elatines floreplena* has double blue blooms.

Green Thumb Tips: Prefer a well-drained soil (⅓ each of sand, peat and loam), kept uniformly moist. During winter withhold water. In summer, trim back lengthy growth and keep on bright sun porch.

Propagation: Cuttings taken in spring and rooted in sand and peat moss.

Troubles: Red spider mites: use Kelthane. Failure to flower: lack of light.

BIRD-OF-PARADISE (*Strelitzia regina*)

The bird-of-paradise makes a poor houseplant, although many gardeners do have luck in forcing it to bloom. It has large banana-shaped foliage, and the blossom itself is quite a novelty. They are orange-petaled with a bluish tongue, and with a little imagination, appear like a bird perched on top of the plant. There's even a dwarf type growing about 20 inches tall.

Green Thumb Tips: You have to grow this item in a tub since it seldom sends forth a flower until it reaches a certain size. Those you see in flower shops are shipped in from California or Hawaii and not raised in greenhouses as is commonly believed. The plant must develop a dozen or more healthy leaves and needs full sunlight for flowering,

Bird of Paradise (Strelitzia)

which is usually in winter and spring, although I've seen plants blooming in later summer and fall. In winter give it a moderate amount of water, good drainage and rich, humusy soil. During the summer, leave plant in tub or pot and sink it to the rim in the garden in a shaded spot. You can divide the plant to start new ones, or just take off suckers in the spring and root them in sand. These plants do best if undisturbed. It takes 3 or 4 years for the bird-of-paradise to bloom after it has been divided or even repotted, so be patient. They are heavy feeders and need pot room to encourage flowering.

BOUGAINVILLEA

Here's a handsome tropical plant not grown enough in American homes. It has tiny flowers appearing in dense clusters, but the main show is the paper-like bracts which surround the blossoms and it's the long life of these tissue-like parts which make the plant the eye-stopper that it is. The plant is vine-like and can be readily trained to grow up a window.

Green Thumb Tips: Keep it trimmed slightly for bushiness. Grow plant in a bright sunny window, average house temperature. Soil should be well drained and kept uniformly moist at all times. Snip off dead floral parts, to extend the blooming period even further. Plants will go into a semi-dormant stage for a few weeks but will come on with more buds. In summer put the pot on sun porch or outdoors where it can get rest. Keep it watered.

Propagation: Sow seeds in sand, peat moss mixture in spring, or start new plants by rooting 4-inch cuttings of half-ripened wood taken in spring or summer. Root in sand and peat. Takes 3 or 4 months for rooting.

Troubles: Red spider mites, control with Kelthane. Failure to flower, lack of light or poor soil. Dropping of leaves due to poor drainage.

BROWALLIA (*Browallia speciosa major*)

Florists use this blue-flowered plant for hanging baskets, window boxes and pot plants indoors. A member of the nightshade family, it grows with the same care petunias would get if grown indoors.

Green Thumb Tips: Prefers bright window, cool temperature. Apt to get sprawly if the top is not pinched back.

Propagation: Start from seed sown in February for Decoration Day use. Or take cuttings from plants and root them in water or moist sand.

Troubles: Aphids and spider mites, spray with Malathion, which is also good for white flies and thrips.

CALCEOLARIA (Pocketbook Plant—*C. herbeohybrida*)

A popular plant sold by florists for Easter and Mother's Day. Flowers are pouch-shaped, hence the name pocketbook plant.

Green Thumb Tips: Keep plants in cool window, out of direct sun.

Calceolaria or Pocketbook Plant

Keep soil well moistened. After flowering is finished, cut the plant back about half its size and it will send out new growth. Many discard the plant after flowering. Must be grown cool or buds won't form. Requires a temperature of below 60° for flower-bud formation.

Propagation: Start seeds in spring in sand, peat moss mix. Keep seed cool or it won't germinate.

Troubles: Failure of seed to germinate due to hot temperature. Aphids, spray with Lindane or Malathion. High temperatures and poor light indoors cause the flowers to be faded in appearance.

CHENILLE PLANT (*Acalypha hispida*)

Has showy chenille-like spikes hanging from leaf axils, pinkish-white or red. Leaves are attractive.

Green Thumb Tips: Likes bright window, and a loose well-drained soil which must be kept moist at all times. Avoid overwatering as it causes leaves to yellow and drop.

Propagation: Cuttings taken in late summer and rooted in sand and peat moss.

Troubles: Dropping of leaves, overwatering or red spider mites.

CHRYSANTHEMUM

The florist's potted mum plant is now available to homeowners every month of the year. By shading the plants with black cloth, the plants can be made to bloom. The shade shortens their day artificially and they will bloom out of season. They normally bloom in the fall when the days are short.

Green Thumb Tips: The indoor mum needs lots of water and a bright window. Best night temperature is 65°, day 73°. A loose soil mixture is ideal because it provides good drainage. After the plant finishes flowering, keep it watered, cut tops back and place in cellar or sun porch until "shirt sleeve" weather approaches. Then place it outdoors. If you have the plant in fall, keep it watered in cellar window. Or place it outdoors, next to the foundation of your home where ice will not kill it and mulch with evergreen boughs. The following spring, take cuttings from the shoots which have come up. A 4-inch cutting in spring will be a big plant ready to bloom by fall. Pinch the tips of the plant out (with your thumb and forefinger) before July 1st, not later, as later pinching will delay bloom. Pinching makes plants more compact and bushy.

Starting mum plants by tip cuttings in sand.

When mum cuttings get too tall, pinch the tips to make them bushy.

My neighbor, Louise Warren, gets her mums to blossom in February indoors. She takes cuttings in the fall and roots them in plain tap water, then grows the plants in a bright window. By the time February rolls around, the plants have buds and blooms on them Some of the blossoms are as large as the florist's mums and just as pretty.

Most of the florist's potted mums are not hardy, but some can be kept and made to bloom again in fall. Some would bloom too late and are caught by the freeze. There are two things you can do to get around this: (1) Dig the plant up in fall, move it indoors and grow in bright window. It will bloom for you at the proper time. (2) Protect blossoms and buds from frost by covering with plastic garment bags.

Cascade Mums: The newest fad is to train mums so they'll have cascade or hanging effect. This is done by pinching out the growing tip when the young plant is about 6 inches tall, then select one to three of the new shoots for leaders. Tie these to wire stakes set at a 45° angle and pinch back all side shoots to three leaves as they develop.

Wires are bent downward gradually each week, and no pinching is done after August. Wires are then replaced by a piece of chicken wire hanging down from the pot, and stems are tied in to give a good cascade effect. The stem should be handled carefully to avoid breaking. Plants should face south when hanging so that the flowers will show to best advantage. While you can train almost all mums to cascade, certain varieties are best suited to such training.

Propagation: Take cuttings from your plants in spring. Those which have just come up are ideal. Just cut them off, stick them in water. They'll root in two weeks and after that can be potted up in sand and peat moss mixture.

Troubles: Mildew (fuzzy white growth on foliage), avoid wetting the foliage. Dust with sulfur or Karathane. Aphids, spray with Malathion or aerosol can. Red spider mites spin webs on tips of shoots, cause yellowing of foliage. Spray with Kelthane. Nonflowering is due to late varieties being frosted before they have a chance to bloom. Can be made to flower out of season by use of black cloth. Florists shade the plants in late afternoon to shorten the daylight hours. By manipulating the amount of light the plants receive, it's possible to have mums flower any month of the year.

CINERARIA *(Senecio cruentus)*

This is the old florist plant sold at holiday times. Heads are showy and daisy-like, blue, red, pink and even white. A coarse plant that gobbles up water like mad. It also gives off ample moisture into the room, thus is beneficial in that respect.

Green Thumb Care: Needs daily watering, bright sunlight and cool room temperature, 50° to 60°. Needs 6 weeks of temperature below 60° for flowering. Soil, equal parts sand, peat and loam or perlite.

Propagation: Seed sown in summer, in sand and peat. After seedlings are up, transfer them to 3-inch pots of good soil mixture.

Troubles: Wilting due to lack of water; give good soaking daily. Aphids, cause sugary crystals, yellow foliage. Spray with Malathion or nicotine sulfate. Also white fly, cyclamen mite, leaf tier, cabbage looper and thrips; Malathion checks them all.

CLERODENDRUM *(C. thomsoniae)*

Glory bower or cashmere bouquet. A twiny shrub ideal for sun porch or small greenhouse. Grows best as a tubbed plant. Flowers are fragrant and handsome, crimson with large white calyx in branching racemes.

Green Thumb Tips: Likes a bright window; preferably a conservatory plant. Cool temperature (60°) and ample humidity. Soil should be well drained, ⅓ each of sand, peat and loam. Keep uniformly moist, except during winter when plant is dormant

Troubles: Red spider mites; spray with Kelthane.

COLUMNEA

A trailing plant with showy flowers borne in axils of leaves.

Green Thumb Tips: Likes a well-drained, humusy soil, half peat or compost and loam. Keep uniformly moist but never soggy wet. Temperature 72°.

Propagation: Seed sown in sand-peat mixture, given bottom heat. Also by cuttings rooted in sand in summer.

Troubles: Mealybugs; wash plant with old soft toothbrush, using soapy water plus Malathion.

CRINUM

A bulbous, evergreen plant flowering in white and shades of pink to rose red. Some crinums are non-evergreen.

Green Thumb Tips: A coarse grower, ideal for tubs on patios, sun porches. Likes cool room in winter (50°), when plant is dormant. At that time, give less water. In shirt-sleeve weather, move plant to patio, and keep soil uniformly moist. Feed liquid plant food once every 4 weeks. Soil should be well drained, using ⅓ each of sand, peat, loam mixture. In fall and winter, grow on dry side.

Propagation: Divide offsets every 3rd year, in fall.

Troubles: A large coarse grower, making it difficult to handle as pot or tub specimens.

CROSSANDRA *(C. infundibuliformis)*

Florist's pot plant which is catching on with the public. Plant is constantly in bloom, noted for tubular salmon-orange blossoms.

Crossandra

Green Thumb Tips: Prefers bright window, 72° temperature. Soil must be well drained, ⅓ each of sand, peat and loam, with vermiculite or peat moss added.

Propagation: Seeds sown in sand-peat mixture in 80° temperature.

Troubles: Non-blooming due to lack of light. Red spider mites; spray with Kelthane.

CROWN OF THORNS *(Euphorbia milii)*

Same family as the Christmas poinsettia. Plant resembles cactus, with thick stems which are covered with spines; leaves are small and unattractive.

Green Thumb Tips: Likes a bright window, well-drained soil, and essentially the same care as the Christmas poinsettia. Because plant resembles cactus, many erroneously treat it as such, withholding water until it shrivels. This is a wrong practice. Place plant outdoors in summer, in full sun and keep well watered. Bring indoors in fall and grow in cool bright window. If plant gets too much light in fall, flowering is delayed. Each day move to dark hall or cover with black cloth at 6 P.M. and removing at 8 A.M. next morning. (For culture of Christmas poinsettia, see poinsettia.)

Propagation: Cuttings rooted in moist sand.

Troubles: Dropping of buds due to dry air, dry soils or lack of light. Non-blooming due to too much light at night.

CYCLAMEN *(Cyclamen periscum giganteum)*

Shooting star plant. The florist's cyclamen is one of the showiest of all plants.

Green Thumb Tips: Likes lots of water. Grow in bright window and coolest room possible. At night it needs temperature of 50°. High day temperatures shorten life of plant, causing yellowing of foliage and blasting of buds. Water daily. If you happen to forget to water the plant, leaves and blooms will wilt. Don't panic. Once drooping sets in, place the plant in a pan of warm water for ½ hour; leaves will perk right up. Pull out spent blooms, rather then cutting them; reach down and pull up stem with quick jerk. After the plant has finished flowering, dry the corm by withholding water gradually until June. At that time, place pot in cellar and forget it until fall. Then scrape off upper two inches of soil and replace with a fresh mixture. You can grow the corm in the same

Shooting Star or Cyclamen

pot year after year. Just make sure the pot is large (8 inches) enough at the beginning.

In fall, before frost, bring the cyclamen indoors, water it and keep in a sunny window.

Propagation: Seed sown in sand-peat mixture. Takes the plant 18 months to flower from seed.

Troubles: Blasting of buds due to dry air, dry soil or cyclamen mites. Give plenty of moisture, grow in cool window, and if mites are a problem, spray with Kelthane. Yellowing of leaves due to lack of light.

CYRTANTHUS SPECIES

A newcomer that may become as popular as the common amaryllis. Flowers are yellow, white or orange-red. Foliage is smaller than, yet similar to, that of amaryllis. Greenhouse fragrant flowering plant of bulbous nature.

Green Thumb Tips: Same care as amaryllis (*hippeastrum*). Pot bulbs in October using 2 parts loam to one of sand and peat.

DEVIL'S TONGUE *(Hydrosme rivieri)*

Also commonly called voodoo lily, sacred lily of India, and even has a common "botanical" name of Amorphophallus. There is another voodoo bulb called Monarch of the East, *Sauromatum guttatum*, which is a different plant. Actually all these items are closely related and take the same culture. Don't be concerned with the botanical classification.

Green Thumb Tips: In summer place outdoors under a bush and keep it watered to encourage good foliage growth. Bring indoors in autumn before frost and dry top off, as you would caladium. Store pot in cellar at 60° temperature, without watering. In February or March, start watering tuber and place pot in bright window at 72° temperature. These plants should be watered sparingly at first. In fact, they often start best without much water. Buds start to open within 4 weeks and before long you'll have a maroon calla-like bloom with a repulsive odor. Flower is borne atop a long marble-like stem 4 feet high.

Propagation: Sever offsets from main tuber in fall and pot up.

Troubles: Weak stem; support with stake and avoid too much fertilizer. Drying of leaves due to dry air, dry soils.

EPISCIA (Red or Flame African Violet)

A handsome trailing greenhouse and houseplant that resembles the African violet except that it is vine-like or trailing, with bronze-green foliage and orange-red blooms. It's a striking plant, ideal for hanging baskets or growing on totem poles. Pronounced e-pisk-kee-ah or epy-see-a or e-pis-ee-a (last one most common).

Green Thumb Tips: Being a member of the gesneria (jes-nay-ree-ah) family, it has the same cultural requirements as the African violet. Prefers rich fibrous loam, mixed with peat, leaf mold and sand. Has same light requirements as the violet. Episcias are very touchy about being chilled and should never be exposed to temperatures less than 60°. Likes semi-sunny window. Feed liquid plant food once every 4 weeks. Water from top or bottom. Not as touchy about getting foliage wet as violets, but still prefers to have warm water. Make sure leaves are dry before night. Avoid dry rooms, lack of humidity will cause the buds to "just sit." Force stubborn buds to bloom by setting the pot in a tray of warm water. Treatment works fine for African violet also. Many home gardeners have tried to make a fortune crossing the episcia with African violet to produce a red-bloomed violet. The scarlet "African" violet is not any kind of an African violet. The genus *Episcia* is in the same family as the genus *Saintpaulia* African violet but they are still far apart, and genetically they are incompatible.

Propagation: Root single leaves in water, sand, or vermiculite, just like African violets. Mature plants send out frequent runners with little new plants on the ends. Cut these off and pot them in sand, peat and loam mix.

Troubles: Red spider mites, mealybugs, thrips; spray with Malathion.

ERVATAMIA

Common names: Crepe jasmine, fleur d'amour, butterfly gardenia, East Indian rose bay, Adam's apple and Nero's crown. Still listed also as *Tabernaemontana coronaria.*

Green Thumb Tips: An evergreen plant grown best in tubs. Bears waxy fragrant flowers in summer. After blooming, keep outdoors in shaded spot until fall, bring in before frost. Grow in bright window. Soil should be constantly moist the year round.

Propagation: Cuttings rooted in sand, any time of year.

Troubles: Drying around edges of foliage; dry air or dry soil.

EUCHARIS (Eucharis Lily)

This item has white flowers resembling the narcissus, blooming repeatedly in spring or winter.

Green Thumb Tips: Likes a sunny window and a cool temperature, 60°, in fall and winter. Use the ⅓ sand, ⅓ loam, ⅓ peat mixture, with pebbles in the bottom of pot for drainage. Keep soil uniformly moist, avoid overwatering from fall to spring. Blooming periods must be preceded by a dry cool rest in order to assure flowering.

Propagation: Seeds started in sand and peat in spring; give plenty of bottom heat for germination. Or, divide bulbs in spring every 4th year.

Troubles: Red spider mites; spray with Kelthane. Non-blooming due to dry soils.

FIRECRACKER PLANT (*Manettia bicolor*)

So-called because of tubular flowers borne on short stems and somewhat resembling firecrackers. There is also russelia which is very similar to manettia and takes much the same care.

Green Thumb Tips: Likes semi-shaded window, 72° and a well-drained soil. Use ⅓ sand, ⅓ loam and ⅓ peat mix.

Propagation: Tip cuttings rooted in sand in spring and summer. Mist foliage while rooting.

Troubles: Aphids and spider mites; spray with Malathion or Kelthane; also syringe plants from time to time in bath tub to keep down insects.

FLAME OF THE WOODS *(Ixora coccinea)*

A shrubby pot plant with red tubular flowers produced in abundance almost every month of the year.

Green Thumb Tips: Likes sunny to semi-sunny window, 72° temperature and a well-drained soil. Use standard mixture of ⅓ each of sand, peat and loam, with pebbles in bottom of pot for drainage.

Propagation: Cuttings in spring; set in sand or sand-peat. Provide bottom heat to hasten growth.

Troubles: None.

FLOWER OF A DAY *(Hibiscus rosa-sinensis)*

A close relative of the hardy rose of Sharon (*H. syriacus*) or althea, and the herbaceous perennial rose mallow, *H. moscheutos.* Chinese hibiscus or rose of China has blooms similar to those of hollyhock, single and double and many colors. (See Hibiscus).

FRANGIPANI *(Plumeria rubra)*

Frangipani or red jasmine is a summer flowering plant with fragrant pink, white or rose-purple blooms, excellent for tub specimens. Soil should be well drained, evenly moist from spring till fall. Place plant outdoors in summer. Before frost, bring indoors and keep soil barely moist until February; then water sufficiently to get plant to grow; place in bright window, temperature of 72°. Feed in winter, using liquid plant food such as Ra-pid-gro.

Propagation: Stem cuttings in spring or summer, root in moist sand.

Troubles: Red spider mites, spray with Kelthane; also syringe plant regularly!

FUCHSIA *(Fuchsia speciosa)*

Lady's eardrops or fuchsia is one of the most fascinating houseplants.

Bell-shaped pendulous flowers that can be pink, white, or violet, single or double.

Green Thumb Tips: Does not like hot temperatures. Above 65° in the home, plants will not flower at all. Grow in bright window and give uniform supply of water. Too much water or water standing at the roots will cause plants to wilt and never recover. After blooming indoors, set plant outdoors and give semi-shade or sun. They like it outdoors and should be fed regularly every 3 weeks. In fall, take cuttings from the parent and forget the old mother plant as it will be full of old wood.

Propagation: Starting cuttings in fall, spring or winter, in sand or sand-peat moss.

Troubles: Wilting due to excess watering. Flower drop due to high temperature or poor light. Aphids and white flies, spray with DDT or aerosol bombs. Mealybugs, rub cotton dipped in alcohol over the cottony masses.

Can be trained into a tree-type plant. Start with a straight-stemmed plant growing in a 10-inch pot. Remove side branches and tie the trunk to a wood stake. Continue to remove side branches until the growing tip reaches the top of the stake. When you get through you'll have a single trunk plant with leaves at the top only. Some gardeners fasten a circular wire frame at the top for support.

GARDENIA

Gardenia jasminoides or common florist's gardenia is one of the fussiest of all houseplants.

Temperature: The gardenia is a semi-tropical plant. That means it grows best in a warm, humid atmosphere and in a location that affords plenty of sunshine. During the winter months, give the plant a southern exposure where the temperature is 70° to 80° F. during the day. The night temperature should range between 62° and 65° F. If lower than this, the plants will grow slowly and the foliage is likely to become yellow-green. Temperatures at night above 65° seem to be partially responsible for the buds dropping—a common difficulty with gardenias. According to Cornell University, ANY CHANGE IN TEMPERATURE WILL CAUSE THE BUDS TO DROP.

Watering & Feeding: Regular watering is essential. Never let the plants grow dry. Occasional fertilizing is helpful. Use ammonium sulfate, 1 level teaspoonful in a quart of water. Apply one cupful of the solution to the soil once a month from March to November. Fertilizing during the dull, short days of the winter months is not recommended.

Summer Care: From June 1st to September 1st, gardenias may be handled outdoors in cold sections of the country. Plunge the pots to the rim in the ground in a location affording morning sunshine and afternoon shade. Care must be taken not to neglect watering during this period. If repotting is necessary, use a mixture of equal parts peat moss and good garden soil. Do not repot later than August 1st.

Propagation: Tip cuttings rooted in sand or sand and peat moss in summer.

Troubles: Yellowing of gardenia foliage may be caused by factors other than low temperature. A deficiency of iron in soils that are not acid in reaction will also cause yellow foliage. Soils that are not acid may be made so by scratching into the surface a small amount of any *one* of the following materials: iron sulfate, aluminum sulfate, or sulfur dust. Repeat at six week intervals.

A disease known as gardenia canker may also be responsible for yellow foliage. A portion of the stem becomes dead. There is no cure for this condition and the plant should be destroyed. Yellow foliage may also result from the activity of nematodes, minute worm-like organisms, that work inside the roots and produce knotted, swollen areas. Destroy the infested plants as there is no cure.

Mealybugs are the insect pests that most commonly plague gardenias, appearing as white, cottony masses in the leaf axils and other protected places. They are difficult to control. Patient washing of the plants with a soft cloth or sponge wet with plain water is helpful. Aphids may be troublesome at times. You can control them easily by using Malathion. Red spider mites may also cause trouble. Spray with Kelthane.

GERANIUMS (*Pelargonium*)

Geraniums are perhaps the most popular plant at Memorial Day and are being grown more and more as houseplants. *P. hortorum* is the florists' or zonal geranium, and has the brown-green foliage. It's the easiest of all geraniums to grow.

Trailing geraniums: If you're looking for a handsome plant for a hanging basket, you'll like the ivy geranium because of its trailing habit, glossy ivy-shaped leaves and bushels of blossoms. You can grow the ivy-leaved kind in semi-shade indoors and outside under overhangs where not many other plants do well. The flowers range from red, pink, lavender, to white. The soil for this geranium and all others should be well drained. Use our standby, ⅓ sand, ⅓ loam and ⅓ peat. A little vermiculite or perlite can be added to make the soil more porous.

Pelargonium peltatum Leopard

Geraniums cannot tolerate "wet feet" or poor drainage. This causes the leaves to turn yellow, also a result of overcrowding. While geraniums will tolerate dry soils, they flower earlier and better if given ample moisture.

Pinching the tip out of the vines from time to time will cause the plants to become bushy and bloom better. Grow plants in a bright window if you want the leaves to color up. In the shade, foliage remains a dark green. Hot, dry rooms and dry soils will cause the leaves to scorch around the edges. Keep the plants away from hot air registers, hot windows and be sure the soil gets a uniform supply of moisture.

Scented geraniums: Few things are more fascinating to gardeners than the scented-leaved geraniums. The old-fashioned rose geranium (*P. graveolens*) is the one most gardeners know best. Then there're the lemon-scented types, fruit- or spice-scented, the peppermint-scented and many others with pungent scents. There's even a pine-scented geranium to add interest to your collection. These items are less demanding and need less sun than do the regular geraniums. Actually their culture is about the same. Start new plants from slips rooted in plain tap water.

After rooting, pot them in mixture of ⅓ sand, peat and loam.

I'll name some sweet-scented geraniums for those of you who want to try your hand at raising these old-fashioned beauties.

The rose-scented group (*Pelargonium graveolens*) has deeply cut foliage and lavender blooms.

Oak-leaf group (*P. quercifolium*) has a pungent scent and showy pink blooms.

The peppermint group (*P. tomentosum*) has large soft, deeply-cut foliage.

The pine-scented type (*P. denticulatum*) has deeply-cut leaves, pink blooms.

The apple, nutmeg and old-spice group (*P. fragrans*) has smaller leaves and a strong scent.

The lemon-scented group (*P. crispum*) has small ruffled leaves and pink blooms.

Culture for these is practically the same as for other geraniums. They need plenty of light for bud formation, a loose well-drained soil and a good house temperature.

Green Thumb Tips: Indoors, geraniums like a cool temperature, 55° to 65°. The time-honored practice of growing them on the dry side is erroneous. Give them plenty of water. Grown with ample water, the plants flower earlier and produce better blooms and foliage than those grown dry throughout their life. Plants grow best in full sun. Too much shade and high temperatures cause spindly growth. You can correct the growth habit of geraniums by pinching out the tips of the growing shoots, or you can prune the stems back to force new growth. Pinching back leggy plants is a common practice which results in nice bushy growth, although it does cause the plants to flower later. Failure to flower is due to a lack of light, improper feeding, low moisture content of the soil, or excessive pinching. Browning around the edges is often due to a shortage of plant food, especially potash. You can correct this plant food shortage by scratching a little 5-10-5 fertilizer into the soil surface, or by applying liquid plant food (23-19-17). If the leaves of your geranium turn brown and drop off, it may be due to dry atmosphere, lack of water, too much water or too much fertilizer. Indoors, geraniums will not blossom if temperature is too high. Ideal temperature is around 50° to 60°. It is difficult to grow the Martha Washington type in the home because high temperatures often prevent flowers from forming. Geraniums are a bedding plant, and they all do best when grown outdoors in full sun. In a heated room with a diffused light the growth becomes soft and plants become spindly. All geraniums need lots of light, but they'll do well in a bright cool window.

Geraniums like a loamy soil, well drained with plenty of humus. Bone meal is OK or sprinkle some 5-10-5 fertilizer in the soil; ⅓ sand, ⅓ loam, and ⅓ peat or compost is a good mix.

A tree geranium supported by a green
stake. The variety is Enchantress Fiat.

Wintering Over: Geraniums are one of the most useful plants for the
porch and window box, cemetery urns and bedding plants. Gardeners
who use plenty of them each spring need not pay 70 cents or more per
plant, if they're willing to nurse along their own plants each winter.
Here are a few tricks gardeners passed along to me for increasing
geranium plants each spring:

Hanging upside down: Digging up plants in fall and hanging them upside down by roots is an old-fashioned method for saving geraniums.
Some cellars are too dry but you can get around that by encasing the
plants in plastic bag (with a few air holes in it) and adding some peat
or moist sphagnum. It takes a tiny amount of moisture to keep the
plants alive during winter. About 2 times a month you can add a tiny
amount of moisture. Some people soak a rag in water and slide this
inside the bag once a month or so. Sometimes they even bloom in the
bag! In March you take the plants down, soak them in a pail of water
for half an hour, cut the tops back and pot them up in ⅓ sand, ⅓ peat
and ⅓ loam.

Cut plants back: Cut your potted plants back and store them in a
bright cellar or attic window, sun parlor or kitchen window, where the
temperature is as cool as possible. Geraniums prefer a cool temperature,
around 55 to 60°. Keep the soil moistened and let the plants grow as
houseplants. If they start to get leggy, just cut the top back (root it,

too!). Yellowing of leaves and drying of foliage can mean too high a room temperature, dry soil or a lack of light. When spring comes the plants can be shortened a bit and set outdoors where they'll produce scads of buds and blooms.

Storing plants in tubs: Many gardeners store geraniums in tubs filled with peat. Pots are set in the peat which is kept moist and tub is kept in a bright cellar or attic window, or sun parlor. Attics which do not freeze make a fine place for geraniums in winter. DO NOT FORGET TO WATER THEM A LITTLE. The old mother plants can be brought indoors and forced to bloom again all winter if you trim back the tops. Then in spring, set the plants outdoors in beds, boxes or urns. They can be left in pots which are set in the soil. In fact, geraniums do just as well outdoors in pots as in the ground without pots. Cutting back the tops in spring seems like a brutal operation but you'll be surprised to see how quickly new growth appears. Even the dead stalks you see when plants are hung in plastic bags will send forth new growth in full light and with ample moisture. Your plants may not be as shapely as florist's geraniums in spring, but they'll catch up fast when planted out.

Propagation: Take cuttings from healthy mother plants in the fall. These should be 3 to 4 inches long. Cut can be made anywhere on the branch. Take all leaves off lower half (they'll only rot) and insert cuttings into rooting material. Clean sharp sand, vermiculite or perlite, or just plain tap water are used for rooting. If you use purchased rooting materials make sure holes are in the bottom of the pot or box to provide drainage for excess water. Place cuttings into rooting material to a depth of one inch to hold cutting upright. Cuttings are watered well and kept moist, but not too wet, until rooted. A 6- to 8-inch clay florist pot makes a good "greenhouse;" and to keep cuttings fresh, place the container with cuttings into a plastic bag and close the top. The plastic bag reduces water loss, hastens rooting. Keep cuttings out of direct sunlight. They'll root in 3 or 4 weeks.

After rooting, pot the cuttings up in 3- or 4-inch clay pots, using a ⅓ sand, ⅓ peat and ⅓ loam mixture. Grow the plants in a bright, cool window and keep the soil moist. If the cutting starts to get a bit tall, pinch the tip back to get a bushier plant. Feed them once a month with Ra-pid-gro, and make sure they get plenty of light. Other garden plants can also be started the same way—coleus, fuchsia, begonia, ageratum, dusty miller, bloodleaf, vinca, patience or sultana. These can be used with geraniums for your window or porch box next spring. Plants started from cuttings will be a better size for the home and will adjust to house conditions more readily than if you bring the entire mother plant indoors. A final word: If your cuttings rot in sand, it may be due to the fungus disease blackleg. To control this, sterilize the sand by pouring boiling water over it and allow to cool.

You can get nice plants from seed, either purchased from a good firm or from your own plants. Seed is gathered in late summer and stored so you can sow in May. Seed germinates in 2 weeks, produces flowering plants in 4 to 6 months. Scatter the seed in a sandy mixture, using sand, leaf mold and loam. Cover the seed with thin layer of sand, or firm it with your hand or block of wood. Keep in a room at 60° temperature. When seedlings are large enough to handle, move them to small pots. You can make a very simple propagating pot, using a large pot and a small one, as shown in the photograph. You can root cuttings or start new plants in these pots of sand.

Troubles: If geraniums make good growth but no blooms, chances are the soil is too rich in nitrogen. Avoid heavy feeding with too much nitrogen. Sometimes when plants fail to bloom it's due to botrytis blight, associated with wet, damp weather. Botrytis attacks all parts of the plant. Spores spread mainly by splashing water and air currents. Control: Remove all dead leaves and burn. Keep all infected flower heads picked and burn. Give good ventilation; keep plants dry. Avoid sprinkling the foliage. Spray with Zineb or Captan, 1 teaspoon to a gallon of water, applied weekly.

Bacterial stem rot: Troubles the leaves. Look for large yellow to brown spots which cause death of leaf from the margins inward. Control: Grow plants in cool window. Spreads by water, cutting knife or fingers.

Verticillium wilt: causes leaves to wilt, wither and die. Control: None.

Pythium (blackleg): These plants have shiny, coal-black, slimy, wet appearance. Rot develops fast and plants die within a week. Control: Disease is spread by infected rooting and potting materials. Bake soil before rooting and potting geraniums.

Rhizoctonia: A soil-borne fungus that attacks plants at soil line, causing brown lesions or cankers on stem. Stems are completely girdled, rot and entire plant dies. Control: Sterilize soil by baking in oven at 180° to 190° for half an hour. Avoid overwatering.

Viruses: A number of viruses affect geraniums but to date no cure has been found.

Sometimes red spider, white flies and mealybugs are troublesome. Spray with Malathion, 1 teaspoon to a quart of water. Oedema causes water-soaked corky eruptions on lower leaf surface in cool, dark, cloudy weather. Keep foliage dry and it will disappear in warm weather. Control: Take cuttings from healthy plants. Root them in sand treated with boiling water, and repot in soil that is well drained. Don't grow in plastic or glazed pots. Clay is best for drainage.

GLORIOSA LILY (*Rothschildiana*)

Climbing lily or glory lily, blooms in spring or summer, rests, and blooms again in fall and winter.

Green Thumb Tips: Bright window, humusy soil, well drained. Prefers uniform supply of water during growing season, less water after flowering has stopped. Plants need trellis or wires to climb on.

Propagation: Cut tubers in spring and pot into 4-inch pots of sand, loam and peat mix. Also by seeds in winter. Sow in loose mixture.

Troubles: None.

GLORY BOWER (*Clerodendron fragrans pleniflorum*)

Sometimes listed as cashmere bouquet, or bleeding heart vine. Flowers, white or pale pink, 1 inch across, resemble the hydrangea and grow on twining vines. Grow as potted or tub plant in sun parlor or small greenhouse. Flowers are fragrant.

Green Thumb Tips: Likes soil loose and well drained. Keep cool in winter and grow in sunny or semi-shaded window. Plant is dormant in winter so avoid heavy feeding or watering then.

Propagation: Cuttings taken in summer and rooted in sand or water.

Troubles: Red spider mites, spray with Kelthane and syringe with tepid water. Non-blooming due to lack of light. Move to bright window.

GLOXINIA (*Sinningia*)

The common name of gloxinia will never change although it should be correctly called sinningia. Our modern hybrids are a great improvement over the old gloxinia and some will bloom all year long without the required rest period. *Sinningia speciosa* are improved forms advertised as *gloxinia hybrida grandiflora*.

The so called slipper-type gloxinias are a different group of present-day hybrids. These include the white slipper flowers (*Sinningia eumorpha*), a miniature (*S. pusilla*) with half-inch lavender flowers on 1-inch stems, and there's one with maroon-green leaves and reddish-purplish flowers.

GLOXINIA, HARDY (*Incarvillea*)

This is a hardy garden plant, blooming from June through July. It belongs to the *Bignoniacea* family and is useful in the garden border. It's not a gloxinia but is listed here because so many gardeners grow it as a gloxinia. Flowers are trumpet-shaped, 2 inches across, and resemble the indoor potted gloxinia. Foliage resembles the fern rather than that of the indoor gloxinias. This plant is hardy enough to stay outdoors in winter, although we've grown them indoors with fair success. The slipper gloxinias have scads of white or lavender slipper flowers and to me are much showier than the common gloxinia. These are tender and grown only as a houseplant.

Green Thumb Tips: Start the tuber in a pot of humusy soil containing compost, sharp sand, woods soil, muck, perlite or vermiculite. The secret is to start with a loose soil. Add some broken charcoal to sweeten the mixture. Pot them up in the spring and water them cautiously, until roots and leaves become established. Too much water at potting time may cause the tubers to rot.

If your gloxinias grow tall and spindly, they are not getting enough light. However, these plants do need shade from direct sunlight. Although related to the African violet, they need more light than their cousins. Gloxinias will grow into well-rounded, bushy plants. Turn the plants every 2 or 3 days to prevent one side from stretching out farther than the other for the sun.

Propagation: Start from seeds sown any time of the year in sand-peat mixture. Also by leaf cuttings. Insert leaf stalk (petiole) in a glass of plain tap water or in box of moist sand. After roots are formed and a tiny tuber is produced at the stem end, pot the rooted leaf in a loose soil mixture. It will go into a rest period, so allow the leaf to die down and withhold water until signs of growth are apparent. You can also start new plants by dividing the tubers.

GLOXINIA, CREEPING (*Asarina erubescens*)

Creeping gloxinia is a misnomer since this is not a gloxinia, although it does have trumpet flowers.

Green Thumb Tips: Light soil with ample peat is best. Uniform moisture. Does well in semi-shaded window.

Propagation: Start by seed or cutting in vermiculite, perlite or plain tap water.

GLOXINERA

Gloxinera is a hybrid which requires the same care as *Sinningia*. A question we receive repeatedly from gloxinera fanciers is: "What makes the buds blast?" There are several reasons for this.

Buds that suddenly shrivel and turn brown without developing is a common complaint among growers of lilies, gloxinias, geraniums and other plants. We used to think it was due mainly to botrytis disease, but there are other causes for the death of well-developed flower buds: root injury from dry soil or too much fertilizer, root rot, poor light, crowding, high temperature, or rapid changes in temperature. Bud blast is common when plants are dry during the period of bud formation.

Green Thumb Tips: Keep the soil of your plants moist at all times. One drying when the buds are forming can cause bud blast.

Most houseplants like a well-drained soil and you can't beat the basic mixture for houseplants—⅓ sand, ⅓ loam and ⅓ peat moss. You can add perlite or vermiculite to this in place of sand, or use it with sand.

Also botrytis, a gray mold fungus, causes buds to blast. The disease is associated with poor ventilation and too much moisture. Uniform soil moisture and ample humidity will do a lot to prevent buds from blasting or drying up. Where botrytis is present, ventilate often and dust with Fermate.

Some growers have trouble with buds "sitting still". This can be corrected by increasing the humidity around each plant. Set the plant inside a large pot, and pack peat moss between the two pots. The wet peat moss gives off enough moisture to open the buds. Also, since gloxinias are rather fast growers, you can move them along by feeding them superphosphate, 1 teaspoonful to a gallon of water. Water the plants with this solution. The phosphorous encourages fast bud formation and often helps overcome stubborn, mulish buds which won't budge.

When the leaves curl and get floppy, it's usually a sign of too much water. After the plants finish blooming, reduce the amount of water you give them until the leaves die down. Gloxinia leaves die down after flowering. Then store the plants (leave the bulbs in the soil) in the cellar.

Troubles: If thrips or aphids bother plants, spray with DDT or nicotine sulfate, 1 teaspoonful to 2 quarts of water (warm & soapy). If crown rot or bulb rot sets in, keep the moisture content down.

HABRANTHUS *(H. brachyandrus)* Rain Lily

Green Thumb Tips: Plant will flower several times during the year. Likes a sunny window, cool temperature and a soil mixture of ⅓ each of sand, peat and loam. Do not overwater. Drying out between waterings seems to be what this item prefers.

Propagation: Divide offsets any time and grow in 4-inch pots of sand and peat.

HAEMANTHUS (Blood Lily)

One of the showiest blood lilies is *H. katherinae*, bearing showy salmon-red flowers, clustered in a large ball, in May and June. Leaves are ever-green and handsome.

Green Thumb Tips: Grow in sunny window while buds are forming, move to semi-shaded window to increase life of flowers. Best soil is ⅓ sand, peat and loam with chipped charcoal, gravel or pieces of pots in bottom. Must have good drainage. We grow our bulbs in 6-inch clay pots. During fall or winter rest period, scrape off the upper inch or two of soil and add a new layer. Yearly repotting is not advised. Add a spoonful of bone meal to each pot of soil.

Propagation: Divide offsets in fall and replant in small pots.

Troubles: Rotting or lack of bloom due to poor drainage. Leaves develop red spider mites. Spray with Kelthane. Excessive number of leaves is from too much nitrogen. Feed only when in active leaf growth.

HOYA *(Hoya Carnosa)* Wax or Parlor Plant

This oldtime favorite is related to the milkweed (*Asclepia*) and is a real challenge to indoor gardeners

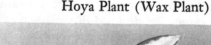

Hoya Plant (Wax Plant)

Green Thumb Tips: Prefers ⅓ sand-peat-loam mixture or 1 part each of peat, perlite and fir bark. Plant needs to be pretty much potbound to bloom well, therefore do not overpot it (that is, don't use too large a pot). Feed it liquid plant food in summer, fall and early winter, but not in mid or late winter as a partial rest is needed.

Needs full sun (won't bloom in shade) and good drainage. Give it plenty of moisture in summer, spring and fall, but in winter keep it on the dry side. Best temperature in winter is 50° to 55° at night and 60° to 65° in daytime.

Propagation: Take tip cuttings in spring and root in pots of sand or layer the plant any time. (See Plant Propagation.)

Troubles: Failure to flower due to lack of light. Needs bright window for buds. Plants are naturally slow to flower, takes 3 or 4 years before they will blossom. If yours won't bloom, even in full sun, allow plant to become potbound. This will force it into blooms. Too large a pot will discourage blooming.

Red spider mites cause mottling of foliage. Spray with Kelthane. Mealybugs, thrips and aphids, spray with Malathion.

HELIOTROPE (*Arborescens*)

Many gardeners pot the heliotrope from the garden in summer and grow it indoors in winter, planting it outdoors again the following summer. It makes a good hanging-basket item or can be shaped into a tree. For winter-blooming indoors, keep the plant pinched back, grow in a sunny window and give uniform supply of moisture. In fall, after the plant has finished its outdoor growing season, take it up and grow it in a bright window. Prune back any long branches from time to time. To grow a heliotrope tree, start new plant from seed or use a slip from the parent plant. Remove the bottom leaves and train the branch to a stake as it grows up.

Propagation: Start seeds in sand and peat in winter or spring, or by tip cuttings rooted in sand.

Troubles: Red spider mites and white flies; spray with Kelthane outdoors for spider mites and Malathion for white flies.

HIBISCUS (*Rosa-Sinensis*)

Chinese hibiscus or rose of China, *H. rosa-sinensis*, makes a fine indoor item. Related to the rose of Sharon (*H. syriacus*) and the perennial rose mallows (*H. moscheutos*).

Green Thumb Tips: Full sun is needed for buds. Plants need ample water to prevent bud drop. Flowers last for few hours, but new ones keep coming on. Plants are everblooming. Soil should be well drained and uniformly moist. If plants get too tall, pinch the tips back, and root the cuttings in water or moist sand.

Propagation: Seeds in sand-peat, or root cuttings.

Troubles: Bud drop due to dry soils and dry air, a common difficulty in the mallow family, of which hibiscus *rosa-sinensis* is a member.

HYDRANGEA (Florist's Hydrangea)

Greenhouse Hydrangea: The common greenhouse hydrangea, also called "florist's hydrangea" or French hydrangea (*H. macrophylla*), is the one hydrangea we receive most inquiries about. There are white-flowered varieties, also pink and blue, color depending on soil acidity. Plants growing in an alkaline soil will have pink flowers; an acid soil will produce blue flowers. Plants in soils of intermediate acidities develop unpleasant mixtures of muddy pinkish and bluish flowers.

Green Thumb Tips: It's easy to change the color of your blooms. Blue blooms can be had by watering plants with alum, at rate of one teaspoonful to a gallon of water, or you can use aluminum sulfate, three ounces to a gallon of water. If you want pink flowers, add limestone to the soil. You can't make the white-flowered hydrangea change color because it lacks coloring pigment.

This Easter hydrangea likes a light window and plenty of water. Don't be alarmed if the leaves and blooms wilt from lack of water. The plant will spruce right up if you submerge the pot in a pail of water for 30 minutes or so. After your plant finishes flowering, the tops should be pruned back to two or three inches, and the plant repotted. In May, plunge the plant, pot and all, in a semi-shady spot in the garden. Leave there all summer. In September, bring plant in and keep in a cool place, water occasionally. All the leaves may fall, but don't be alarmed. In January, put the plant in a warm sunny room and water it frequently, giving it a spoonful of common fertilizer.

Propagation: Stem cuttings rooted in sand.

Troubles: Unlike the hills-of-snow hydrangeas, the florist's hydrangea blooms on wood of the previous season. The flower buds originate near the tips of the canes formed. This hydrangea must be pruned right after blooming; later pruning removes the flower buds and gets no flowers. Spring is the best time to move these.

Cold injury is another reason why the florist's hydrangea does not bloom outdoors. In many areas, the stems freeze or are injured enough to destroy the flower buds for the next season. Suggestion: Build a small rack of poles around your hydrangea outdoors and wrap burlap around it, filling insides with leaves. Or you can cover with a bushel basket—anything to protect the buds.

Another trick is to dig up the plant in fall, bring it indoors and store in the cellar, near a fairly bright window. Keep it slightly watered during the winter, and in spring, when warm weather rolls around, set the plant outdoors where it will bloom freely for you. The cellar treatment prevents the buds from winterkilling.

If the leaves of your hydrangea get yellow or mottled, it means the soil is too alkaline or sweet. Add aluminum sulfate to reduce the soil acidity to pH of 6.5 or so. Sometimes the hydrangea stops flowering after blooming for 2 or 3 years. This may also be due to heavy shade, poor soil, too much nitrogen, bad pruning, winter injury. Do not prune your florist's hydrangea in spring or fall—but immediately after blooming (about late July). By the way, you cannot make the outdoor hydrangeas turn colors by adding the above-mentioned chemicals—just the greenhouse or French hydrangea. The greenhouse hydrangea gets its colors due to pesence of aluminum in the tissues. Rusty nails, etc. have no effect on colors. Use aluminum sulfate solution, 5 to 8 times at weekly intervals.

Hydrosme *(H. rivieri)*

Voodoo lily, sacred lily of India, see Devil's Tongue.

Hylocereus *(H. unadatus)*

One of the large red-flowered night-blooming cacti (see Cactus).

Ice Plant *(Aptenia cordifolia)*

A hanging-basket plant, commonly called ice plant. Another genus, *Mesembryanthemum*, is also one of the ice plants. All have daisy-like flowers blooming in spring and summer.

Green Thumb Tips: Prefers a bright sunny window, well-drained soil, uniformly moist. Another so-called "ice plant" is Lampranthus.

Troubles: None.

Impatiens (Impatience Plant)

Impatiens holstii and *I. sultanii* ideal for indoor pot plants and hanging baskets.

Green Thumb Tips: Does fine in sunny or semi-shady window. Soil should be well drained and full of peat moss.

Propagation: Take cuttings and root them in sand or plain tap water. Also by seed in sand-peat mixture.

Troubles: Red spider mites cause yellowing or mottling of foliage. Spray with Kelthane, or syringe foliage in bath tub weekly. Aphids cause honeydew secretion. Spray with Malathion. Sometimes the sugary crystals on leaf edges are from the leaf secretions, not insects. Wash them off with soap and water.

JASMINUM *(Jasminum grandiflorum)*

Jasmines are touchy houseplants grown for their fragrant flowers.

Green Thumb Tips: Does best in a bright or sunny window, soil mixture of ⅓ each sand, peat and loam. Treat as you would gardenia.

Propagation: Tip cuttings rooted in sand in summer.

Troubles: Bud drop due to changes in temperature. Yellowing of foliage due to lack of acidity. Add a pinch of sulfur to soil to correct it. Red spider mites, spray with Kelthane.

Another plant, known as night jessamine (*Cestrum nocturnum*), has wonderful fragrance from its tubular white flowers. Its care is similar to the jasmine, semi-sunny window, soil mixture of sand, peat and loam, uniform supply of moisture. Pinch plant back at tips to keep it from getting scraggly. Start new plants by rooting in sand.

JERUSALEM CHERRY *(Solanum pseudo-capsicum)*

Christmas pot plant of the florist trade. Prized for orange fruit, size of a sweet cherry, NOT edible, very poisonous.

Green Thumb Tips: Bright window, night temperature 50°, day time 72°. Uniform supply of water at all times. After flowering, continue to water plant, keep in bright window. Set outdoors in bright spot in garden for summer. Cut plant back about half and keep it watered until fall when it should be brought indoors and kept cool for a week or so. Then move to bright window for fruits to form.

Propagation: Seeds saved from fruits and planted in spring. Also by cuttings rooted in sand.

Troubles: Leaf drop and fruit drop due to age of plant, poor light, too much water, or even dry soil. Aphids, mealybugs, and red spider mites, spray with Malathion and Kelthane. Syringe plant in summer.

Joseph's coat (Miniature)

Alternanthera bettzickiana, a close relative to the outdoor Joseph's coat (*Amaranthus tricolor*), see Foliage Plants section.

Kalanchoe (Kalen'-*ko*-ee)

K. blossfeldiana is the variety sold by florists at Christmastime.

Green Thumb Tips: Full sun for flower formation. Will grow in shade but produce nothing except green leaves. Florists force plant to flower by covering it with black cloth at 6 P.M. and removing cloth at 8 A.M. following day, starting in September and continuing for four weeks. Keep soil moist, but not saturated. Care after blooming makes a good foliage plant. Will not flower again indoors due to high temperature and lack of light.

Propagation: By leaf or tip cuttings. Place leaf on soil surface and rooting will take place. Also by tip cuttings in sand. Seed in sand-peat mixture.

Kohleria amabile

KOHLERIA (*Kohleria amabilis*)

Still listed incorrectly as *Isoloma hirsutum*. Decorative orange-red, tubular blooms.

Green Thumb Tips: Produces scaly rhizomes similar to those of achimenes. Plant in loose soil, mixture of sand, peat and perlite or vermiculite. Likes warm temperatures and bright window. After flowering, dry off and store in cool basement, watered just enough to keep it alive. Allow to rest for winter.

Propagation: Division of scale rhizomes. Nearly constant bloom can be maintained by keeping a rotation of cuttings in a pot or basket.

Troubles: None.

LANTANA (*Lantana camara*)

Common lantana makes a fine hanging-basket item, valuable for green foliage and lavender blossoms. Foliage rough, like sandpaper. There's also a weeping lantana (*L. montevidensis*) which is much better for the house than the plain *Lantana camara*.

Green Thumb Tips: Needs good light. Soil well drained, equal parts of sand, peat and loam. Soil must not be soggy. May turn out to be a poor houseplant if you don't give it a bright window. After plant finishes flowering, cut it back and plant outdoors in the border.

Propagation: Start new plants from cuttings any time of the year.

Troubles: Mealybugs and white flies, spray with Malathion, top and bottom of foliage.

LILY, JACOBEAN (*Sprekelia formosissima*)

This is a member of the amaryllis family and is not a true lily nor an orchid, but sometimes called orchid lily because of the shape of the flower.

Green Thumb Tips: Grow in bright window 72°. Water well to get good growth in summer. In fall, bring indoors before frost. Dry off foliage and keep in same pot in cellar for winter. Store at 60° all winter.

Propagation: Divide bulbs in spring prior to planting.

Troubles: None.

Lily, Easter (*Lilium longiflorum eximium*)

Common Easter lily or Bermuda lily.

Green Thumb Tips: Likes lots of water. Make sure drainage is good. Sometimes the florist's pot will not let water drain through the bottom. Punch hole in foil at bottom for drainage. Place in bright, cool window. Remove the yellow floral parts (male elements or anthers) to keep the white blooms from becoming soiled with yellow pollen. This also helps to make the blooms last longer. After the plant has finished blooming, plant it (pot removed) in the garden and leave it permanently. You may be surprised to find it will bloom again for you in fall. Don't attempt to force the Easter lily to bloom again indoors.

Propagation: Dig up every 3 or 4 years and separate bulbs. Or plant seed.

Troubles: Yellowing of foliage due to age of plant, overwatering, lack of light, high room temperature. Plant lice (aphids), spray with Malathion or use aerosol spray can.

Lily of the Valley (*Convallaria majalis*)

This hardy item is forced indoors by florists who use the sweet-scented flowers for weddings.

Green Thumb Tips: You buy the "pips" (storage buds) from your local florist or you can dig plants in the fall. Plant in sand-peat mixture and store at 32° for 3 weeks, keep soil uniformly watered, and give them ample humidity. Then place in bright window at temperature about 72°. Some florists keep the pips covered with plastic sheets in a dark room for the 3-week period. Florists buy the roots already "storage-treated", ready to grow. Care after flowering: Continue to water and feed, keep in a bright window. When warm weather comes, plant them outdoors in permanent spot.

Troubles: None.

Maple, Flowering (*Abutilon*)

Sometimes called parlor maple, this item is prized for its hollyhock-like blooms of orange, pink, white, red or salmon. This is not a true maple, but gets its name from its maple-like leaf. A shrub-like plant of graceful habit. *Abutilon megapotamicum variegatum* has small leaves with ivory to yellow variegation and small pendulous flowers, lemon-yellow with a lantern-like red calyx. It's an ideal hanging-basket plant.

Green Thumb Tips: Flowering maple is apt to get tall if you don't prune back. A fast grower, it requires repotting at least once a year. Does best in sunny window and in a ⅓ sand, peat and loam mixture. Keep soil uniformly moistened.

Propagation: Take tip cuttings and root them in sand any time. Also by seed, grown in sand-peat mixture.

Troubles: Red spider mites, spray with Kelthane. If grown outdoors, syringe plant with hose.

MORNING GLORIES *(Ipomoea horsfalliae)*

Did you know that you can grow morning glories indoors and get scads of blooms from them? If you sow the seed in a pot full of sand, peat and loam, you'll have blossoms within two months. You'll need a wooden trellis or strings to support the vines in a south window where they'll bloom profusely against a background of snow outdoors. Morning glory seed has a tough coat on it, and you'll get quicker germination if you soak seed first in warm water for 24 hours, or nick the tough coat with a file, just enough to show a speck of white meat inside.

Troubles: Red spider mites cause yellowing of foliage. Spray with Kelthane. Poor drainage also a cause of yellowed foliage.

NERINE (Guernsey Lily—*Nerine sarniensis*)

A handsome group of flowering bulbs noted for their show from fall to winter. Flowers, in red, salmon or scarlet shades, are borne on long spikes.

Green Thumb Tips: Likes sunny window, cool temperature (60°). Well-drained soil, sand, peat and loam, with perlite or vermiculite added. Repot in autumn, leave neck of bulb ⅓ above soil. Go easy on water after repotting. Apply just enough to keep moist. When buds show, keep soil uniformly moistened. Feed Ra-pid-gro, 1 teaspoon to a quart of water, once every 3 weeks in fall, winter and spring. In May, place pot outdoors, let it dry and go dormant. In August repot or remove one inch of top soil and replace with fresh mixture, fortified with peat.

Propagation: Divide offsets and repot in 4-inch pots in fall. Repot every 3rd year.

Troubles: None.

NERIUM *(Nerium oleander)*

Rose bay or common oleander, *(Nerium oleander)*, is an evergreen, grown as a tubbed plant indoors in winter. This item has a poisonous juice in the leaves, and children should be warned against chewing the foliage. Flowers come in white, pink, reddish and purple, sometimes double forms. Flowers poisonous to eat, also.

Green Thumb Tips: In warm weather, place outdoors in full sunshine. Keep the foliage syringed, and plants watered. In September bring indoors and keep in bright window. They need full sun to bloom. They prefer a rather rich soil for abundance of blooms. A good mixture is ⅓ sand, ⅓ peat, ⅓ loam. Repot anytime during the summer. If your plant grows too tall, nip the tips back to shape and size desired.

In September bring indoors and place in brightest window. Do not keep soil too wet, just uniformly moist. They bloom anytime from February to May, so in February start giving the plant more water and apply a liquid feeding.

Propagation: In summer you can start new plants from slips in sand. Keep moist constantly, cover with glass in cold frame or use a glass-covered box. Some gardeners start slips in water and pot them up in soil when rooted. (See Plant Propagation)

Troubles: Failure to flower can be due to lack of sunlight. Oleander needs plenty of sun for flower-bud formation. After plants have flowered, cut them back to encourage new growth. Do not prune hard. During early winter a rest period is desirable; that is, not too much water and no plant food. Water just enough to keep stems moist or flower buds will drop. Don't forget to set the plants outdoors in summer in full light.

Aphids, scale and mealybugs are a problem. Spray with Malathion, and in winter syringe foliage in a bathtub to keep pests away.

ORCHIDS

Although the air in most homes is dry, it's still possible to grow orchids whose natural home is moist jungles. The secret is to start out with the easy types such as the cattleyas (lavender and white florist's orchid) or the long-lasting cypripedium. Some orchids you'll find in current literature include: Brassavola (lady of the night); Cattleya, Cycnoches (swan orchid); Epidendrum (scarlet orchid); Odontoglossum (tiger orchid); Oncidium (butterfly orchid); Paphiopedilum (lady slipper); and Phalaenopsis (moth orchid).

Russell Mott, in charge of the Conservatory at Cornell University, has supplied me with much information on orchid culture. Here are

Cypripedium Orchid   Phalaenopsis Orchid, easy to grow

some easy-to-grow orchids Mr. Mott recommends for the home gardener who wants to grow orchids indoors.

KIND	COLOR	TYPE	TIME OF BLOOM
Brassacola Nodosa	White	Spray	Variable
Cattleya Bowringiana	Dark Purple	Cluster	Fall
C. Dowiana	Yellow	Corsage	Summer
C. Labiata	Rose Lilac	Corsage	Winter
C. Mossiae	Dark Purple	Corsage	Spring
C. Skinneri	Dark Purple	Cluster	Spring
C. Trianaei	Light Purple	Corsage	Winter
Dendrobium Phalaenopsis	Purple	Spray	Fall & Winter
Epidendrum Atropurpureum	Tan, White & Pink	Corsage	Spring & Summer
E. Ciliare	Yellow Green	Spray	Winter
E. Cochleatum	Mahogany & Green	Spray	Variable
E. Fragrans	Cream	Spray	Summer & Fall
E. Stamfordianum	Yellow & Crimson	Spray	Spring
E. Tampense	White, Green & Lavender	Spray	Summer
Laelia Anceps	Purple	Spray	Fall & Winter
Oncidium Ornithorhynchum	Rose & Purple	Spray	Winter
O. Varicosum Rogersii	Yellow	Spray	Winter
Phalaenopsis (Hybrids)	White & Pink	Spray	Variable

Kind	Color	Type	Time of Bloom
Rodriguezia Secunda	Rose	Spray	August
R. *Venusta*	White & Pink	Spray	Variable
Vanda Gilbert Triboulet (Hybrid)	Blue & Purple	Spray	Variable
Vanda Herziana (Hybrid)	Purple & Blue	Spray	Variable
Vanda Rothschildiana (Hybrid)	Blue	Spray	Variable

Cattleyas (florist orchid) are plants of tropical origin and in nature are accustomed to a wet and a dry season. During the wet season, the plants make their new leaves and pseudo-bulbs; in the dry season, the plants are resting. Flowering occurs during the rest period just before new growth commences. To assure annual flowering, the plant must have these periods of rest and growth.

When the rest period comes to an end, new shoots and roots appear at the base of the pseudo-bulb. Growth should be encouraged by gradually increasing the amount of water supplied to the plant. When growth is completed, a new pseudo-bulb and leaf will have been formed. A thin leaf-like sheath appears at the top of the pseudo-bulb where it is joined to the leaf. This is the flower sheath. At this time, the plant is more or less dormant and requires water only when the potting mixture becomes very dry. But as soon as a bud appears with the sheath, gradually increase the watering until the flower is fully open. Once the flower opens, water the plant less frequently until a new shoot appears. Caution: Never allow the potting mixture to become dry enough during the rest period to cause a shriveling of the leaves of the pseudo-bulb.

Watering: Do not overwater any orchid. Either too much or too little water is detrimental, but overwatering causes the greatest harm. Plants do best when given a quick dipping rather than a soaking. Allow the fiber to become dry between each watering to encourage proper aeration about the root system. A light overhead spray with an atomizer is beneficial. A good point to keep in mind is that orchid plants do not all have the same water requirements. Also, plants growing in the osmunda potting fiber may need watering every three or four days; while plants growing in one of the new potting materials such as fir bark may need water more often, probably every two or three days.

Humidity: A moist atmosphere with a relative humidity of 70 percent or more is essential for successful orchid culture. To maintain such a damp condition in the home, use a special glass case, a miniature greenhouse, for your orchids. Put a 6-inch deep tray on the bottom of the glass case. Fill the tray ⅔ full of small pebbles. Then build a wooden rack of thin slats ½ inch apart. Put this on top of the pan, leaving the extra 2 inches above the 4 inches of pebbles for free air circulation. The pots of orchids are placed on this rack. By keeping the pebbles and rack wet, air within the case surrounding the plants is kept quite humid. Do not close the glass cover completely or the plants will not get enough air. Leave the cover just slightly open, say ⅛ inch on one side.

Temperature: Maintain a 60° F. night temperature in winter, and a daytime temperature of 68° to 80°. Most of the orchids in the table will grow where a day and night temperature averages about 70°.

Light: Sunlight is as necessary for the manufacture of plant food in orchids as in other plants. Successful flowering of cattleyas seems dependent upon the amount of direct sunlight the plants receive during the winter months. However, protection from direct sunlight should be provided from April 1st until October 1st; during these months the sun may cause the foliage of orchids to become yellow. Plants grown in the home in a south or west window in the winter should be moved to a north or east window during these months.

Orchids that are getting ample sun, as well as proper amounts of plant food and water, will be grass-green in color, husky and growing upright. Those not getting sufficient sun will produce darker green slender twisted leaves. New growth pushing out horizontally, instead of upright, is also an indication of too little light. Too little light causes lack of flowers and buds whereas excessive light causes light green leaves and injury to the leaf tissues.

Feeding: Orchids are not heavy feeders. We feed ours a liquid plant food (23-19-17) at the rate of a teaspoon to two quarts of water, applied once every 3 weeks in fir bark, and about once a month when osmunda is used.

Potting Material: The material usually used for potting cattleyas is known as osmundine. It is composed of roots of the osmunda fern and makes a good potting mixture because of its porous character. Orchids require an abundance of air as well as moisture around their roots. Shredded bark (fir, pine, cedar or birch bark) is being used by florists who find osmunda fiber difficult to obtain. Prepare the bark by soaking in water overnight. A small amount of household detergent added to the water makes the bark easier to wet. Any potting material should be coarse and allow fast drainage and good ventilation so that the roots can dry out between waterings. Charcoal, coarse bark or large gravel seem to do best unless your growing conditions are very dry.

Repotting: Like other plants, orchids will outgrow the pot and need repotting about every 2 or 3 years. The time to repot is usually when the roots start to push out from the base of a mature bulb or from the base of new growth.

Take a sharp knife and cut the roots loose from the inside surface of the pot. A large clump can be divided into several plants, each with at least four or five pseudo-bulbs. Fill ⅓ of the pot with broken pieces of crock. Place small pieces of osmunda on top of the crock to fill it half way. Then, holding the plant in position, place small pieces of osmunda next to the root or rhizome. Continue this operation by inserting more osmunda until the plant is firmly and tightly held in place. Use a wooden wedge-shaped potting stick for packing the osmunda.

Insects: The principal insects which attack orchids are scale, slugs, thrips, sowbugs and garden centipedes. Any nicotine preparation used according to directions on the container is effective. The insecticide may be conveniently applied with a small camel's hair brush. Malathion is a new insecticide effective against most insects that attack orchids.

Summer Care: Orchid plants may be grown out-of-doors during the warm summer months, but they should not receive full sunlight. Suspend the potted plants from a tree or vine-covered pergola. Here the plants will receive the proper light conditions. However, water and syringe the plants much more frequently while the plants are outside. In dry weather, water daily.

Brassavola Orchid	Dendrobium Orchid	Oncidium Orchid

OXALIS

When it comes to houseplants few are more interesting than a group called oxalis (pronounced ox-alice or ox-a-lis). There are over 300 species and all are sour-juiced. The common wood sorrel is an oxalis member and is also one of the plants known as shamrock. As houseplants, oxalis are either bulbous, semi-bulbous or fibrous-rooted. The bulbous types need a rest period when the foliage dies down. The semi-bulbous grow and bloom continually if you divide the plants when they appear to be potbound. The fibrous-rooted types need pinching to keep them bushy. At night or in dark cloudy weather, the leaves of the oxalis tend to fold up ("go to sleep"). A few worthwhile varieties are: *O. cernua*—Bermuda buttercup, *O. cernua florepleno*—a desirable variety suitable for hanging baskets. Bulbs are dormant in summer. *O. hedysoroides rubia*—fire fern, shrubby plant, wiry stem and thin fern-like foliage of satiny wine red. Many small bright yellow flowers. *O. ortgiessii*—tree oxalis, leafy succulent stems, olive-green to brown-red leaves, flowering at all seasons. *O. rubra*—old-fashioned, free-blooming type for hanging baskets.

Green Thumb Tips: As a houseplant, oxalis likes a cool and bright window sill. Soil should be well drained. Allow plants to get a bit dry before watering. When you do water, give oxalis a good soaking with tepid water. Too dry a soil will cause the leaf stems to bend over, but once the plants have been watered again the leaves will perk up. Yellowing of foliage is due to nitrogen shortage. Feed the plants with a liquid plant food every 3 or 4 weeks, and about once a year divide the plant. To divide, we take a sharp knife and thrust it down through the center of the roots and tubers. Each section can be divided again if you want extra plants for your friends.

Troubles: Yellowing of foliage due to excess water, poor drainage, dry soil or red spider mites. Improve drainage; spray plants with Kelthane if red spider mites are present.

PASSION FLOWER *(Passiflora)*

A flowering vine that's difficult yet challenging. *Passiflora alto-caerulea* is a free-blooming hybrid found in the trade. A climber, whose large, fragrant, showy flowers are about 4 inches in diameter, with white sepals and pink petals, and a fringed purple crown. *Passiflora edulis*, the purple granadillo, is a sturdy climber with edible fruit.

Green Thumb Tips: Likes a bright window and loose soil mixture. Best temperature 65° to 72°. Good drainage is important, as well as plenty of room for roots. Scraggly vines can be prevented by nipping the tips now and then. All passifloras are planted outdoors in summer, then lifted, potted and brought indoors for the winter.

Propagation: Seeds sown in sand-peat mixture. Also by cuttings rooted in sand and peat or vermiculite and peat moss.

Troubles: Failure to bloom due to age of vine. Takes up to 4 or 5 years to flower. Needs sufficient light for bud formation. Syringe the plants in bath tub once every 2 weeks as they are susceptible to red spider mites.

Peacock Plant (*Kaempferia*)

Kaempferia roscoeana is a summer-blooming pot plant with attractive flowers and foliage—wide fleshy bronzy leaves, zoned pale green like a peacock tail, fleeting flowers, pale purple with white eye, appearing day after day in summer.

Green Thumb Tips: Likes soil mixture of ⅓ each sand, peat and loam. Semi-sunny window, uniform supply of moisture. In late fall and winter give less water. Give more water again in spring.

Propagation: Start from cuttings in spring, rooting in sand.

Troubles. None.

Pepper (Christmas Pepper—*Capsicum frutescens*)

Fruits are cone-shaped, purple or red. Plants grow about 15 inches tall and are sold by florists at Christmas time. Peppers are hot but edible and make the plant very showy.

Propagation: Start seeds from old peppers. Sow in sand-peat moss in spring or summer. Grow plants outdoors in summer, bring in before frost. Trim back any long shoots to give plant a shape. Likes bright window or full sun, and ample amount of moisture. After old plant has finished bearing, cut it back to about half its previous size and new growth will come.

Troubles: Aphids and spider mites, spray with Malathion or Kelthane. Dropping of bud due to dry soil, age of plant, or lack of light. No peppers due to lack of light.

Poinsettia (*Euphorbia pulcherrima*)

Christmas poinsettia. This plant is in the same family as crown of thorns (*E. milii*).

Green Thumb Tips: If you received a poinsetta for Christmas, here are a few tips on handling it so it will bloom again next Christmas. This plant likes plenty of light. It prefers a temperature of 70° F. by day and not less than 60°, at night. Dropping of leaves is caused by poor light, high temperature, too much water, not enough water or drafts. Cold draft is the plant's worst enemy. Wilting due to lack of water is next. Sometimes poinsettias have to be watered 2 or 3 times a day in the home. Avoid any practice that injures the roots such as over-watering, heavy feeding or breaking roots when transplanting.

When the plant begins to fade, you can plan on growing it again for next year's show. Dry the soil by witholding water gradually. Set the potted plant in a dark, cool cellar where the temperature will be about 50° F. or lower. Then you cut it back 5 or 6 inches in April or May and allow new growth to start. You can easily start new cuttings taken from the mother plant. These cuttings, 3 or 4 inches long, are stuck in moist sand or tap water. They root within a few weeks and make fine plants for Christmas bloom. Cuttings can be taken through August and still make fine Christmas flowers.

In spring after danger of frost is over, set the mother plant outdoors, pot and all, also the young plants, which should be in 4- or 5-inch pots. Keep these watered during the summer months, giving them an occassional feeding of a liquid plant food such as Ra-pid-gro. That's all the care they need until September 1, when you should bring them into the home. At that time, they need a special day-night treatment for Christmas flowering.

Remember that the poinsettia is extremely sensitive to light and darkness. It should be put on a short-day, long-night schedule starting in September and ending around Thanksgiving Day. In the subtropics nature takes care of this by providing the short days and long nights required. But in a living room that's lighted, the plant is likely to get just the reverse and will be retarded. So you should limit the poinsettia's day to about 10 hours and put it to bed for the rest of the night. Even a very dim but continuous light will delay flowering, so a dimly lit hall is not dark enough.

It's an interesting fact that even in greenhouses, many plants which received a small amount of light from a distant street light flower too late for Christmas. Thus, for handsome blooms do this: Place the poinsettia where it will get as much light as possible during the day, then move it to a completely darkened room at night. Protect the plant from drafts and extreme temperature changes and keep it watered. This gay Christmas flower requires a fairly high and uniform temperature if its maturing is to be successfully controlled. Without adequate warmth indoors, it will not flower until January or later. Applications of liquid manure at weekly intervals will help, but Ra-pid-gro will do just as well, especially after the plant becomes potbound. Indoors, try to maintain a temperature of around 60° after early September, with a leeway of 2°, above or below. Higher or lower temperatures will often cause the leaves to drop and plant will not flower. WHEN PLANT IS OUTDOORS, GIVE POT A TWIST ONCE A WEEK SO ROOTS WILL BREAK OFF. IF YOU DON'T LEAVES WILL DROP WHEN YOU BRING POT IN.

How to Shorten a Tall Poinsettia: Commercial growers use an ammonium compound (CCC or Cycocel) a growth retardant which keeps the plants shortened. It's sold as an 11.8% solution and you pour it on the soil, not later than late September. You can also shorten a tall plant by using a trick florists use, known as bending or folding of stems. The time to bend or fold your poinsettia is from November 15 to December 1. The stem has to be just at a certain hardness, not too soft and not too hard. With your index finger and thumb, seize the stem where you want to make a bend on the branch, and, in a space of 1½ inches or so, mash it with the fingers. This softens the spot where you want to make the bend. You have to make two bends on stem, to fold it down, and then back up again. You get the height of the plant desired by the length between the two bends. In other words, the distance between the two bends is what shortens the height of the plant. The branches have to be staked and tied. IMPORTANT: Do not break the stem off, but really bend the areas where you mashed them with thumb and finger.

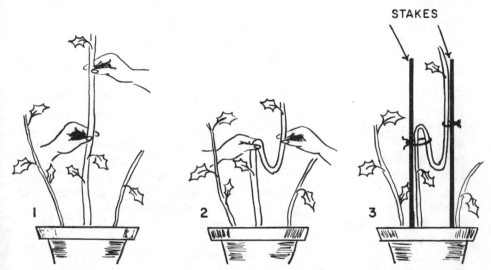

Homeowners who raise their own poinsettias are often dismayed to find the plants are tall and gawky. Don't let this discourage you. Try a trick commercial growers use to shorten a tall plant. (1) Mash stems gently with thumb and index finger for a distance of one inch at two points shown above. (2) Gently fold down, then up, (3) Stake and tie stem.

Propagation: Take cuttings anytime in summer or early fall and root in moist sand.

Troubles: Failure to flower due to excess artificial light at night. Place in dark at 5:00 P.M. and bring to light at 8:00 A.M. the next morning. Yellowing of leaves due to poor light, dry soil, high room temperature or root injury. Give brightest window possible and keep soil uniformly moist. Mealybugs, remove with cotton swab dipped in alcohol.

PRIMROSE *(Primula)*

Primula obconica can cause a skin rash. *P. malacoides* does not bother allergic people and should be used if you are prone to primrose poisoning.

Green Thumb Tips: Grow in sunny window in soil kept uniformly moist. Feed liquid plant food. Keep old blossoms snipped off. After flowering discard plants as they are hard to carry over the summer and grow the next year.

Propagation: Seeds sown in sand-peat mixture in spring.

Troubles: Leaf margin burn or scorch due to dry soils or fertilizer burn.

ROSE, MINIATURE *(Rosa chinensis minima* or *R. roulettii)*

These miniatures are the only roses which can be successfully grown indoors.

Green Thumb Tips: Plants received from nursery are dormant, ready to plant in 4-inch pots. Use soil mix of 2 parts good loam, 2 parts peat and 1 part coarse sand. Water thoroughly. Also advisable to set pot in tray of gravel with ½-inch water at all times. Give maximum sun, away from hot radiator. Temperature 65° to 70°. Feed liquid plant food, such as Ra-pid-gro, every 3 weeks. Spray with Sevin and Captan. Blooms within 5 weeks. As soon as flower fades, pinch it off to promote more blooming. In late spring, plant the rose outdoors in garden or in window box. (For more detailed information, see section on How To Grow Miniature Roses Indoors)

Miniature tree roses can be grown outdoors, and their culture is same as for regular miniature rose. Select a good cane and remove shoots from it, letting the top grow. Trunk will be a good foot high, and treetop covered with blooms.

Propagation: Cuttings rooted under glass.

Troubles: Yellow leaves due to poor drainage, dry soils, excess water. Black spot, dust with Captan or Phaltan, also Malathion to check aphids and thrips.

SHRIMP PLANT *(Beloperone guttata)*

This is a wire-stemmed plant constantly in flower. Blossoms are borne in long drooping spikes with red and green bracts, resembling a shrimp. True flowers themselves are scarcely visible. Long after the small inconspicuous flowers have faded the green and red bracts remain to put on a show.

Green Thumb Tips: Plants like light in winter. Pinch young plants at the tips when about 8 inches high to cause branching. Keep soil uniformly moist. After plant has finished flowering, put it outdoors for the summer. When fall comes, take cuttings and start new plants. Old mother plant will be too large to bring indoors. Feed every 6 weeks with liquid plant food, such as Ra-pid-gro.

Propagation: Take cuttings about 4 or 5 inches long and root them in plain tap water or sand.

Troubles: Mealybugs and red spider mites, spray with Malathion, 1 teaspoon to a quart of soapy water.

SPREKELIA

Jacobean lily, St. James lily, or orchid lily (*S. formosissima*) has flowers that resemble the florist's cattleya orchid. Blooms in spring or early summer, usually in June before small narrow leaves appear.

Green Thumb Tips: Light window, 72°, from January on when growth is active. Use ⅓ sand-loam-peat mixture for good drainage. Repot in late winter or early spring. Plant can be grown dry from September until February when growth starts again. Otherwise, care is similar to that of amaryllis.

Propagation: Division in late winter or spring.

Troubles: None.

STEPHANOTIS (Steff-ann-oh-tus)

Stephanotis floribunda (bride's flower), the florist's stephanotis, is often grown in the greenhouse or as a houseplant. It's a twining vine with shiny, deep green leaves and clusters of tubular white flowers, waxy and highly scented.

Green Thumb Tips: Grow in a bright window with average house temperature. Soil should be humusy and well drained, moist at all times. From February through fall, apply liquid plant food once every 3 or 4 weeks.

In winter, water just enough to keep soil moist and prevent drying. Does not flower during winter months due to short days and low light intensity.

Propagation: Take 4-inch cuttings and root in moist sand in spring or early summer. Syringing helps hasten rooting.

Troubles: Failure to flower due to lack of light, poor soil. Red spider mite, spray with Malathion. Yellowing of foliage due to poor drainage or red spider mite.

STREPTOCARPUS (Cape Primrose)

A member of the gloxinia family with about the same cultural requirements, many species and hybrids. English and German strains are highly rated. Semi-shaded window, 72° room, humusy soil that's well drained and uniformly moist.

Propagation: Seed sown in peat-sand mixture in winter; also by dividing old tubers.

Troubles: Same as those of gloxinia. Failure to flower due to insufficient light. (See Gloxinia)

TIBOUCHINIA (Princess Flower—*T. semidecandria*)

A winter-blooming plant which can be trained to grow on a trellis or into a tree form.

Green Thumb Tips: Needs bright window. Soil mixture, ⅓ each of sand, peat and loam, kept uniformly moist.

Propagation: Cuttings made in spring or early summer, stuck in sand or sand and peat.

Troubles: Brown leaf edges due to poor drainage or spider mites. Spray with Kelthane.

VOODOO LILY (*Amorphophallus*)

Sometimes called sacred lily of India, devil's tongue, stinker plant. The flower is perched on a leafless stalk, has a green spathe, and is red and yellow outside, greenish inside. Blossom gives off a disagreeable odor, hence the name stinker plant. Some gardeners cut out the spadix with a sharp knife to remove the scent glands. This is a close relative of the hydrosme (*H. rivieri*), which is also called by the above common names. To confuse you even further, the voodoo bulb is another name given to *Sauromatum guttatum*, sometimes referred to as the monarch of the east.

Green Thumb Tips: They all like a bright window and a soil with equal parts of sand, peat and loam or peat. Plant the crown of the bulbs in a 6-inch pot just below the surface. Water the bulb in the pot when planted to settle the soil. After the sprout is up 3 or 4 inches, apply more water. For all practical purposes hydrosme and amorphophallus take the same culture. After all the leaves are out, plant can be watered daily. After bloom period is over, the decorative palm-tree foliage on marble-like stems grows quickly. Support should be given with bamboo stakes. When shirt-sleeve weather comes, move the bulb outdoors, grow in shaded spot and leave until fall, about October 1 or before frost hits. At that time pot it up and keep dry until January when you can start growth again by watering. None of the voodoo bulbs is hardy and they should not be left outdoors in cold regions.

Propagation: Cut offsets from mother tuber and pot them in a sand-peat-loam mixture.

CHAPTER III

Foliage

Plants

In recent years homeowners have turned to "hard-leaved" foliage plants to brighten drab corners and add distinction to the modern interior. This group is referred to as foliage plants, in contrast to the flowering plants mentioned in the preceding chapter. Foliage plants are grown for their leaf effect rather than flowers. They thrive under conditions of warm temperature, diffused light, high humidity and moist soil. Most homes do not have high humidity, but foliage plants on the whole are tough and will flourish as long as they are warm and have adequate moisture.

Foliage plants should be selected with as much care as you'd select plants for the outside foundation of your home. Some foliage plants are large specimens suited for spacious rooms. Of these, *Monstera deliciosa* is the most common, others include *Philodendron hastatum,* various kinds of dracaena and ficus, and old favorites such as aspidistra. Dish gardens, a relatively new kind of adventure in indoor gardening, are making use of the smaller foliage plants such as Chinese evergreen, syngonium, peperomia and scindapsus.

The requirements of most foliage plants are simple: a humusy, well-drained soil, diffused light and the highest humidity possible. Probably more foliage plants die in dish gardens and planters from overwatering than underwatering. Plastic or metal containers are trickier to use because they do not dry out as fast as clay pots and, therefore, are usually overwatered. Water standing in plastic or metal containers causes stunted growth, yellowed leaves and musty soil. For the most part, the soil and water requirements for foliage plants are similar to flowering plants. The big difference in culture is that the foliage plants need less light than do the flower-producing plants.

CULTURE

Pots

Does it make any difference if you use glazed or clay pots for growing houseplants? Actually, you can grow good plants in both types of pots if you understand what each will do. There is more danger of overwatering the glazed pots because they do not "breathe" as the clay pots do. Water your plants when the soil feels slightly dry and you won't overwater. If you water them as often as you do the clay pots, the water builds up around the roots, leaves turn yellow and the plants suffocate from a lack of oxygen to the roots.

Incidentally, many ask me if castor oil is a good plant fertilizer. It's neither a fertilizer nor a stimulant for plants and there is no good reason for applying it to the soil. Use a good liquid plant food.

Here are a few general cultural directions for foliage plants:

Lights above make it possible to grow plants even in dark room.

If your room is too dark to grow plants, try growing them under artificial lights as shown here.

LIGHT

On the whole, most of them do not like direct sunshine; diffused light is better.

SOIL

One reason why gardeners have bad luck growing foliage plants is poor soil mixture. A potting soil can be loaded with harmful organisms which pounce on the tiny seedlings and young plants. Also, if it happens to contain clay, drainage will be poor and growth will be spotty. If you have your own soil mixture, be sure to sterilize it by baking in oven (messy job!) at 180° for ½ hour. If you have large amounts of soil to sterilize, use formaldehyde, 2½ tablespoons to a cup of water. Sprinkle this on to a bushel of soil, mix well and cover with plastic sheet. After two days, remove sheet and sow seed or make your transplants. If you don't want to bother with this type of soil sterilization, then try a method developed at Cornell University and used by commercial growers. Use the "peat-lite" mix. Here's the recipe for a peck: vermiculite, 4 quarts; shredded peat moss, 4 quarts; 20 percent superphosphate (powdered), 1 teaspoon, and 1 tablespoon of ground dolomitic lime-stone. Add either (not both) 1 tablespoon of 33 percent ammonium nitrate, or 4 tablespoons of 5-10-5 fertilizer. Moisten this mixture well before using. We water the young plants with an extra feeding of liquid plant food (23-19-17) about a month after growth has started.

WATERING

On the whole, it is better to give plants a good soaking, then let them dry out a bit between waterings. "Wet feet" is harmful to plants.

TEMPERATURE

Most foliages like it warm, however, too high a temperature is harm-ful (over 80°) and will cause leaves to turn brown at edges (so will excess fertilizer) or to turn yellow.

DUST

Dust slows down the growth of most foliage plants. Wash glossy-leaved plants off with soap and water, or damp cloth.

A cross-section view showing how smaller pots can be supported in a planter. A layer of gravel is placed on bottom of the planter. The area between the pots is filled with peat moss.
If a plant dies, remove pot and all, without disturbing rest of the planter.

University of Minnesota

GROOMING HARD-LEAVED FOLIAGE PLANTS

If you've wondered how to make foliage on your vines and other indoor plants look shiny and well scrubbed, try a trick that florists use. Put a few drops of glycerine on a cloth and swab the leaves. This gives the plants their desired natural color and appearance, and at the same time eliminates the dull dusty look found on most plants. Glycerine is safe to handle and does not harm plant life. It can also be used on gourds for brighter effect. Never use olive oil as it collects dust and plugs up the pores in the leaves.

Homeowners often daub the leaves of their hard-leaved foliage plants weekly with plant shining and cleaning materials. Research at state colleges find that some of these new plant-shine or cleaning materials are harmful to plant growth when overused. In fact, treating houseplants too often with the cleaning or shining materials will slow down their growth noticeably. We've found that heavy applications will cause brown patches in the "skin" of some foliage plants. Once a month is plenty when it comes to adding plant-shine materials.

The old-fashioned method is to wipe leaves with skim milk, but since milk contains fats it's apt to clog the pores.

If you use any kind of polish, never use it on the underside of the leaves. There are more pores (stomates) on the underside and the plants do most of their breathing through the bottom of the leaves. It's more critical to clog the bottom pores than those on top.

GREEN PLANTS IN PLAIN WATER

Many homeowners who cannot grow good plants in soil have excellent luck growing green plants in plain tap water.

The Society of American Florists has some good tips for those who want to have fun with flowers indoors and I'm grateful to them for their suggestions which I have drawn on freely.

GREEN PLANTS IN WATER

Arranged in a variety of containers, green plants become the constant decor for dining table, mantelpiece, window ledge, desk and entrance-hall table. Fresh flowers, added on a moment's notice, can transform each arrangement into a charming welcome-the-guest piece.

First choice for plants which will grow well in water are Chinese evergreen, philodendron, pothos, (see Pothos) and nephthytis. Ivy may also be used. Sprays, clusters or a grouping of single flowers of an informal type—chrysanthemums, daisies, cornflowers, lilies, jonquils, narcissi and many others—blend gracefully with green plants. There is no end to the charming changes-of-face which can be achieved in a flash.

To make basic plant arrangements, remove plants from their pots and break the dirt away from the roots gently. Hold the roots under warm running water until all dirt is washed away. Arrange the plants in containers, using non-rusting needle holders. Place small rough stones, shells or clinkers around the needle holder. Roots will curl around them and find extra nourishment. Odd stones and shells also may be added.

Plant roots like to reach out for water. Plants should never stand in deep water no matter how deep the container. Like humans, they can take cold from wet feet, their leaves then turn yellow. Water should come no higher than the top roots on the plant.

Change water in the containers occasionally during the first few months while the many small curling roots are shedding. When the main root water is clear, the water in the container need not be changed. Simply add fresh water regularly, keeping the water level constant. A piece of stick charcoal, purchased in an art store, will keep water sweet and clear. Ask your florist for advice about the frequency of adding a liquid plant food to the water. For glossy leaves, wash each leaf with plain water, or use one of the special liquids carried by your florist.

THE PROBLEMS OF INDOOR GARDENS AND PLANTERS

I'm often asked why leaves turn yellow, buds and blooms blast or drop off, or why vines and foliages turn brown and dry up. Usually, there is no one answer to these questions, but here are a few green thumb notes on caring for your indoor gardens and planters.

TEMPERATURE:

Some plants like it hot, some cold. During the winter months the best day temperature for most plants is about 70° and 55° at night. There are a few exceptions, such as African violets. A high night temperature causes the food in plants to be used up with the result that the plants yellow off and die. One reason why grandmother grew better houseplants than we do now is because the room temperatures then were lower, especially at night. In those days, bedrooms were seldom heated. That meant that houseplants saved their food during the night, thus were big and husky. If your foliages are making spindly growth, color is pale, buds blast, or drop prematurely, you can blame it, for one thing, on high room temperatures.

WATERING

It's safe to say that more plants in dish gardens, planters, etc. are overwatered than underwatered. Plants in plastic or metal containers suffer when given too much water because there is then lack of oxygen around the roots. If water stands in the bottom of a container, growth is stunted, leaves turn yellow, and buds and blooms blast or fall off. Avoid constant soakings; also avoid teasing with small dabs daily. If clay pots are set in ceramic, copper or brass jardinieres they will grow better than if they are planted directly in these containers. When soils take on a musty odor or green appearance, it's because of poor drainage. The musty smell is due to gases given off by soil organisms which are in the oxygen-starved soil. Improving the drainage will eliminate this trouble.

LIGHT

While all plants vary in their light requirements, it can be safely said that they all need some light for energy. When your plants do not get enough light to make food, the leaves turn yellow, buds fail to form; eventually the plant is starved to death, regardless of how much chemical plant food you feed them. No set rule can be given for all plants, but, on the whole, most foliage plants and vines do best in a window without direct sun. Most other houseplants do best in a window getting full sun at least a half day. Without maximum light, a geranium will fail to bud. When a houseplant becomes leggy or spindly it's because not enough light is reaching it. Pinching, feeding, etc. will not offset or overcome the bad effects of poor light. Often the leaves on the shaded side of houseplants or the lower leaves will yellow and die. The reason is that leaves with more light exposure have more sugar and can take up more water than older shaded leaves. Roughly speaking, a south window in winter is about equal to an east or west window in summer. Half a day's full sun in winter will usually give plenty of light.

WEEKLY CARE

Wipe off the accumulation of dust, using a cloth dipped in glycerine. Look your leaves over for round, tan colored spots, with a water soaked margin. This is leaf spot disease and is worse in wet soil. Leaves will turn yellow and drop from the plant.

CONTROL

Remove the diseased leaves and burn. Use care in watering to avoid wetting the foliage. Dust the plants with Captan or Ferbam. Another cause of yellowed foliage is too much light or poor soil drainage. Plastics make poor containers for these subjects since they allow very little passage of air to roots. For all indoor foliage plants, it's a good idea to avoid overly wet soil. Use a mixture that allows for good aeration or you're apt to get stem-rotting or root-rotting diseases. (See Soil Section.)

HUMIDITY

The higher the room temperature, the more water your plants give off. Hot, dry air causes the foliage to burn at the tips, and, since the air in our homes is drier than the air in the Sahara Desert, we should do all we can to increase the humidity. Set plants on pebbles in a pan of water or syringe the foliage with an atomizer a few times a day. Water on the foliage won't do any harm if plants are in sunny widow. If globs of water remain on foliage for long periods, diseases are apt to flare up. If the tips of your ferns or vines have dried up, look for dry air as cause.

CONTAINERS

Growing plants in television lamps, small glass jars, plastic dishes, or metal containers is a hard job. One reason is that no provision has been made for drainage of water, and water remains around the roots. Also, such plants are usually neglected when it comes to watering. The tighter the container, the more care you need in watering. Put some pebbles in the bottom so that water has a chance to drain off. Clay pots produce the best growth, but are not as pretty. One way to overcome this is to wrap them with aluminum florist's foil or set them in ceramic, copper or brass jardeniers.

How to Diagnose Your Plant Troubles:

If leaves are curled and twisted, look for red spider. They leave a cobweb growth on the foliage. Control: Wash under faucet, then spray with Kelthane, 1 teaspoon to 2 quarts of water plus a little detergent. If your plants are stunted, look for nematodes on roots. They are microscopic, but do great damage. No control, but you can test by putting a few squash or melon seeds in soil of your sick houseplants. Let the seed germinate, then pull up young plants in a couple of weeks. If nematodes are present, you'll see galls on the roots. Take cuttings near top of plant then burn the old plant.

Leaf scorching on ferns, begonias, foliages may be a sign of lack of water, sun burn, not enough humidity or gas heat. Bud drop is due to too much water, dry air, thrips, traces of gas or sudden changes of temperature.

Wilted leaves can be caused by worms in the soil. Dust some Chlordane on soil and water in. Might also be due to too much water. Rot at the crown causes the leaves to wilt or go limpy. In some cases you can cut off the rotted part at the crown and reroot it. Rot is usually associated with too much water or poor drainage.

Scorched edges or drying up along the edges is a physiological disease and is usually due to dry air. Water-soaked areas in leaves is also a physiological condition and is often associated with too much water.

THE MOST COMMONLY ASKED-ABOUT FOLIAGE PLANTS
(Description and care)

ACHIMENES

A member of the *gesneriaceae* family. Plants are velvety leaved with bell-shaped blooms, resembling a petunia flower. Flowers are tubular, single or double, pink, rose, red, violet, blue or purple. Achimenes produce small rhizomes or tubers, resembling miniature pine cones. Leaves and stems are purplish and covered with hairs.

Green Thumb Tips: Grow in same window as gloxinia or African violet, meaning a bright but not sunny situation. Avoid temperatures below 65°, and in winter keep away from cold window pane. Soil should be 1 part each of peat, loam and sand for good drainage. Keep soil unifomly moist during growth period. In late summer, start drying the plant by withholding water. Allow the roots to remain in the pot in a dry state until about February. At that time, remove the soil from the roots, and, if plant is large, divide it and repot. If plant is small, do not disturb but leave in soil for another year's growth. Repotting and division is not necessary each year. Feed plant liquid plant food such as Ra-pid-gro, a teaspoon to a quart of water once every 3 or 4 weeks. After flowering is over, dry off the plant and place pot in cellar.

Propagation: Divide the cone-like storage roots.

Troubles: Aphids, spray with nicotine sulfate, 1 teaspoon to a quart of water. Rotting off at surface of soil due to excess water, poor drainage, especially in non-clay pots. Repot and use florist's pot for best growth.

ADAM'S APPLE

East Indian rosebay or Nero's crown (*Ervatamia coronaria*) although still listed as *Tabernaemontana coronaria*. A handsome evergreen shrub ideal for tubs or pots indoors.

Green Thumb Tips: In spring should be pruned back for shape. During summer leave it on enclosed porch and keep it watered. Flowers are waxy white and fragrant, almost like gardenia blossoms.

Propagation: Cuttings rooted in sand and enclosed with plastic sheet to maintain humidity.

Troubles: None.

AGAPANTHUS

Commonly called agapanthus, or lily of the Nile. *A. africanus* is called blue African lily, whereas the white flowering type is *A. orientalis albus*, the lily of the Nile. A tuberous-rooted plant handled in redwood tubs.

Green Thumb Tips: Grow in well-drained soil in large tub. In winter water sparingly to let plant grow in semi-dormant state. Strap-like leaves remain green in winter. In spring move to bright window and keep soil uniformly moist. Apply liquid plant food once every four weeks. Grow in bright window and plant will have either the blue or white flowers all summer. There is a miniature lily of the Nile, *A. orientalis*. *A. pendulus* drops its foliage in winter and also needs a rest period.

Propagation: Divide the plant in spring.

Troubles: Failure to flower could be due to forcing in winter, lack of light, need for repotting, or too rich a soil.

AIRPLANE PLANT

Chlorophytum comosum is often called spider plant. All varieties have leaves similar to day lily, and are interesting items to grow. *C. bichetii* has white-margined foliage, *C. comosum madaianum* is white-striped, *C. comosum picturatum* has yellow-striped foliage, as does *C. elatum vittatum*. Small white flowers are borne on slender racemes which are followed by new plants, hence the name spider plant. While the white stripes in the center of the leaf have attraction, the small plants borne near the tip of the foliage are remarkable. When the grass-like leaves bend over (due to weight of the baby plants), the new plants, in contact with the soil surface, take root.

Green Thumb Tips: Does best in semi-shaded window, with a moist soil. Use ⅓ sand, ⅓ loam and ⅓ peat.

Propagation: Offsets formed on the flower branches, cut aerial plantlets off as soon as rooting has taken place and pot them up.

Troubles: Scorched tips due to hot dry room, lack of water in soil.

AIR PLANTS (Kalanchoe)

Homeowners have a choice of several air plants, plants which bear baby plants along the scalloped leaf edges. These belong to the kalanchoe (kalen-ko-ee) family. The most common air plant is K. *pinnata*, and this is the one that's pinned to a window curtain or laid on moist soil. It's so rugged it even grows when pinned on the curtain. In my greenhouse I have an unusual air plant called multiplication plant, monkey plant, and other common names. It's real name is K. *daigne-montiana*, and it bears baby plantlets along the scalloped leaf edges. If you touch these baby plants they drop to the ground or soil in a pot and grow like mad. It's probably the easiest plant there is to grow. Air plants are sometimes listed as Bryophyllums.

Green Thumb Tips: All kalanchoe or air plants like a sunny window. Without light the leaves grow well but plants will not flower or bear plantlets. Soil should consist of sand, peat and loam, equal parts. Water only when the surface is dry.

Propagation: Rooting the baby plants in soil or sand-peat mixture.

Troubles: None. (For more information on kalanchoe, the kind florists sell at Christmas and Valentine's Day, see section on Kalanchoe.)

ALLAMANDA *(A. cathartica hendersoni)*

A tender perennial used as tub plant for porch or patio. Flowers are trumpet shaped, brass colored and often reach a diameter of 3 or 4 inches.

Green Thumb Tips: Prefers bright window, temperature 70° or so, and a good well-drained soil. In fall and winter, plant becomes dormant and should have just enough water to keep it green. In spring, start growth by feeding and watering regularly.

Propagation: Division.

Troubles: None.

AGLAONEMA *(Commutatum)*

C. V. White Rajah, a Chinese evergreen, is properly known as

Kwantung Wan Nien Ch(ing), literally "ten thousand years green of Canton." A free-growing Chinese evergreen that will grow in shade as well as sun. Its leaves are dark green with accents of light green and white. Grows in soil or water.

Propagation: Division of root stalks anytime.

Troubles: Drying of edges due to dry air or poor drainage.

ALUMINUM PLANT *(Pilea cadierei)*

A handsome plant with silver markings. This silver-marked effect results from the air space between the tissues of the leaves. A close relative is the artillery plant *(pilea microphylla)*. This item has a reddish appearance if grown in bright window. Blossoms are small and globular, opening with a sudden burst, throwing the pollen out in small clouds of smoke, hence the name artillery plant. The best way to get this effect is to place the plant in a sunny window for half-day, then sprinkle it with water and leave it in the sun.

Green Thumb Tips: Grow in sunny window in winter, semi-shade in summer. Old plants get spindly and leggy, so start new ones from cuttings. Grow them in a soil that's continuously moist in a 4-inch pot.

Propagation: Cuttings rooted in sand.

Troubles: Shedding of leaves due to poor light or improper drainage. Mealybugs, spray with Malathion, or scrape off the pests with cloth.

ANTHURIUMS

These are arums (calla lily family) grown both for flowers and foliage effect. Anthurium has no common name. Florists use the *A. andreanum* in their arrangements which last for many days. Flowers resemble wax and are often taken to be artificial, due to their patent leather spathes of red, white or pink. One group has suede-like foliage. In their natural habitat in Hawaii, anthuriums grow treelike or shrublike.

Green Thumb Tips: As a houseplant they aren't easy to grow. Give them a bright window, a warm room and humidity as high as possible. In a dry room, flowers are small and leaves take on a scorched appearance. You may grow them in a loose soil with plenty of humus, half peat and half loam. If the plants send out aerial roots you may want to grow them on a totem pole of sphagnum moss or tree fern which is kept moistened. This is one of the secrets of getting them to flower.

Propagation: Cuttings rooted in water or sand. Take them any time of year. Some anthuriums send out offsets which can be rooted in sand.

Troubles: Failure to flower due to lack of light, dry air or dry soils.

Aphelandra Squarrosa

Here's one of showiest "undiscovered" plants you can get. Its spike of waxy flowers and shiny green leaves veined in white make it a striking plant.

Aphelandra squarrosa

Green Thumb Tips: Likes a loose soil and a uniform supply of moisture. Avoid hot sun, but keep in bright window. Average room temperature.

Propagation: Start new plants by tip cuttings rooted in moist sand, peat, vermiculite or perlite, or plain tap water.

Troubles: Drying of leaves due to dry soil, hot dry room. Set pot in tray of pebbles. Insect and disease free.

Ardisia

A good house plant is the false holly or coral-berry (*Ardisia crispa*). It may grow to quite a size before producing sweet-smelling white blooms and berries.

Green Thumb Tips: Likes a bright or semi-sunny window (not direct sun) and a temperature of 72° or less. Soil should be well drained, and made of equal parts sand, peat and loam. Avoid over-watering or drying of soil. It prefers a uniform supply of moisture at all times.

Propagation: Start new plants by rooting tip cuttings in moist sand or a mixture of sand and peat moss, or by seed started in sand-peat mixture.

Troubles: Failure to produce berries due to hot, dry rooms. Shedding of berries is due to dry soils.

Asparagus (*A. plumosus* and *A.sprengeri*)

There are two kinds of asparagus grown indoors, and sold by florists. *A. plumosus* has fine fernlike leaves and its foliage is used in vases, sprays, corsages, boutonnieres and other floral arrangements. It's also the one that sheds its growth if kept dry for any length of time. *A. sprengeri* has bright green inch-long needles which also shed if kept dry. Both have red berries and are easy to grow. We use them in hanging baskets, window boxes, cemetery urns and in combination pots.

Green Thumb Tips: Grow in semi-shady window. If *A. plumosus* starts to climb, prune it back so it can grow bushlike. They like a soil that's loose and humusy, such as our standby, equal parts of sand, peat and loam. Keep soil uniformly moist. Hot sun will turn leaves yellow. Give liquid plant food once a month to maintain green color.

Propagation: Sow seed in spring or early summer At these times the seed is fresh and has a much greater germinating potential. The older the seed, the lower the germination. Sow in sand-peat mixture, and keep in 72° temperature. Takes 30 to 35 days for germination. You can also divide the root clumps any time of year.

Troubles: Shedding of foliage due to dry soil, hot sun. Keep plenty of humus in soil mixture, feed liquid plant food to prevent yellowing.

Baby's Tears (*Helxine soleirolii*)

Also called Irish moss or Paddy's wig, is a creeping vine that will take over the home greenhouse if you let it. Baby's tears forms a dense intertwining mass of leaves. Each leaf is about the size of a pinhead but when they are matted together you get a green carpet effect.

Green Thumb Tips: Baby's Tears likes ample humidity. Grow it in a pot of peat moss and loam, and syringe the plant from time to time. It likes plenty of moisture in the soil and on the foliage. It'll do fine in a semi-shaded window out of direct sun.

Propagation: Divide clumps or root cuttings in pot.

Troubles: Drying out in the center and outer foliage due to dry soils or direct sun.

BLOODLEAF PLANT *(Iresine)*

All the *Iresines* have deep crimson-red foliage which accounts for the name bloodleaf. *I. herbstii* is a broad leaved bloodleaf plant; *I. lindenii* has pointed leaves. This is in the amaranth or Joseph's coat family.

Green Thumb Tips: Grow them in full sun, temperature around 65° to 70°. During the winter, growth is poor due to insufficient light. They do best in full sun in porch or window box. Pinch out the tips to promote branching and bushiness. Soil can be standard equal parts mixture of sand, peat and loam.

Propagation: Cuttings taken any time of year and rooted in sand, peat or plain tap water.

Troubles: Mealybugs and aphids, spray with Malathion once every two weeks. Hand pick mealybugs and destroy. Dropping of foliage is due to poor light.

BROMELIADS

Bromeliads are foolproof houseplants anyone can grow. They are ideal for people who do not have a green thumb but still love plants.

Bromeliads on a windowsill.
Cutak Photo

They have no common names. Some have foliage that is green, pink, white, or variegated. Have long flowering period, although the foliage is their greatest value. They will grow in semi-shaded window, but you get best colors from window with bright light. Prefer a loose soil, good drainage. If drainage is poor the tips turn brown.

Some bromeliads are among the most stubborn plants grown, when it comes to producing flowers. Most gardeners grow them for foliage effect. An example is the pineapple, a common bromeliad which seldom flowers indoors. Other good ones have jaw-breaking names such as aechmea, vriesia, billbergia, cryptanthus, all lumped together as attractive foliage plants, which do not flower.

Aechmea fasciata

If you have bromeliads growing in your window and want to force them into bloom, try a trick suggested by H.M. Cathey of the U.S. Department of Agriculture. This consists of placing a plastic bag over the plant; add an apple inside, then tie the bag at the base. Leave it alone for 4 days. Then remove the bag and the apple and take care of the plant as usual. In 1 to 6 months, depending on the species, the plant will produce beautifully colored blooms and fruit.

How does the apple force stubborn bromeliads into bloom? It gives off ethylene gas (harmless to humans) which acts as a growth regulator. They use the same principle in Hawaii to make field-grown pineapples bloom and form fruit. By the way, ethylene gas shortens the life of cut flowers such as roses, carnations or snapdragons. That's why it's a good idea not to keep apples, potatoes or bananas near cut flowers.

The pineapple of commerce is a bromeliad grown indoors for its foliage effect. The most common bromeliad is the *Aechmea fasciata*, an urn-shaped plant with silvery-striped, gray-green leaves. The leaf rosettes of all aechmeas are vaselike and will hold water, hence their name "living vase plants." *Cryptanthus bromelioides* is a fine bromeliad with bright green leaves. *C. zonatus zebrinus* has bronzy leaves with cross-bands, and the stiff leaves are more or less star shaped from a bird's eye view.

Billbergia is a bromeliad with strap-like leaves resembling those of the sansevieria or snake plant.

Aechmea chantinii

Neoregelia has colorful foliage with spiny edges. *N. carolinae tricolor*, found in floral shops, is one of the best; it has green leaves striped with parallel bands of yellow-white.

Vriesia is a bromeliad with spectacular flowers on a long spike. It too has been called the living vase plant because the cups formed by the whorls of leaves are tight enough to catch and hold water.

Green Thumb Tips: All bromeliads require about the same care. They like a bright window, even sun if possible, and a soil containing sand, peat and loam; good drainage is essential or the plants will rot. A good soil mixture for bromeliads is ⅓ peat moss, ⅓ perlite, ⅓ fir bark. Add to one bushel of the soil mixture: 5 ounces dolomitic lime, 3.5 ounces superphosphate, 1.8 ounces 12-12-12 fertilizer.

Propagation: By cuttings or offsets stuck in loose soil.

Troubles: Brown tips due to dry air, dry soils. Improve drainage. Failure to flower is due to insufficient light.

CALATHEA

Often erroneously called maranta, has colorful leaves resembling the maranta (prayer plant) leaf. Plant has rhizomatous roots.

Green Thumb Tips: Prefers shaded window, 72° temperature, and a soil that's humusy, well drained. Feed liquid plant food, such as Ra-pid-gro.

Propagation: Divide the roots any time of the year and pot them up.

Troubles: Scorched leaf edges due to dry soils, hot dry room, or direct sun. Red spider mites: Control with Kelthane.

Red Hot Cattail Plant (Acalypha hispida)

Chenille Plant (*Acalypha hispida*)

Called chenille plant because of the showy chenille-like spikes which hang gracefully from the leaf axils. This showy plant is red or pinkish-white and is an eye-stopper.

Green Thumb Tips: Does best in a bright window with loose soil, ⅓ each of sand, peat and loam. Likes ample moisture at all times and ample pot room. Shift to larger pot before plant becomes root bound.

Propagation: Easily rooted by cuttings in fall or spring. Insert in sand and peat moss, perlite or vermiculite.

Troubles: Failure to form chenille stems due to lack of light. Move to brighter window. Dropping of showy flower spikes is due to poor soil, poor drainage or overwatering.

Cissus Rhombifolia

See Grape Ivy.

Coffee Tree (*Coffea arabica*)

Grown in Florida from coffee seed gathered in Central America. Plant is a real conversation piece for the home. Hardy with dark green shiny leaves, it will grow as much as 8 feet in height.

Green Thumb Tips: Grows in bright window, well-drained soil. Seedlings grow best at 70° to 75°. Later on plants need 55° to 58° night temperature for flowering and producing beans.

Can be topped at desired height. Encourage horizontal growth by keeping all terminal growth cut off. Flowers and beans are produced on horizontal growth.

Propagation: Seed.

Troubles: None.

Coleus

When it comes to foliage plants, few are as striking as the coleus (*C. blumei*), native of Java. These highly-colored items do well in shade, sun or semi-sunny situations.

Green Thumb Tips: Give loamy soil, we use equal parts sand, peat and loam. Likes uniform supply of water. Avoid dryness. Keep flower spikes picked off for bigger and better foliage. In hot sun, leaves will bleach out, therefore, provide a semi-shaded window.

Propagation: Stem cuttings taken any time of year. Root in plain tap water. Also by seed sown in sand-peat mixture. Keep seed moist and in a warm temperature (80°).

Troubles: Spindly plants due to lack of pruning flower spikes. Mealybugs, handpick and feed to your goldfish. Bleached foliage due to hot sun or dry soil. Sudden wilting due to low temperatures, excess water, or poor drainage.

COLOCASIA

Elephant's ears, *C. esculenta*, has large heart-shaped foliage, similar to caladiums. Grows 3 feet high and is grown mostly for foliage effect.

Green Thumb Tips: Care is same as for anthuriums.

CORAL VINE (*Antignon leptopus*)

This member of the buckwheat family forms a tuber and is easy to grow indoors. It climbs by means of tendrils which latch on to anything in sight. Bright rose-pink flowers are showy from spring until early winter.

Green Thumb Tips: Give it your brightest window. Any good humusy soil will do as long as it's kept uniformly moist.

Propagation: Start new plants from seeds sown in sand-peat mixture in spring.

Troubles: Develops a leaf spot disease. Dust with Captan.

CRAPE JASMINE (*Ervatamia coronaria*)

Common names: Crepe or crape jasmine, fleur d'amour, butterfly gardenia, East Indian rosebay, Adam's apple, and Nero's crown. Still listed as *Tabernaemontana coronaria.*

Green Thumb Tips: An evergreen plant grown best in tubs. Bears waxy fragrant flowers in summer. After blooming, keep outdoors in shade until fall, bring in before frost. Grow in bright window. Soil should be constantly moist the year round.

Propagation: Cuttings rooted in sand, any time of the year.

Troubles: Drying around the edges of foliage due to dry soil. Needs full light or it won't bloom.

CROTON (*Codiaeum variegatum pictum*)

Crotons are grown for their striking foliage which is equally as colorful as that of the coleus. *Codiaeum interruptum* is a red-yellow type that draws a lot of attention. *C. spirale* has green leaves dotted with yellow and red. This is the corkscrew plant, twisted like a corkscrew. Leaf shapes are quite varied, as are the color markings.

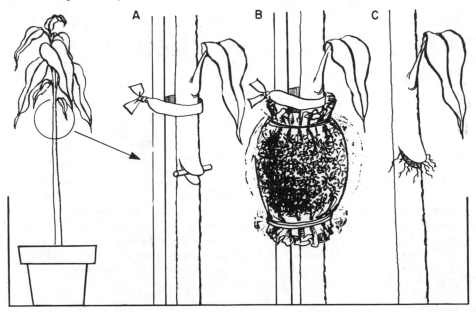

Simple steps in air-layering leggy houseplants: (A) Select spot where you want to shorten plant. Make a slit in it and insert piece of toothpick. (B) Wrap wound with sphagnum moss and enclose with plastic sheet, tied at both ends. (C) Later, after rooting has occurred, remove the plastic wrap and sphagnum. Cut off stem, below roots and pot up in clay pot.

Green Thumb Tips: Does well in average temperature (72°), grows in sun or semi-shaded window. Soil should be loose and humusy. If plants are poorly drained, yellowing occurs. Use ⅓ sand, ⅓ loam and ⅓ peat, with charcoal in bottom of pot for drainage.

Propagation: Take cuttings and root in moist sand in warm room. Plastic bags over cuttings trap moisture and heat. Rooting cuttings need warmth and high humidity.

Troubles: Drying of foliage, or yellowing due to poor drainage or

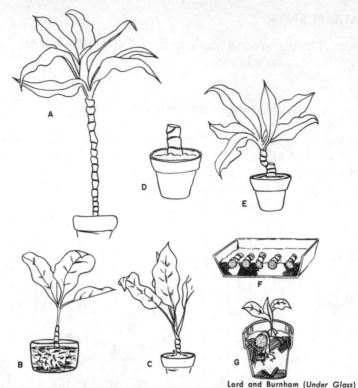

(A) Dieffenbachia (Dumbcane) gets tall and leggy and can easily be shortened. (B) Top cut off and placed in container of plain tap water to root. (C) Rooted top potted in soil. (D) Stump of old plant after top is cut off. (E) Stump breaks out with new top and forms new plant. (F) Or you can take the long trunk and cut it into four-inch pieces. Place them in a mixture of sand and peat moss. Each piece will form new roots and top shoots. (G) When rooting has occurred, pot up each piece separately in 4-inch pots and you'll have a lot of new plants to give your friends.

excess sunlight. Best plants grow in bright window without direct sun. Rotting at base due to poor drainage or excess water.

DEVIL'S BACKBONE (*Pedilanthus tithymaloides*)

Called devil's backbone because of its bizarre stems zig-zagging back and forth, bearing lance-shaped foliage.

Green Thumb Tips: Prefers semi-shady window, 72° temperature and well-drained soil, ⅓ sand, ⅓ loam and ⅓ peat.

Propagation: Snip cuttings in spring, root in sand.

Troubles: Dropping of foliage due to excess water or poor drainage.

Dumb Cane *(Dieffenbachia)*

This item gets its name from the fact that its acrid juice (contains calcium-oxalate crystals) will cause partial paralysis of the tongue if the cane is chewed. Makes a fine foliage plant.

Green Thumb Tips: Likes a sunny or semi-shaded window, temperature 72° or higher, and a soil containing equal parts of sand, peat and loam.

Propagation: Cut top off and root it in water. Or take stem cuttings and root them in sand. Tall plants can be handled by cutting the top and growing it in a jug of water. Also take 4-inch pieces of the bare stem and root them in sand-peat mixture.

Troubles: Plants often give off water which drops to the floor (process called guttation). Place plastic sheet beneath to catch the water. Plant tends to get tall and main trunk is bare. Cut top off and root it in water. Scorched leaves are due to excess sun. Poor leaf color is due to lack of light. Excess water (poor drainage) will cause the bottom leaves to turn brown and drop, also rank, weak growth. Water the plant well and let it dry out slightly before watering again.

Fig *(Ficus)*

The fig family includes the common fig with handsome foliage, and the rubber plant with green leathery foliage, or variegated leaves. *F. lyrata* is the handsome fiddle-leaf rubber plant. There are also creeping figs grown for ornamental effect.

Many homeowners have good luck growing the edible fig as a tubbed plant or as an outdoor specimen, even in areas where temperatures go below zero.

For more information see Tropical Fruit.

Green Thumb Tips: As foliage plants, figs or rubber plants do best in semi-shaded rooms, out of direct sun. They do not like wet feet and will develop brown spots on leaf edges if overwatered or if soil is poorly drained. Use pebbles in bottom of pot and grow in ⅓ sand, ⅓ loam and ⅓ peat.

Propagation: By cutting tops off and rooting in gallon of tap water. Also by air layering (see Propagation).

Troubles: Tall growth. Remedy by cutting out top and rooting it in water to form new plant. Yellowing of bottom leaves due to overwatering. Plant grows better with soil on dry side rather than soggy.

Brown spots on edges due to anthracnose disease. Dust with sulfur and keep soil slightly on dry side.

Flame Vine

Senecio confusus is a close relative of the German ivy or parlor vine, *S. mikanioides*. Flame vine has orange-red flowers.

Green Thumb Tips: Semi-shady window, 65° or so, and almost any soil that's well drained. Likes uniform supply of moisture at all times, needs no rest period. A very profuse vine, needing a support, wire trellis.

Propagation: Tip cuttings rooted in water or washed sand. Start new plants yearly.

Troubles: Aphids and mealybugs, spray with Malathion.

Flame Violet

See Episcia.

Flaming Sword (Living Vase Plant)

Vriesia is a handsome bromeliad with sword-like flower spike. Leaves grow in rosettes and will catch and hold water, hence the name living vase plant.

Green Thumb Tips: Semi-shady window, well-drained soil, ⅓ each of sand, peat and loam. Spray foliage with warm water in bathtub every 3 weeks, but do not overwater plant as it cannot tolerate wet feet.

Propagation: Cut out top and root in water or pot of soil or sand. Suckers can also be rooted. Snip off young shoots and root in soil.

Troubles: Rotting of foliage due to excess water. Failure to flower due to lack of light.

Flamingo Flower

Pigtail plant, see Anthurium for culture.

Gasteria

Ox-tongue plant, so-called because of the stiff tongue-shaped leaves.

Green Thumb Tips: Does best in semi-shaded window, well-drained soil. Grow on dry side in winter as it requires less watering then. Use ⅓ sand, ⅓ peat and ⅓ loam mixture.

Propagation: Seed sown any time in sand-peat mixture. Also by removing the offsets and potting them.

Troubles: None.

GEOGENANTHUS

Commonly called the seersucker plant because of the silvery-gray metallic sheen on the foliage. A fast-growing foliage plant.

Green Thumb Tips: Grow in bright window, 72° temperature. Use a soil mixture of ⅓ sand, ⅓ peat and ⅓ loam, with pebbles in bottom of pot. Needs good drainage.

Propagation: Suckers or offshoots, potted in above mixture.
Propagate often because younger plants do best.

Troubles: Rotting due to excess water or poor drainage. Leaf scorch due to direct sun.

GERMAN IVY *(Senecio mikanioides)*

Yellow-green fast-growing vine with small maple-like foliage and yellow florets.

Green Thumb Tips: Grows in sun or shade, ideal for trailing baskets, window boxes. Will grow in plain tap water alone.

Propagation: Take tip cuttings and root in water any time of year.

Troubles: Blackening of foliage due to poor drainage, poor light. Plant lice, mealybugs and aphids; spray with Malathion.

GOLD DUST PLANT *(Aucuba)*

If you're looking for a handsome item that will grow in a bright or shaded window, try the gold dust plant *(Aucuba japonica variegata)*.
This is a tender shrub with stiff waxy foliage spotted with yellow.

Green Thumb Tips: Give it plenty of water. Best soil mixture consists of sand, peat and loam, equal parts.

Propagation: Start new plants by taking tip cuttings and rooting them in sand or peat moss. You can set the plants outdoors in summer and bring inside in fall before frost.

Troubles: Leaf scorch due to dry soils. Scale insects, scrub with brush and soapy water. Syringe the foliage occasionally to give them the waxy, glossy effect.

GRAPE IVY *(Cissus rhombifolia)*

Cissus is the Greek name for ivy. Since this plant grows by leaps and bounds it is aptly referred to as the kangaroo vine. Also called grape ivy. It is a tendril-climbing vine originating in South America.

Green Thumb Tips: Grape ivy is a most popular houseplant. Give sun until some growth is made, then grow in any convenient location. Cut off long growths, root in water or rooting mixture. Related kangaroo vine from Australia has large oval leaves. Both flourish with little or much light, in most soil mixtures, tolerate drought and require very little attention.

Propagation: Cuttings taken from tips and rooted in plain tap water.

Troubles: None.

GYNURA *(Gynura aurantiaca)*

Purple velvet plant is covered with purple hairs and always a conversation piece because of its handsome color.

Green Thumb Tips: Does well in sunny window, or even semi-shaded, soil should be humusy (⅓ each of sand, peat and loam). Likes ample moisture, but never soggy soil condition. Plant is fragile and tends to grow crooked unless staked. Pinch the top back to make the plant bushier. Grows best when treated as annual. Goes into a flowering and semi-dormant condition in winter.

Propagation: Tip cuttings rooted in plain tap water. Start in spring.

Troubles: Spindliness. Just the nature of the plant. Keep it staked and pinched back and you'll eliminate this condition.

HAWAIIAN TI

Cordyline terminalis is also listed as dracaena, a relative of the florist's spike. Actually there is very little difference between the cordyline and the dracaena, and you find them used interchangeably.

Green Thumb Tips: The Hawaiian ti likes a rich loose soil, ⅓ sand, ⅓ loam and ⅓ peat. Some gardeners grow it in water alone, but in most cases this isn't too satisfactory as it often dries up and dies. Pot yours in soil mixture mentioned. Grow in bright window and in a room temperature of 70°. Do not overwater.

Propagation: Divide the roots or take tip cuttings and root in sand, sphagnum moss or plain tap water. Sphagnum is preferred.

Troubles: Yellowing of foliage and dropping due to overwatering.

HAWAIIAN WOOD ROSE

The Hawaiian wood rose you see in flower shops is not a rose, but morning-glory seed pods. It is called ipomoea (ipp-po-meo-ah) and is a close member of the morning glory family.

Ipomoea tuberosa or wood rose blooms twice a year and the flowers are greenish-yellow, with the appearance of an ordinary rose. As the petals open and the rose reaches maturity, it turns to a rich golden brown, making it ideal for use in a centerpiece arrangement or corsage. The flowers look like parchment paper, and you can even spray them with gold paint. The wood rose is the dried seed pod and inside the pods are black seeds the shape of an acorn having a hard shell similar to our Brazil nut.

Green Thumb Tips: You can grow it indoors on a sunny porch. All the vine needs is a sunny window and a temperature of 72° or so.

Propagation: File a notch in the hard seed coat, enough to expose the meat, for faster germination. Seed is sowed in a sand-peat mixture and kept in 72° F. room. Germination should be within 3 weeks. Growth is fast, as much as 3 inches in 24 hours. The plants need as much as a quart of water a day. It takes the wood rose a year to flower, but it's worth waiting for, if you like to grow things out of the ordinary.

Troubles: Indoors, red spider and aphids may become troublesome. Spray the vine with Malathion. Grow in a ⅓ sand, ⅓ peat, ⅓ loam soil mixture, in a 6-inch pot. Water daily but do not allow the pot to stand submerged in a jardiniere, as this may cause leaves to turn yellow. Leaf spot disease sometimes pops up, dusting with Captan will check it. Grow the wood rose in a small greenhouse or on a sunny, heated porch and you'll have a tropical vine right in your own home.

HYPOESTES

See Measles Plant.

ICE PLANT

Aptenia (*A. cordifolia*) is a trailing plant in same family as other ice plants, such as *Mesembryanthemum*.

Green Thumb Tips: Bright window, 72° temperature. Any loose soil mixture kept uniformly moistened.

Propagation: Stem cuttings rooted in sand.

Troubles: Red spider mites, spray with Kelthane.

IRESINE

Most common form of "chicken gizzard plant" or bloodleaf is *I. herbstii*, which has rounded leaves, brightly colored red.

Green Thumb Tips: Likes a bright sunny window, average temperatures found in the home. Will grow in shady spots and useful for urns, porch boxes. Sand, peat and loam mix suitable, kept uniformly moist. Grow outdoors in summer, indoors in winter.

Propagation: Cuttings rooted in plain tap water any time.

Troubles: None.

JADE PLANT (*Crassula argentea*)

The jade plant is found in the majority of American homes. It's leaves are fleshy and the plant resembles a cactus. While there are hundreds of crassulas, the most common is the jade plant.

Green Thumb Tips: It likes a bright, sunny window, but will do well in a semi-shady one; best temperature 72°, and a soil mixture of ⅓ each sand, peat and loam. In summer set plant outdoors, then bring in before frost.

Propagation: Take cuttings from tips and root them in moist sand. Or try this trick: take just a leaf (all by itself) and place it on a window sill. Leave it there for a period of 3 to 6 weeks, and pretty soon you'll notice it has small leaves and roots, all ready to plant in a pot of soil. Or, root the tip cuttings in box of moist sand.

Troubles: Withering of leaves and stems due to too much water, or poor drainage. Let plant get dry between waterings. Leaf drop due to poor light or too much water. Non-flowering is due to age of plant. Take tip cuttings and grow plants in bright window. Older plants seldom flower.

Joseph's Coat (Miniature alternanthera)

This member of the tender amaranth family, like the rest, has beautifully colored foliage and striking flower heads. *A. bettzickiana* grows about 3 inches tall and has distorted leaves marked in salmon and creamy-yellow colors, hence the name dwarf Joseph's coat. *A. ramosissima* grows 12 inches high and has pointed leaves of red with purple underneath. Flowers are similar to clover blossoms, smaller and white, thus the common name indoor clover. *A. versicolor* is another dwarf alternanthera, having bronzy-red and purplish veining, with yellowish-white edge. This indoor plant is called Joseph's coat, as is the garden annual *amaranthus tricolor*.

Green Thumb Tips: Needs bright sun for good foliage effect. Soil should be ⅓ sand, ⅓ loam, and ⅓ peat and kept uniformly moist.

Propagation: Take slips any time and root them in sand or plain tap water.

Troubles: None.

Lipstick Plant

Aeschynanthus lobbianus (still listed by some as *trichosporum*) is a trailing-type plant with green leaves placed opposite one another. Clusters of flowers form on stems and each scarlet flower resembles lipstick, hence the name. However, lipstick plant is known more for its handsome waxy green foliage. Some people also apply the name lipstick plant to *A. pulcher*.

Green Thumb Tips: Avoid direct sun but bright window is necessary for bud formation. Prefers soil mixture of ⅓ sand, ⅓ peat and ⅓ loam.

Troubles: Apt to get spindly. Pinch the tip out to make it stronger. Lack of flowers is due to poor light.

Madeira Vine

Some friends gave me a slip and I've been fascinated by this handsome climber. Commonly called mignonette vine, due to the fragrance of the tiny flower. Its botanical name is *Boussingaultia baselloides*.

Here's a tall, fast growing item which is ideal for adorning porches and arbors or for climbing up indoor windows. The foliage is leathery, clean and attractive, and in summer the plant throws out long spikes of small white fragrant flowers. The leaves are oval or heart-shaped, and in the area between the leaf stalk and stem you'll find small tubercles which will produce new plants if planted in moist sand.

Green Thumb Tips: The Madeira vine can be grown indoors, and, while a tropical item, it does fine on outdoor porch or window boxes in the north. The tuberous roots, which sometimes live over in warm winters, can also be lifted and stored in the cellar or some frost-free place. You can also root slips in plain water.

Propagation: Also called manetti vine, this handsome subject is propagated by seed, root divisions, small tubercles found along the stems in the leaf axils, and by slips rooted in plain tap water. Ours does well in a sunless window and, since it is so free from troubles, I heartily recommend the Madeira vine to our friends.

Troubles: None.

MAURANDIA

Actually should be asarina, sometimes called creeping gloxinia. Prefers a bright window, well-drained soil kept uniformly moist. Start new plants from seed, or cuttings rooted in plain tap water. (See Gloxinia)

MEASLES PLANT *(Hypoestes sanguinolenta)*

This plant is also called freckle face and pink polka dot plant because of the rose-colored markings on the oval foliage. Ideal for hanging baskets and planters.

Green Thumb Tips: Needs full sun to bring out the colorful dots. If grown in shade, plant will not develop freckles. Prefers loose soil, ⅓ each of sand, peat and loam, with vermiculite added. Uniform moisture at all times. After blooming is over, plant dies back and that's the time to withhold moisture, just enough to keep it alive. When new growth starts, cut plant back and give it plenty of water.

Propagation: Cuttings rooted in sand.

Troubles: None.

MOSES IN THE BULLRUSHES or MOSES IN THE CRADLE

Rhoeo spathacea or *R. discolor*, so-called because each straplike leaf has a number of small white flowers at the base. Prefers a bright window, and soil that is well drained and uniformly moistened.

Propagation: Start the plants from offsets, in a pot of sand and peat moss. Also by seed found in the pouches.

Troubles: None.

Musa Rosacea (Flowering Banana)

M. acuminata (also listed as *M. cavendishii*) is a dwarf ladyfinger banana. All bananas are easy to grow. Prefer a well-drained soil, ⅓ sand, ⅓ peat and ⅓ loam. Do best in semi-sunny window. Feed liquid plant food in spring. Grow superbly in peat-like mix. Feed weekly and give plenty of room Should have 24-inch tub at least. Will produce bananas in one year.

Propagation: Seeds or plant suckers formed at base of plant. Cut when not more than 1 foot high and use to start new plants.

Troubles: Blackening of foliage due to poor drainage.

Nasturtium Vine

A reader told me that she has a nasturtium plant that has reached a height of over 10 feet indoors, and loaded with blossoms in the home! Nasturtiums are climbers, ideal for training up and around windows. They'll tolerate semi-shade, have few problems. Aphids might be a problem indoors, as they often are outdoors, but spraying with nicotine sulfate will check them. For a fast-growing vine indoors, try this one.

Propagation: Seed sown in pots.

Troubles: Aphids (plant lice), spray with Malathion or nicotine sulfate.

Onion (Climbing)

Bowiea volubilis is a twining green succulent plant grown as a curiosity. Likes a semi-sunny window, cool, and uniform supply of water. In fall and winter bulb is dormant.

Propagation: Offsets planted in spring.

Palms

Palms are not the easiest houseplants to grow. Once you understand their wants, you can grow them well. The commonest palms include the Belmore sentry palm (*Howea*); Forster sentry palm (*Bel-*

moreana H. forsteriana); Roebelin palm (*Phoenix roebelenii*); yellow
palm or butterfly palm (*Chrysalidocarpus lutescens*) and the Weddell
palm (*Cocos weddelliana*). The dwarf palm is *Chamaedorea* or parlor
palm, and has bamboo-like canes. The Weddell is enough of a dwarf to
be grown in fern dishes for table decorations. Here are some species
of the *Chamaedorea* or parlor palm to try: *C. elegans*, *C. erumpens* and
C. seifrizii (very common in hotels), *C. metallica* (house palm) and *C.
ernesti angusti*, another fine house palm.

Green Thumb Tips: Palms like a fairly heavy garden soil enriched
with humus. They don't need frequent potting and should not be
exposed to direct sunlight. During summer months they like a lot of
water, but should be watered sparingly during the winter. Frequent
syringing and washing of the leaves to remove the dust is beneficial.
A common fault is to overpot palms, inviting too much water. This
causes a checking of growth and leads to yellowing of foliage. We like
to keep our wedding palms on the edge of being potbound. In winter
they are partly dormant and should not be watered heavily, just enough
to keep them from drying out. Best temperature is 65° to 80°, in a semi-
shaded window.

Propagation: Start from seed, but it takes many months or even years
to grow suitable plants. Best bet is to buy plant directly from a florist.

Troubles: Mealybugs, scale, lice and red spider mites, spray with Malathion or dip entire plant in solution of soap suds plus 1 tablespoon of
Malathion. Tip burn is due to hot dry room, dry soil or fertilizer injury.
Cut out the dried or dead leaves. Syringe plant in bath tub from time
to time.

PELLIONIA

If you're looking for something unusual to put in the hanging basket
or for a planter, try the pellionia (no common name). This item has
pairs of silvered leaves edged brownish-purple.

Green Thumb Tips: It prefers a semi-shady window, temperature of 72°
or more, and a good porous soil mixture, such as ⅓ each of sand, peat
and loam. Plant likes to be kept uniformly moist, but the soil should
never be soppy wet.

Propagation: Take tip cuttings anytime and pot them in moist sand.
Cuttings 3 or 4 inches long will root within 5 to 6 weeks.

Troubles: Drying of edges due to hot dry room, dry soils or fertilizer
injury. No insects to trouble this handsome item.

PHILODENDRON

A few years ago, the most important houseplants we had were the snake plant, Boston fern and the rubber plant. These are no longer in the lead. The aroid family with its many tropical genera is ahead. The genus philodendron is way out ahead of them all. Here are some tips for growing the most common types of philodendrons.

Some Philodendrons You Can Grow: The list is endless. Try *Philodendron hastatum.* Stands quite a bit of abuse. It is a climber with

Philodendron panduraforme

arrowhead leaves. Glossy green, fast growing, one of the best for homes. *P. cordatum* is really *P. oxycardium,* a heart-shaped glossy-leaved type, found in any 5 & 10 store. Does well in soil or water, ideal for pot and wall pocket. *Philodendron dubia* or *dubium* has shield-shaped leaves. *P. panduraeforme* is fiddleleaf philodendron, popular, an excellent keeper under adverse conditions. There are philodendrons which do not climb and these are worth looking into.

How To Use Philodendrons: In using philodendrons, make sure they are in a place suited for them. Dark halls or rooms are not good, unless you can have constant artificial light. Don't grow them with dry plants such as cacti or with plants that can take a lot of water. If you do, you may either overwater or underwater them. The non-climbing philodendron does not need pruning, and may work into your scheme better than climbers. You should ask your florist for the various types.

Soil: Most philodendrons are climbers or trailers, so their soil should be moist, open and well drained. A mixture of ⅓ sand, ⅓ loam and ⅓ peat is good, and you can add wood shavings, charcoal, vermiculite, perlite or well-rotted compost. Remember that the denser the mix, the smaller the leaves, and poorer the growth. The soil mix should be highly organic.

Water: Water should drain fast, never accumulate. The soil should never be allowed to dry out. Most philodendrons can take a lot of water if the drainage is good. Occasional spraying of leaves is good. Better still, turn the hot water on in the bathroom and get it nice and foggy. Leave the plant in the bathroom overnite; it will help a lot. When you water the plant, be sure to water the bark slab so the roots can draw moisture from bark. This helps keep leaves from getting smaller.

Avoid Too Much Water: Excessive yellowing and leaf drop means water around roots.

Light: Some feel that light is even more important than soil mixture. Philodendrons need intense though FILTERED light if kept at high temperatures, or the leaves will grow smaller and smaller and vines stringy. A weak-yellowish color in leaves in an otherwise healthy plant indicates too much light. However, if the same condition exists and the whole plant seems wilted and soft-bodied, that means too much heat and not enough humidity. Small leaves and/or long, leggy vines can be caused by too little light. Monstera, sold under the name of *Philodendron pertusum*, needs more light than true philodendrons or the leaves will not split as profusely as they should. This is the Swiss cheese plant or fruit salad vine. At first the leaves are bright green and tightly rolled up but soon unroll into heart-shaped blades deeply slashed from the margin halfway to the broad midvein. In its juvenile stage, with solid or partially indented leaves, it's often sold as *P. pertusum*. Keep in mind that young plants of both monstera and philodendron have quite different characteristics from mature ones, and, if you aren't acquainted with both forms, you might think two species were involved. That is why so much confusion exists in the philodendron listing. The *Philodendron pertusum* of the trade is nothing but one of the horticultural selections of *Monstera deliciosa*. All the *Philodendron pertusum* sold on the market today are rightfully *Monstera deliciosa*, the Swiss cheese plant.

Feeding: All philodendrons respond to a balanced liquid plant food, once every 4 weeks. We use Ra-pid-gro applied on foliage and on the moss-covered totem pole. Always feed and water the bark pole as the vines have aerial roots which penetrate and attach themselves to it, absorbing moisture and nutrients. Avoid dry fertilizer, as it may burn, discolor or spot leaves. If this does happen from feeding, flush the pot with running water to leach out salts, or repot the plant.

How To Prune Philodendrons: All philodendrons need pruning from time to time. Train them to grow on a totem pole, using twistems. If the tips grow above the pole you have a choice of two things: (1) Train the top to grow back down again, or (2) cut the tip out, root it in sand or water and make a new plant. Do not allow the tip to grow past the pole because it needs support. Aerial roots grow into bark to gather moisture and nutrients. Prune off those ugly aerial roots which stick out in mid-air. Try to get them to grow into the moss bark, if you use a totem pole. Some gardeners feel that you get smaller leaves when growth is made beyond the top of the totem pole. NEVER cut a philodendron back completely as it is apt to shock the plant and kill it. Prune off any leaves which are diseased and yellow.

Repotting: Plants seldom need repotting, although you can replenish the upper 2 inches of soil from time to time, adding peat, compost or loam. Feed liquid plant food. Also scatter 1 teaspoon of DDT or Chlordane in soil if you see tiny white worms in the soil. This kills symphilids, springtails and other soil pests.

Tips On Caring For Leaves: (1) give bath in a tub once every 2 or 3 weeks. (2) For gloss, don't use olive oil or vaseline. Use a half-and-half mixture of milk and water, applied with soft cloth; or use a commercial leaf shine sold by florists. Do not apply commercial leaf shiners too thick or too often. Glycerine on cloth gives good shine. (3) Cut off yellowed, or spotted leaves and burn. (4) Keep plants out of cold drafts and away from passageways where people will rub against them.

Propagation: Tip cuttings rooted in water. Tall plants can be cut back and the cuttings rooted to make a new plant.

Troubles: Aphids, red spiders, mealybugs and scale are pests to reckon with. Malathion will check these. Also syringe plants regularly to keep pests down. Browning at tips and edges is due to dry soil, being pot-bound, low humidity, or waterlogging. If the leaves of the monstera or Swiss cheese plant do not split, plants are not getting enough light, enough nutrients or enough moisture. Be sure your plant is not in a dark room. When tips or edges turn brown, it may be due to salts concentrating in soil. This may be alkali from water or residues from excessive fertilizer. In areas where water is highly alkaline, use rain water, distilled water or water you get from defrosting refrigerators for watering, and any burning of leaf tips will cease.

Leaves that get smaller and smaller or which tend to return to juvenile form may be due to a separation of the organic matter from the soil, leaving the rooting medium in a hard cement-like condition which the roots cannot penetrate readily. Such soils are hard to keep moist and the water merely runs down the inside of the pot, leaving the core dry. Or it might be that you aren't giving the plant enough water. Another cause of reduction in leaf size, or plain leaves is simple starvation. Philodendrons are gross feeders and should be fed once every 4 weeks. Incidentally, the irregular holes or cuts in the older character leaves are really a protection provided by nature against the heavy rains or winds. Most philodendrons bloom at some time but in many living rooms, they are often shy bloomers.

PICK-A-BACK PLANT (*Tolmiea menziesii*)

Also called piggyback plant or youth and old age, this item gets its name from the fact that young plants arise on the older leaves. Foliage is heart-shaped and hairy, and the plants themselves are nearly stemless.

Green Thumb Tips: Plant does well in a bright window or in full sun and prefers a uniformly moist soil. Good mixture consists of ⅓ each of sand, peat and loam.

Propagation: Start new plants by taking the young baby plantlets which arise on the leaves and root them in a pot of soil.

Troubles: Death of leaves due to poor light, improper watering, or dry soils.

PITTOSPORUM (*P. tobira*)

The pittosporum (*P. tobira*) is a handsome foliage plant with shiny leathery foliage with fragrant clusters of white flowers. There's a variegated form with grayish-green and creamy-margined leaves.

Green Thumb Tips: It likes a bright or semi-sunny window, cool temperature (around 72°) and you'll do it a favor if you mist the foliage regularly with warm water. Soil should be well drained; we use a mixture of ⅓ sand, ⅓ peat and ⅓ loam. Keep soil uniformly moist, allowing it to dry somewhat between waterings.

Propagation: Start new plants from tips rooted in a mixture of sand and peat moss.

Troubles: Scorched edges due to dry soils or dry air. No insect problems with this item.

POTHOS (Devil's Ivy)

The pothos sold by florists is really *Scindapsus aureus*, a handsome item with dark green leaves, splashed with yellow or cream. Marble queen is a popular variety and is listed as *Scindapsus aureus* Marble queen in the trade. To me, it's much more handsome than the philodendron. Technically pothos (or scindapsus) is actually *Epipremnum aurea.* However, the common name for epipremnum is accepted as pothos, and it looks like pothos is going to be with us for a long time to come.

Green Thumb Tips: Likes same culture as philodendron, takes ⅓ each of sand, peat and loam, with pebbles in bottom of pot for good drainage. Let plants become nearly dry between waterings. Likes a warm room and ample light. The better the light the better the foliage variegation.

Propagation: Take tip cuttings and root them in water or moist sand.

Troubles: Scorched edges, due to dry soils, dry air. Yellowing of leaves due to excess water or poor drainage. Small foliage due to lack of light.

RESURRECTION PLANT

I'm often asked for information regarding the care of the resurrection plant. It took me a little while to find out just what this plant really is since common names are often misleading. The plant listed as resurrection plant is *Selaginella lepidophylla.* It gets its name from the fact that it can be dried into a compact brownish ball and be brought back to life merely by placing the roots in a pan of water. The only care it needs is a bright or semi-shady window, and a soil mixture of sand, peat and loam. Give it plenty of water, but do not overwater.

RUBBER PLANT (*Ficus*)

A member of the fig family. *F. elastica decora* (common in flower shops) is the tough, wide-leaved rubber plant. A variegated leaf type (*F. elastica doescheri*) oftentimes called *F. pandurata,* or fiddleleaf rubber plant is very durable and popular. Creeping fig (*F. pumila*) has tongue-shaped leaves and may climb. (Ficus rhymes with "my-kuss")

Rubber Plant

Rubber comes commercially from the *Hevea braziliensis* or the true rubber tree. Some varieties of the household rubber plant were formerly an important source of rubber, but today the true rubber tree is hevea.

Green Thumb Tips: While the rubber plant does well in a warm, moist atmosphere, it will stand a surprising amount of abuse. One main trouble in growing this item is overwatering. This shuts off oxygen from the roots and the leaves start to turn yellow and drop off. The type of container the plant is in makes a big difference, a glazed pot is not usually satisfactory. Poorly drained soil also shuts off air to the roots and causes the leaves to turn yellow.

The best soil is a mixture of ⅓ sand, ⅓ peat and ⅓ loam. Don't overfeed the plant. Probably once every 3 or 4 years, usually a weak solution of liquid plant food is best.

Full sun is not necessary, although a partially-shaded window is helpful. Too much direct sun will scorch the leaves. The room temperature can be anywhere from 60° to 80° for this item.

If your rubber plant starts to stretch up and get too tall, don't hesitate to cut the tip out. This tip can be rooted in sand. Cut any dried or dead-looking leaves out.

Propagation: The rubber plant is best propagated by air layering. This is used to shorten a tall plant also. Simply make a slanting cut halfway thru the stem, then insert a toothpick or matchstick to keep it open. Bind the wound with a ball of damp sphagnum moss. Wrap a sheet of plastic film around it and fasten securely with string, wire or rubber band. Moss will fill with roots in 4 months. Cut it from the parent plant and pot the new plant up in a good soil mixture. To keep the leaves shiny, wash them with a mixture of half milk and half water. Never use olive oil or grease.

Troubles: Diseases: Rustlike spots on the leaves, appearing as a scorching and tip burning; indicates a fungous disease is present. Dust some good fungicide, such as sulfur, Captan or Ferbam, on the spots. Also remove the severely spotted leaves and burn them. Do not allow drops of water to remain on the foliage, as this will cause the disease to spread, especially along the edges. Rubber plants usually have no insect pests, although scale and aphids are known to attack them. Spraying with Malathion two or three times will check them. Swab a piece of cotton in alcohol and dab it on scales or mealybugs.

SCHEFFLERA (Umbrella Tree)

Originally from Australia, it is an ideal house, porch or patio plant. Its upright habit of growth and the ability to flourish in various situations have contributed to the popularity of this plant. It has light green, naturally shiny leaves. Growth is rapid and strong.

Green Thumb Tips: This item does get a bit tall and needs to have the top cut out. Start a new plant by rooting the top in a gallon jug of water. Save the mother plant as it will send out new growth and be a bushier plant. Schefflera likes a light or semi-shady window, out of direct sun. Water by soaking the soil well; let it dry out a bit between waterings. Poor drainage or too much water will cause leaves to drop off and new ones to curl inward instead of remaining rigid and flat. Best soil mixture consists of equal parts of sand, peat moss and loam. Start new plants any time of the year by taking cuttings from the top or tips. Growth is strong and rapid.

SNAKE PLANT or MOTHER-IN-LAW-TONGUE

The snake plant is a hardy item that will grow for the poorest green thumber. (Listed as *Sansevieria trifasciata laurentii*).

Green Thumb Tips: When the sansevieria or snake plant blossoms it causes quite a stir. Usually the snake plant is tucked away in some room where it gets no sunshine, little food or water, and that is why it doesn't bloom. If you give it full sun, regular feeding and watering it will flower reliably. During the summer this item can be put outdoors in sun or shade. Keep it watered regularly and bring indoors before fall. You'll be rewarded with greenish-white flowers with spider petals on a wire stem. The blooms are fragrant and dripping with honey.

The *S. laurentii* has yellow edging. Bright sun brings out the bright color whereas a little shade is conducive to darker green color. *S. hahnii* is a patented sport, vase shaped, dwarf and most ornamental.

Propagation: You can start new plants from divisions or cuttings of leaves stuck in moist sand. The white-striped forms propagated by cuttings produce plants with no striping. The striped plants are multiplied by dividing the plants.

Troubles: Failure to flower due to adverse growing conditions.

SPATHIPHYLLUM

Here's an easy-to-grow item with narrow leaves and calla lily-like flowers that are pure white.

Green Thumb Tips: Does well in semi-sunny, or semi-shady window in average room temperature. Soil mixture should be well drained, and can be equal parts of sand, peat and loam. Keep soil uniformly moist at all times.

Propagation: Start new plants by division of the rootstocks. You can even start the plants from seed formed in the flowers (spathes), sown in sand-peat mixture.

Troubles: Leaf scorch due to dry soils or dry air. Plant likes ample humidity and moisture.

VENUS FLYTRAP (*Dionaea muscipula*)

This is an oddity that always attracts attention, especially among children.

Green Thumb Tips: Likes a rich, humusy soil, ample humidity. Grow it in an aquarium filled with sphagnum moss. Has tiny hairs on two hinged jaws. If the hairs are touched (by finger or insect) the jaws will snap shut and enzymes from the plant will digest the insect. Instead of fertilizing, feed the "traps" insects or raw hamburger.

Propagation: By started plants from specialists.

Troubles: None.

WANDERING JEW

If you're looking for a good houseplant, try the old-fashioned standby, the wandering Jew, sometimes called the inch plant or the joint plant. One of the wandering Jews is *Tradescantia fluminensis,* having green or green-and-white leaves. Another wandering Jew is *Zebrina pendula,* having purplish leaves. For hanging baskets and window boxes these are among the easiest to grow in sun or shade.

Green Thumb Tips: They like a loose well-drained soil and ample moisture at all times. A cool temperature suits them fine. In full sun, the colors are more intense and you get a better show. You can start new plants from cuttings any time of the year. Just place them in a glass of water. Pot them up in a soil containing ample amounts of peat.

Troubles: Scorched leaf tips due to hot dry rooms and dry soils. Plants grow fast and should be clipped if growing on porch or in hanging baskets. Red spider mites, spray with Kelthane.

WAX PLANT (*Hoya Carnosa*)

The hoya or wax plant is a popular houseplant, but getting it to bloom in the average home is quite a chore. Leaves are leathery, glossy and handsome, some are variegated. Flowers are waxy. *H. carnosa variegata* has pink-tinged leaves bordered in creamy white.

Green Thumb Tips: Likes a loose soil mixture (1/3 each of sand, peat and loam) for good drainage. It should be pretty much potbound to bloom well, therefore do not overpot (that is, don't use too large a pot). Feed it liquid plant food in fall and early winter, but not in mid or late winter as a partial rest at that time is beneficial.

Prefers full sun and will not bloom in shade. Give it plenty of moisture in summer, spring and fall, but in winter keep it on the dry side. Best winter temperature is 50° to 60° at night and 60° to 65° in daytime.

If you can get your vine to flower do not remove the stem or "spur" on which flowers have been produced, since next season's flowers will appear from the same place.

Propagation: To start new plants, cut out tips and root them in sand.

If insects such as red spider, scale, mealybugs or thrips bother, spray with Malathion.

Troubles: Failure to flower (see above). Also keep in mind that these plants are naturally slow to flower. In fact, they seldom bloom unless they're 3- or 4-years-old and grown in full sun. If yours won't bloom, even in full sun, allow the plant to become potbound and see if this won't force it to bloom. Red spider mites, spray with Kelthane outdoors.

Tough Foliage Plants Anyone Can Grow

Many a homeowner has wished he had a houseplant that would take all kinds of abuse. These are some tough plants you can use: arrowhead, Australian umbrella tree, cast iron plant, Chinese evergreen, crown of thorns, devil's ivy, fiddleleaf fig, grape ivy, heartleaf philodendron, India rubber plant, jade plant, oval leaf peperomia, snake plant, trileaf wonder, dracaena, Veitch screw pine and zebra plant. These toughies will take all kinds of punishment and we suggest you use them if you do not have a green thumb.

Vines and Trailing Plants for Totem Poles

Arrowhead
Black Pepper
Creeping Fig
English Ivy and Varieties
Grape Ivy

Kangaroo Vine
Pellionia
Philodendron
Scindapsus (Pothos)
Wax Plant

Plants Useful for Tubs

Australian Umbrella Tree
Dracaena
False Aralia
Fatshedera
Veitch Screw Pine
Tuftroot

Fiddleleaf Fig
India Rubber Plant
Palms
Philodendrons
Silk Oak

House Plants Which Take Abuse

Arrowhead
Australian Umbrella Tree
Cast Iron Plant

India Rubber Plant
Jade Plant
Peperomia

Chinese Evergreen
Crown of Thorns
Devil's Ivy
Fiddleleaf Fig
Grape Ivy
Heart-leaf Philodendron

Snake Plant
Syngonium
Tuftroot
Veitch Screw Pine
Zebra Plant

House Plants Which Take Extremely Dry Rooms

Bromeliads
Cacti
Crown of Thorns
Jade Plant (Crassula)

Peperomia
Snake Plant
Wandering Jew

Vines and Trailing Plants for Hanging Baskets

Arrowhead
Asparagus
Creeping Fig
Coleus
English Ivy
Grape Ivy
Kangaroo Vine

Nasturtium
Pellionia
Perlargonium Peltatum
Philodendron
Scindapsus
Senecio
Vinca Major, Periwinkle

Plants Needing Special Exposure

South or West Window

Amaryllis
Azalea
Begonia
Bloodleaf
Cacti and Succulents
Calla Lily
Coleus
Cyclamen
Gardenia

Geranium
Lily
Easter Lily
Oxalis
Poinsettia
Rose
Sweet Flag
Tulip
Velvet Plant

East Window

African Violet
Banded Maranta
Caladium
Dracaena
Fatshedera

Peperomia
Philodendron
Rubber Plant
Scindapsus
Veitch Screw Pine

Fern
Gloxinia
Ivy

Silk Oak
Wandering Jew
Wax Plant

North Window

African Violet
Anthurium
Arrowhead
Baby's Tears
Australian Umbrella Tree
Cast Iron Plant
Chinese Evergreen
Dracaena
Fern
Dumb Cane
Ivy

Mother of Thousands
Norfolk Island Pine
Peperomia
Philodendron
Piggyback
Rubber Plant
Scindapsus
Snake Plant
Tuftroot
Wandering Jew

PLANTS TOLERATING HIGH TEMPERATURES (65° to 70° Night)

African Violet
Aphelandra
Arrowhead
Australian Umbrella Tree
Banded Maranta
Cacti and Succulents
Caladium
Chinese Evergreen
Croton
Dracaena

Episcia
Figs
Gold Dust Plant
Gloxinia
Philodendron
Scindapsus
Seersucker Plant
Snake Plant
Spathiphyllum
Veitch Screw Pine

PLANTS TOLERATING LOW TEMPERATURES (50° to 60° Night)

Australian Laurel
Azalea
Baby's Tears
Boxwood
Bromeliads
Calceolaria
Camellia
Christmas Begonia
Cineraria
Citrus
Cyclamen
Easter Lily
English Ivy
Fatshedera

Flowering Maple
Fuchsia
Geraniums
German Ivy
Jerusalem Cherry
Kalanchoe
Miniature Holly
Mother of Thousands
Ornamental Pepper
Oxalis
Primrose
Vinca
Calla Lily

Plants Tolerating Medium Temperature (60° to 65° Night)

Achimenes
Amaryllis
Arisia
Avocado
Bromeliads
Browallia
Chenille Plant
Silk Oak
Ti Plant
Tuberous Begonia
Velvet Plant
Christmas Cactus
Chrysanthemum
Citrus
Copper Leaf

Crown of Thorns
Easter Lily
English Ivy
Gardenia
Shrimp Plant
Grape Ivy
Hibiscus
Hydrangea
Norfolk Island Pine
Palms
Pilea
Peperomia
Poinsettia
Rose

A QUICK GUIDE TO SOME COMMON FOLIAGE PLANTS

Foliage Plant	Green Thumb Tips	Propagation	Troubles
Acorus gramineus variegatus	Iris-like leaves, useful in terrariums; bright light, lots of water.	Division of clumps.	Drying of tips due to dry soil, dry air.
Aechmea fulgens	Leaves reddish underneath. Flowers red, tipped with blue; berry-like fruits. Bright window, good drainage.	Division of suckers.	Brown leaves due to poor drainage.
Alocasia	Heavily-veined leaves similar to caladium; semi-sunny; use soil mix of peat, sand and loam with charcoal added.	Divide mother plant.	Drying of leaves due to low amount of humus in soil, hot sun, dry soil.
Aloe variegata	Forms rosettes of leaves, reddish flowers, semi-sunny window, well-drained soil; AVOID OVERWATERING OR POOR DRAINAGE.	Divide suckers formed at base.	Rotting at base due to poor drainage, too much water.

A QUICK GUIDE TO SOME COMMON FOLIAGE PLANTS (Continued)

FOLIAGE PLANT	GREEN THUMB TIPS	PROPAGATION	TROUBLES
Amomum	Sword-shaped leaves, with spicy aroma when mashed. Semi-shady window, 72°. Soil ⅓ each sand, peat and loam.	Divide clumps any time of year.	Yellowing due to poor drainage, red spider mites.
Aphelandra squarrosa	Semi-sunny window, soil, ⅓ each of sand, peat and loam. Evenly moist. Syringe foliage every 3 weeks.	Tip cuttings in spring in sand, peat mixture with bottom heat.	Brown leaf edges due to dry air and dry soil.
Aralia balfouriana	Likes warm, bright sun and plenty of water, loose soil mixture.	Divide plant any time.	Yellowing due to dry soil, red spider mites.
Araucaria excelsa	Pine tree, growing up to 5 ft. indoors, cool bright window, lots of water, good drainage.	Take cuttings from top shoot.	Yellowing of leaves due to excess sun. Filtered sun best.
Ardisia crispa	Red holly-like berries and leaves. Light shade, 72° or lower, loose soil, mist foliage.	Sow seeds in sand and peat, or root cuttings.	Dropping of berries, brown spots on foliage due to dry soils.
Asarina barclaiana	Semi-sunny window, sand, peat and loam mix; evenly moistened.	Seeds sown anytime; cuttings rooted in glass of tap water.	None.

A QUICK GUIDE TO SOME COMMON FOLIAGE PLANTS (Continued)

FOLIAGE PLANT	GREEN THUMB TIPS	PROPAGATION	TROUBLES
Aspidistra elatior	Takes all kinds of abuse. Semi-sunny window to shade; any soil that is fairly well drained.	Divide roots any time of year.	None.
Barbados Cherry (*Malpighia*)	Reddish blooms, like leaves. Light window. Soil equal parts of sand, peat and loam, uniformly moistened.	Seeds sown in sand, peat and vermiculite. Or cuttings taken in spring or summer.	Brown spots on foliage, due to poor drainage. Dry soils.
Bertolonia marmorata	Difficult foliage plant to grow, semi-shady window, 75° sand, peat and loam mix.	Seeds in vermiculite and peat or cuttings rooted with bottom heat.	Tip burn of foliage due to dry soil or excess sun.
Billbergia	Plant bushy, ideal for dish gardens; cool temperature dish gardens; good drainage; can take bright sun.	Cuttings rooted in sand.	Yellowing and dropping of leaves due to excess water, poor drainage.
Buxus (Boxwood)	Small-leaved shrubby plant. Tolerates sun or shade.	Cuttings rooted in sand.	Likes well-drained soil. Few troubles.
Cactus	(See Cactus)		
Caladium	(See Caladium)		

A QUICK GUIDE TO SOME COMMON FOLIAGE PLANTS (Continued)

Foliage Plant	Green Thumb Tips	Propagation	Troubles
Century Plant (*Agave americana*)	Sunny window, sandy soil. Do not water heavily.	Division of offsets any time, pot in loose mixture with plenty of sand.	Rotting due to excess water.
Ceropegia woodii	Sunny to semi-shade; sand, peat and vermiculite mixture. Avoid heavy watering.	Cuttings rooted in moist sand, or plant tiny bulblets.	Drying of leaves due to lack of water.
Cestrum nocturnum	Fragrance similar to gardenia blooms; semi-sun.	Cuttings rooted in sand, spring or summer.	Bud drop, leaf scorch due to dry soil.
Chenille Plant (*Acalypha hispida*)	Long flower spikes, resembling chenille stems. Sunny window, 70°; sand, peat and loam soil. Moist at all times and well drained.	Cuttings in fall and winter in sand.	Leaf drop, lack of flower spikes due to improper light, dry soils.
Chlorophytum comosum	Good for hanging baskets; filtered light.	Let baby plantlets root in soil.	Drying of leaf tips due to dry soils, fertilizer injury.
Colocasia esculenta	Heart-shaped leaves take humusy soil, semi-shade, 72°. Uniform supply of water.	Tubers same as for caladium.	Browning of leaf edges, yellowing due to dry soils or overwatering.
Columnea	Semi-sunny window; humusy soil, sand, peat and loam, evenly moistened.	Seeds in peat, vermiculite mixture or cuttings in sand alone.	Leaf drop due to hard soils, dry soils.

A QUICK GUIDE TO SOME COMMON FOLIAGE PLANTS (Continued)

Foliage Plant	Green Thumb Tips	Propagation	Troubles
Cissus antarctica (Kangaroo vine)	Filtered light; prefers to grow slightly on dry side; cool window.	Cuttings rooted in water.	Red spider mites, spray with Kelthane.
Corn plant (Dracaena massangeana)	Filtered light; do not let soil dry out; avoid poor drainage or excess watering.	Cuttings in sand, or by root divisions any time.	Rotting due to poor drainage; leaf scorch due to dry soils.
Crassula argentea	Cool window; soil mix of sand and peat. Will grow fine on dry side.	Stem or leaf cuttings rooted in sand or plain tap water.	Leaf drop due to poor light, dry soils.
Crossandra infundibuliformis	Sunny window, soil—⅓ peat, loam and sand. Kept moist.	Seeds sown in sand and peat, cuttings in sand.	Bud drop, brown tips on foliage due to dry soils.
Hedera helix	Glossy foliage, sunny window, 72°, well-drained soil.	Cuttings rooted in water.	Drying of leaves due to low humidity, dry soil. Red spider mites, use Kelthane. Aphids and scale, use Malathion, plus soapy water.

SOME FOOLPROOF FOLIAGE PLANTS WITH
LOW LIGHT REQUIREMENTS

This includes plants that can be grown in areas not near windows. Plants would do better if growing in indirect bright light, but will tolerate the low-light conditions found in many homes.

BOTANICAL NAME	COMMON NAME
Aglaonema	Chinese Water Evergreen
Aspidistra	Cast Iron Plant
Asplenium nidus	Bird's-Nest Fern
Aucuba	Gold Dust Aucuba
Cissus antarctica	Kangaroo Vine
Cissus rhombifolia	Grape Ivy
Dieffenbachia	Dumb Cane
Dracaena	Striped Dracaena or Corn Plant
Pandanus	Screw Pine
Philodendron cordatum	Heartleaf Philodendron
Pittosporum tobira	Pittosporum
Podocarpus macrophylla	Podocarpus
Sansevieria hahnii	Birdnest Hemp
Sansevieria trifasciata	Snake Plant
Spathyphyllum	Spathiphyllum
Syngonium	Arrowhead Plant

SOME FOOLPROOF PLANTS WHICH TOLERATE A
SEMI-SHADY WINDOW

This means indirect light from the sun. Direct sun will burn the foliage. Dense shade or dark room will not do for these items.

BOTANICAL NAME	COMMON NAME
Achimenes	Flame or "Red" African Violet
Acorus	Sweet Flag
Adiantum	Fern
Aglaonema	Chinese Evergreen
Amomum	Cardamon
Anthurium	Anthurium
Aspidistra	Cast Iron Plant
Aucuba	Aucuba
Begonia Rex	Rex Begonia
Caladium	Fancy-leaved Caladium
Dieffenbachia	Dumb Cane
Episcia	Flame Violet
Fatshedera lizei	Tree Ivy
Ficus	Rubber Plant
Fuchsia	Lady's Eardrops
Hedera	English Ivy

Botanical Name	Common Name
Helxine	Baby's Teardrops
Maranta	Prayer Plant
Monstera	"Philodendron"
Nephrolepis	Boston Fern
Peperomia	Peperomia
Philodendron (Many species)	Philodendron
Saintpaulia	African Violet
Schefflera	Umbrella Tree
Scindapsus (Pothos)	Marble Queen or Pothos
Senecio cruentus	Cineraria
Senecio mikanioides	German Ivy
Sinningia speciosa	Gloxinia
Spathiphyllum	Spathiphyllum
Tolmiea menziessii	Piggyback Plant

SOME FOOLPROOF HOUSEPLANTS WHICH TAKE BRIGHT SUN

Some of these plants may not be able to tolerate direct sun in summer, especially if the soil is dry. However, these will endure 5 or 6 hours of light, if the soil is kept uniformly moist.

Botanical Name	Common Name
Abutilon	Flowering "Maple"
Agave americana	Century Plant
Aloe arborescens	Octopus Plant
Agapanthus	African Lily
Azalea	Florist's Azalea
Begonia	Christmas Begonia and others
Bromeliads	Bromeliads
Bougainvillea	Bougainvillea
Cacti (many genera)	Cacti
Cattleya orchid	Florist's Orchid
Campanula	Bellflower
Capsicum	Christmas Pepper
Chrysanthemum	Florist's Chrysanthemum
Citrus	Orange, Grapefruit, etc.
Codiaeum	Croton
Coleus	Coleus or Foliage Plant
Crassula	Jade Plant
Cyrtanthus	"Earth Stars"
Dracaena	Gold Dust Plant
Fuchsia	Lady's Eardrops
Freesia	Freesia
Gardenia	Florist's Gardenia
Hedera	English Ivy
Hoya carnosa	Wax or Parlor Plant

BOTANICAL NAME	COMMON NAME
Hydrangea	Florist's Hydrangea
Maranta	Prayer Plant
Pelargonium	Geranium
Pilea cadierei	Aluminum Plant
Saxifraga sarmentosa	Strawberry Begonia
Schlumbergera bridgesii	Christmas Cactus

CHAPTER IV

Other Easy-To-Grow

Favorites

Bulbs, Indoor Forcing

Tulips, daffodils, crocus, scilla, grape hyacinths and paper-white narcissus are all forced alike indoors.

Green Thumb Tips: Pot them any time from October to December. Place flat side of tulip bulbs toward rim of pot. The broad leaf grows from this side and makes a better looking pot of tulips.

Set daffodil or tulip bulbs ½ inch apart with tips just showing above soil surface. Hyacinth bulbs need one-quarter of upper part of bulb exposed. Hyacinths can be potted singly in 4-or 5-inch pots or five in an 8-inch pan or earthenware bowl.

After planting the bulbs, water the pots well and store in cold (50°) completely dark place for 10 to 12 weeks. You can even bury the pots outside under a covering of leaves or straw to keep the frost from ground so that the pots can be lifted at any time. Absolute darkness in a cold temperature is needed for a period of 10 to 12 weeks to insure root growth. Bring gradually to light and heat, always avoiding overheated rooms. When roots have developed and buds emerged from neck of bulbs (hyacinth bud should be at least 3 inches tall) put pots in partial light for about a week, temperature 60° to 65°. Then place pots in sunny window and water as needed.

Paper-white narcissus can be forced into bloom without a cold-storage period. Bulb is potted in tray of pebbles covering half the bulb. Water enough to cover the stones and put away in a cool dark room for a short period. (Many do not even bother to do this with paper-

These bulbs have been in cold storage and are now ready to be forced into bloom. After 10-week cold storage period, they are placed in a sunny window and kept watered. Left to right: snow drops, tulips, Easter lilies, narcissi and crocus.

whites, but move it directly to a light place.) Generally roots will form in less than two weeks. Keep temperature about 60°; temperatures above 75° cause weak growth and loss of flowers. One trick used by city dwellers for forcing hyacinth bulbs is to use a hyacinth glass. Fill with water and add a small piece of charcoal. Set bulb in glass so its base almost touches the water. Twist a sheet of paper into a cone, fasten with a pin and cover bulb, then place in a cool dark closet. In 8 weeks (but not before January) roots should be well-developed and bud protrude about an inch or so. Transfer to warm but still dark spot till bud is at least 3 inches. Then place in sunny window. Keep water at original level at all times. After tulips, daffodils, hyacinths and other hardy bulbs have finished blooming, they may be planted in the garden in a permanent spot. Do not attempt to force them again indoors. Let them grow green leaves as long as possible after blooming. It is not necessary to keep them in the cellar, rather it's best to plant them outdoors where they will bloom for you again the following spring.

Propagation: Divide bulbs in fall.

Troubles: Failure to bloom due to lack of cool period for root formation. Tiny flower buds (especially with hyacinths) is the result of forcing too fast after bringing in from cool storage. Bud blast due to hot dry room. Never let pots dry out in storage, always keep soil reasonably moist for strong root system.

DAFFODILS, NARCISSUS AND TULIPS

Pot your bulbs in fall, using a 4-inch clay pot. Do not crowd; allow at least ½ inch between bulbs. Fill pots to within 1½ inches from the top, place bulbs, fill with soil, press soil firmly around bulbs and give good watering. Then bury outside under a covering of leaves or straw to keep frost from ground. If you have a cold cellar you can bury them in there, with an occasional watering to keep soil in good condition. In a nutshell, tulips, daffodils, crocus, scilla and grape hyacinths can be potted any time from October to December. Place the flat side of tulip bulbs toward the rim of the pot. The broad lower leaf grows from this side and makes a better looking pot of tulips.

Absolute darkness in a cold temperature is needed for about 10 weeks to insure root growth with all except the paper-whites. Bring gradually to light and warm room, always avoiding overheated rooms. Temperatures of about 65° are best. The only exceptions are the paper-white and soleil d'or narcissus which can be planted in a bowl of pebbles, enough to cover the bulb only half way. Water enough to cover stones and put away in a cool dark place for root formation. Generally bulbs are rooted in two weeks and can be brought to light in as cool a location as possible. Or bulbs can be brought directly into lighted room as long as it is in a temperature between 60° and 65°. Failure to flower means that roots did not form due to too high a temperature.

AMARYLLIS

Hippeastrum vittatum, commonly called amaryllis, probably the best known of all pot-grown bulbs. The colorful amaryllis can do a lot to brighten up your home in winter. You can buy advanced bulbs (pretreated) which will bloom in one month, or you can resort to the regular untreated bulbs, sold all winter long. One bought in early December will bloom in February. The larger the bulb the more stems ("scapes") it produces. A first-size bulb will produce 2 to 4 stems each 1½ to 2 feet tall, and each with 2 to 5 trumpet-shaped flowers.

Green Thumb Tips: Before potting, check bottom for bulblets. If present, remove and plant them in small clay pots. If left attached, they hinder normal growth. If roots and base of bulb are dry and corky trim off the hard part of base with sharp knife. Four-inch clay pots are OK for even the largest bulbs. Usually, the larger the plant, the more room the roots need, but amaryllis is an exception. They will do well in 5- or 6-inch pots with a mix of ⅓ sand, ⅓ peat and ⅓ loam. Pot bulb so that the neck is exposed down to the shoulder of the bulb. Some plant them so that ⅔ of bulb remains exposed above the rim of the pot. Pack soil around bulb firmly, water just enough to settle it. Place in a cool spot in subdued light for a few weeks, until top growth begins. Then move to a sunny window and water well. Withholding water until growth begins is important with amaryllis. If you

African Amaryllis

give it too much water before the growth begins, the foliage, not the stems, grows first. The bulb then puts its energy on growing leaves instead of flowers. Without the needed energy, the buds rot or are produced on very short stems.

When stems are 4 inches high, feed with liquid plant food once a week until buds show color. Stems shoot up fast once they get started. Stake with bamboo sticks so they won't bend. After flowering period is over, leaf growth becomes vigorous, and bulbs should be left in their pots and watered.

When all danger of frost is over, set pots and bulbs at earth level in a sunny spot outside in garden and give plenty of water and food. In August, scapes or stems appear again and often come into full bloom after most perennials have faded. Before heavy frost in late fall, bring pots into the house and put in a cool basement or closet gradually withholding water until soil in pot is absolutely dry. This will cure them and give bulbs the 60 day rest they need prior to starting into growth again. Leave bulbs in same pots for several years. Merely scrape off two inches of soil and replace with fresh mix.

Propagation: Start new plants from bulbs purchased from garden centers, or divide plant.

Troubles: Non-flowering. Due to lack of rest period (see above).

Caladium (Fancy-Leaved)

These are handsome shade lovers, prized for their showy marbleized foliage. They are frost touchy outdoors, but make a fine tubbed plant on the patio or the dark sunless room indoors, or for the shaded border.

Green Thumb Tips: Requires ample moisture at all times. Good drainage is a must or the leaves will wilt down. Any warm room is ideal. Feed once every two weeks with a liquid plant food such as Ra-pid-gro. After the plant starts to go dormant in fall, withhold water gradually until the foliage has died down completely. Best soil mixture is ⅓ sand, ⅓ loam and ⅓ peat moss, with charcoal in bottom for drainage. Store dormant bulbs in cellar where they won't freeze.

Propagation: Tubers, divided and planted at potting time in spring. Try this trick used by florists. Plant the bulbs upside down in small boxes or flats, since this is a crown-rooting bulb and the roots come out around the top (center) eye. This direct contact with the soil produces roots more quickly than the opposite method. Start them in the usual humusy mixture of 1 part each of leaf mold (or peat moss) sand, and loam. Press the bulb halfway into the soil and place near a warm stove; if you have a home greenhouse, under the bench is fine. Temperature should be 80° or so; the higher the temperature, the better starting results will be. Do not let the bulbs dry out during the starting process. Water sparingly until the bulbs begin to sprout and have roots 4 or 5 inches long. When the sprouts begin to show, place bulbs, right side up, in 5- or 6-inch pots. Water copiously when in full growth, and use a liquid plant food. Bone meal and dried cow manure are good foods for caladiums. You can divide tubers into sections in spring, making sure each section has a part of center or "eye." Dust the cut surface with Ferbam or sulfur, plant in sand-peat mixture, in warm room.

Calla Lily (*Zantedeschia aethiopica*)

This was the funeral flower of grandma's time. There are callas with rose-colored flowers (spathes), some yellow and white.

Green Thumb Tips: Use rich sandy loam, mixed with peat, and give ample water. Pot bulb in a 5-inch pot, keep in a cool room so roots can develop, watering lightly. Plant white calla so neck comes just above the surface of soil. Allow ½ inch of soil over yellow calla (elliottiana). Grow both in bright window, with a uniform supply of moisture, NEVER DRY. Feed liquid plant food every 3 or 4 weeks. After flowering, allow bulbs to ripen off naturally by withholding water. After danger of frost, place pots in a garage (pots on side). In August, take up the dormant bulbs, clean them off and repot in fresh soil. Callas may also be grown outdoors as summer bedding plants,

near the edge of a pool. But be sure to take them up at FIRST SIGN
OF FROST as they are tender.

Propagation: Start new plants from tiny offshoots or tubers. We plant
the tubers in summer for winter bloom in our greenhouse.

Troubles: Failure to flower due to lack of light, overcrowding or lack
of water. Give plenty of water at time of forcing. When plants start
to go dormant and turn yellow, withhold water gradually. Red spider
mites, spray with Kelthane.

Spray callas with Malathion to keep down aphids. If calla leaves
turn yellow and plant makes no growth, it's root rot. Cut off rotted
portion, soak bulbs for 1 hour in 1 ounce corrosive sublimate to 7½ gallons water, or for 2 hours in 2 percent solution of commercial formaldehyde (1 pint to 6 gallons of water). Let treated bulbs dry before
planting in new soil. DURING GROWING SEASON DO NOT
LET THE BULBS GET DRY or it will throw callas into a "molt"
or rest period and the bulb will not bloom.

CLIVIA (*C. miniata*)

Commonly called kaffir lily. A fine bulbous houseplant with clusters
of trumpet-shaped blooms borne on a slender stalk. Leaves strap-like
and similar to those of common amaryllis (hippeastrum).

Green Thumb Tips: Grows well in poorly lighted room if temperature
is kept below 70°. Withstands temperature near 40° in winter. Keep
soil moist. Never dry off completely. Care after flowering: Put in
sunny spot outdoors. Keep in same pot for several years, without disturbing the plant even though roots are crowding badly. Roots will
soon fill the pot and that's the signal to divide the plant. From May
to August, feed with liquid plant food such as Ra-pid-gro. Give the
plant plenty of water at all times.

Propagation: Division when plant fills the pot.

Troubles: Non-flowering due to lack of light or insufficient water.

FREESIA (*Freesia refracta*)

A tender member of the iris family, producing corms, sword-shaped
leaves 6 to 12 inches long, and long bell-shaped fragrant flowers, in
colors of white, yellow, orange and lavender carried on wiry stems.

Green Thumb Tips: Pot corms in September in loose soil (⅓ sand, peat
and loam). Keep uniformly moist until January when flowering commences. Keep in coolest window possible (60°). After flowering, discard or dry the corms and plant them again the following year.

Propagation: Corms. Buy new ones each year for best results.

Troubles: Non-flowering due to poor light or high temperature.

CARE OF TENDER BULBS IN WINTER

Each fall when the time comes to put the garden to bed for the winter many home gardeners are puzzled about what to do with their assorted bulbs, corms and tubers. In fact, they are even sometimes more confused by the terms themselves. Actually, to the rough-and-ready gardener, it makes little difference whether the underground storage organ is a bulb, a corm, a tuber or a rhizome. What is more important is how to handle the organs properly for the winter so they will put on a repeat performance the next year. All are underground storage organs with buds, ready to sprout at the proper time.

Hardy bulbs are rarely a problem, for the earth is usually their best storehouse in winter. But the tender ones must be given protection, either by heavy mulching or storing indoors.

Unfortunately, the modern home no longer has a root cellar with a dirt floor, a perfect storage place for apples, potatoes and bulbs in winter. However, one need not be discouraged; there are other ways to keep bulbs alive in winter.

The dividing line between hardy and non-hardy bulbs sometimes is not distinct. For example, often a gladiolus bulb will winter over outdoors in New York State, and one woman I know does not dig her dahlias. She mulches them heavily with straw each fall, and they come through the hardest of winters. However, the following table contains some suggestions for handling common and not-too-common tender bulbs, based upon years of gardening experience in western New York.

		H–Hardy in many areas	SH–Semi-hardy	T–Tender in cold climates	
PLANT	AFTER-FLOWER-ING CARE	TIME TO DIG	STORAGE TREATMENT	TEMPERATURE	TIME TO DIVIDE
Acidanthera (Scented glads) (SH)	Let foliage die down with glads.	In fall before ground freezes.	Cut off dead tops. Dust with DDT. Store in sand, buckwheat hulls, dry (or only slightly moistened) peat moss.	45–55°	In spring before planting.

CARE OF TENDER BULBS IN WINTER (Continued)

Plant	After-Flowering Care	Time to Dig	Storage Treatment	Temperature	Time to Divide
Anemone (SH)	Let foliage grow.	After first frost, or mulch with 5 in. straw.	If dug, store in perforated plastic bags with peat. Dust with Captan or sulfur.	35–45°	Divide in spring.
Achimenes (T)	Reduce water gradually until plants are dry. Store in pots in boxes with damp peat moss or sawdust around pots.	Before frost.	Keep slightly moist during storage period. Dust with Captan.	50–60°	In spring divide roots or rhizomes.
Agapanthus (Lily of the Nile) (T)	Cut down watering gradually to dry off tuberous roots.	Before frost.	Store in large tub or pot in dry place. Keep soil almost dry.	45°	Divide in spring.
Alstroemeria (Peruvian lily) (T)	Dry off gradually.	Before frost.	Store in sawdust or damp peat moss.	45° or cooler.	Divide roots at planting time.
Amaryllis (T) (Hippeastrum)	Allow foliage to grow in same pot in summer.	Early fall.	Bring indoors and keep soil on dry side for 60-day rest.	Keep in room at 40° during rest or cure period.	Divide and repot any time needed. May be left in same pot for several years.

CARE OF TENDER BULBS IN WINTER (Continued)

Plant	After-Flowering Care	Time to Dig	Storage Treatment	Temperature	Time to Divide
Tuberous Begonia (T)	Dry off in pots in fall.	In fall at first sign of frost.	Cut off tops. Dust bulbs with Captan or sulfur. Store in vermiculite, peat or perforated plastic bags.	50–60°	In spring cut old tubers into 2 pieces with eyes or buds.
Caladium, fancy-leaved (T)	Reduce water gradually in fall.	Before frost.	Cut off tops, remove bulbs from pots, dust with sulfur. Keep in plastic bags with vermiculite or slightly damp peat.	50°	Divide tubers at planting time.
Calla Lily (Zantedeschia) (T)	Withhold water gradually until leaves start to yellow.	Before frost.	Cut off tops. Dust tubers with sulfur or Captan and store like tuberous begonias.	50–60°	At potting time in spring remove offset and repot.
Cannas (T)	Let frost blacken foliage, then cut to within 6 in.	After frost.	Store in cool basement upside down in vermiculite, peat moss, buckwheat hulls or sawdust.	50–60°	Divide rhizomes in spring, each with 2 eyes.

CARE OF TENDER BULBS IN WINTER (Continued)

Plant	After-Flowering Care	Time to Dig	Storage Treatment	Temperature	Time to Divide
Clivia (Kaffir lily) (T)	Keep soil rather dry in summer.	Bring indoors in fall.	Store in same pots, repotting once every 3 or 4 years.	50–60° in winter	Divide at repotting time in summer.
Crinum (Milk & wine lilies) (T)	Let leaves grow.	Dig before frost in fall.	Store in rather dry cellar, in sawdust, peat or vermiculite.	50°	Divide at planting time in spring.
Dahlias (T)	Let frost hit foliage.	In fall before severe freeze, cut off tops, dig up clumps and let rest upside down for a few days.	Store in boxes of peat (slightly dampened) or coat roots with paraffin. Heat water to 90°, pour in melted wax. Then dip tubers.	45°	Divide in spring, make sure each tuber has eye or bud.
Eremurus (Foxtail lily) (SH)	Let foliage die down.	Leave in ground. Mulch with evergreen boughs or straw after hard freeze.	Do not let go into dormant period with water around roots.	——	Divide in fall and plant in well-drained soil to prevent rot. Mulch after dividing.

CARE OF TENDER BULBS IN WINTER (Continued)

Plant	After-Flowering Care	Time to Dig	Storage Treatment	Temperature	Time to Divide
Galtonia (Cape or summer hyacinth) (T)	Water heavily to force extra foliage.	Dig before frost.	Cut off tops, store in peat moss, perforated plastic bags of vermiculite to prevent drying out. May be hardy outdoors if protected.	40–50°	Divide at planting time in spring.
Gladiolus (T)	Let foliage yellow naturally. Bulb growth is made in fall.	Before the ground freezes. The longer foliage remains green, the better for bulbs and bulblets. Leave bulbs in sun day or two, then cure in airy place. May winter over in ground, but don't count upon it.	Cut stalks close to bulb, dry with electric fan. Leave skins on. Quick curing with fan helps avoid disease. After 3 weeks clean bulbs, without removing husks on new. Dust with DDT for thrips and fungicide (Arasan or Spergon). Store in wire basket or shallow boxes.	35–50°	After digging and curing about 3 weeks. Before spring planting soak bulbs in Lysol, 1½ tblsp. per gal. water for 3 hours. Plant while wet.

CARE OF TENDER BULBS IN WINTER (Continued)

PLANT	AFTER-FLOWERING CARE	TIME TO DIG	STORAGE TREATMENT	TEMPERATURE	TIME TO DIVIDE
Haemanthus (Blood lily) (T)	Let foliage mature.	Bring indoors before frost.	Keep in pot in cellar leaving top half of bulb exposed.	50°	Remove offsets at potting time (spring).
Hymenocallis (Peruvian daffodil, ismene, spider lily) (T)	Let foliage mature.	Can be dug in fall before frost. Some leave in ground all winter in mild areas.	Dry off foliage but do not disturb fleshy roots. Prefer heat in storage, especially first few weeks.	60–70°	Remove offsets before planting in spring.
Iris (Bulbous) (T)	Let foliage die down gradually.	May be dug after bloom or (indoors) watering gradually stopped.	Store in cellar or plant in autumn. Must be mulched heavily in cold regions.	50°, if stored.	Dig and divide every 4 or 5 years.
Ixia (Corn lily) (T)	Plant in garden in spring. Let foliage grow all summer, as with glads.	In fall before first hard frost.	Cut off tops and dust bulbs with DDT. Treat like glads.	35–50°	Remove offsets before planting in spring.
Montbretia (Tritonia) (SH)	Let foliage remain green, as with glads.	In fall before first hard frost.	Lift corms and cut tops close. Dust with DDT and Spergon or Captan.	40–50°	Clean and divide at planting time in spring.

CARE OF TENDER BULBS IN WINTER (Continued)

Plant	After-Flowering Care	Time to Dig	Storage Treatment	Temperature	Time to Divide
Nerine (Guernsey lily) (T)	Rest in summer by keeping dry. Keep outdoors.	Bring indoors before frost for fall flowering.	Needs none in winter. Keep plant watered for foliage growth which follows blooming.	——	Divide in summer and repot every 3 or 4 years.
Oxalis (T)	Let foliage remain green as long as possible. When it starts to yellow, place outdoors in pots under bush, or leave on sun porch.	Before frost bring pots indoors.	Keep in cool, dark room with little water until growth begins. Then bring to bright window.	50°	Divide in summer or fall, potting offsets.
Polianthes ('Tuberose) (T)	Let plants remain green in summer.	In fall before severe frost.	Store in dry cellar in vermiculite, sawdust or peat moss.	50°	Divide in spring.
Ranunculus (Florist's ranunculus) (T)	Let growth continue throughout summer.	In fall before frost. In mild areas may be left in ground and mulched.	Store in perforated plastic bags, with peat moss or sawdust, slightly dampened. Dust with Captan.	35–45°	Divide at planting in spring.

CARE OF TENDER BULBS IN WINTER (Continued)

PLANT	AFTER-FLOWER-ING CARE	TIME TO DIG	STORAGE TREATMENT	TEMPERATURE	TIME TO DIVIDE
Sprekelia (Jacobean lily)	Water heavily to get good growth in summer.	In fall before frost.	Dry foliage and keep pot in cellar for winter.	60°	Divide bulbs prior to planting in spring.
Tigrida (Tiger flower or shell flower)	Let foliage mature in summer as with glads.	In fall before severe frost.	Cut tops close to neck. Store in buckwheat hulls, slightly moistened peat moss or soil.	35–50°	In spring before planting.
Zephyranthes (Fairy lilies) (SH)	Let plants continue to grow in summer.	Lift before frost.	Dig up and store in vermiculite, sphagnum or damp sawdust. Dust with sulfur.	45°	Divide in spring or in fall after lifting.

Growing Cactus In The Home

The cactus family is a big one. Cacti (plural of cactus) make interesting houseplants twelve months of the year because their stems and spines are always pleasing to look at, if not to touch. While there are hundreds of cacti, I'll mention a few of the common ones grown as novelties. Rattail cactus (*Aporocactus flagelliformis*) has slender stems with scarlet flowers. Sand dollar cactus (*Astrophytum*) and old man cactus (*Cephalacereus senilis*), which has a snowy-white covering

Rhode Island College of Agriculture

Cacti and succulents make interesting houseplants and dish gardens. Avoid overwatering and use a well-drained soil, ⅓ each of sand, peat and loam.

of hair (spines), are always attractions. Peanut cactus (*Chamaecereus silvestri*) has clusters of short cylindrical branches, covered with soft white spines.

Barrel cacti include *Echinocactus*. One of the easiest cacti to flower is *echinocereus*, a hedgehog cactus. Easter lily cactus is the *Echinops multiplex* with white or pink flowers somewhat resembling the blossom of an Easter lily. One of the best so-called night-blooming cactus, *Epiphyllum oxypetalum*, belongs to a large group of husky, spineless plants (*see Hylocereus undatus*). The group known as *Mammallaria* includes such plants as the long lady finger, old lady, powder puff and thimble cactus. The cactus known best to home gardeners is the *Opuntia*, commonly called rabbit ears or pad cactus; you see these in dish gardens a great deal. Lemon cactus (*Pereksia*) has white flowers with a lemony smell and grows almost vine-like. The crown cactus (*Rebutia*) is another excellent one to add to your collection. The popular and cantankerous Christmas cactus, *Schlumbergera bridge-*

You can bring a welcome touch of the sun country indoors the year round with selections from this clay-potted array of cactus plants. Kept in clay pots, as quality growers do to insure perfect drainage, they are long-lasting if you go easy on watering and give them lots of light. Versatile and durable, they come in all sizes to fit your decorating needs and locations.

sii, is still listed under *Zygocactus truncatus*. Getting it to bloom at Christmas time is the aim of all homeowners. You can do it if you understand that it will not set buds if it gets artificial light at night from September on. It needs a resting period with only scant watering, from spring until fall. Then in October bring it down from a bedroom

Purdue University Cooperative Extension Service

These plants are gaining popularity as house subjects. They are easy to grow and easy to start. Usually, a leaf stuck in a pot of soil will root and form a new plant.

window and grow it in a bright window where it gets ample water and protection from direct sunlight. Full directions for getting it to bloom at Christmas are found under Christmas Cactus.

Green Thumb Tips: The pot you use can mean the difference between success and failure for cactus plants. Use unglazed pots, never glazed pots since they hold moisture. You can repot any time, but keep moisture away from the young plants or they will rot. In spring plants can be set outdoors in pots and left in the ground until September when they are brought indoors. Soil must be well drained, so incorporate a lot of sand in the mixture and less peat moss. Go easy on fertilizer as these plants do not require much feeding. A little lime in the soil will help.

Cacti do best in a temperature of 60° to 75°, so they really aren't too fussy; don't go below 50°. As for light, give them the brightest window possible. Direct sunlight is not needed. These plants are more temperamental when it comes to watering than to other factors. In winter, most cactus plants are in a rest period and should be grown on the dry side.

Propagation: All cacti may be started from seeds, by grafting and by cuttings. Cuttings is the easiest method for multiplying your plants. If you take cuttings, be sure to sear the end so that no moisture can get in or out. A simple way to do this is to place the cutting in the sun for a few days or on a shelf in a dark closet. It takes about a week for a cactus to sear well. Don't be afraid that the plant will die. Plant the cutting in a well-drained soil mixture of sand, leaf mold and loam. A spoonful of slaked lime to a 5-inch pot of soil is helpful to cactus plants. Do not water the new cuttings. No water should be added until you are sure new roots have a start. Seeds may be started in a loose sand-peat mixture, temperature 72° to 75°.

Troubles: Rotting is due to excess water; most of the trouble with cactus plants stems from overwatering, especially during the dormant winter period. Most cacti don't need watering more often than once every 10 days or so. Some kinds last 3 weeks or more without additional water. Wilting is due to excess water; cut plants back and repot. Mealybugs are insects covered with cottony masses, control by mixing up Malathion, 1 teaspoon to a quart of soapy water. Scrub the affected areas with a soft toothbrush, a treatment which will check scale pests as well. Aphids cause sticky substance on plants. Spray with Malathion or nicotine sulfate.

Rotting is due to excess water. Do not water from above, especially those cacti which show a depressed crown. A good watering rule is to keep the soil slightly moist, not wet.

Night-Blooming Cereus: Many plants are called night-blooming cereus and this has caused home gardeners a lot of confusion. The cereus tribe of the cactus family is a big one, but all of them have huge blossoms, many fragrant, and they always open at night. They remain a thing of beauty until dawn. Probably the most outstanding night-blooming cereus is *Hylocereus undatus,* noted for its large flowers. Unlike its brother cacti, it is thornless, but fleshy and succulent. This fleshiness is the plant's secret weapon for storing moisture inside itself. A natural gum prevents evaporation, thus sustaining it through the dry months. Plant grows 3 to 8 feet high and will lean over without some support. Another night-blooming cereus is the *Epiphyllum oxypetalum* which has many day-blooming hybrids known as orchid cacti. Culture is same as for the *Hylocereus.*

Green Thumb Tips: Prefers a loose, humusy soil, good drainage. A potting soil mix of equal parts of sand, peat and loam is fine. Give overall syringing with tepid water from time to time. Best temperature is 72° to 82°. Low temperatures (below 50°) cause it to wilt.

Grow in a bright window. In winter do not water or feed heavily, just keep soil moist enough to prevent wilting.

Propagation: Take root cuttings and start in water or sand.

SOME EASY TO GROW CACTI

BOTANICAL NAME	COMMON NAME
Aporocactus flagelliformis	Rattail Cactus
Astrophytum myriostigma	Bishop's Cap, Sand Dollar

Cephalocereus senilis	Old Man Cactus
Chamaecereus silvestri	Peanut Cactus
Coryphentha runyoni	(No common name)
Echinocereus	Hedgehog Cereus
Echinopsis multiplex	Easter Lily Cactus
Epiphyllum oxypetalum	Orchid Cactus
Lemaireocereus marginatus	Organ Pipe Cactus
Mammillaria	Pincushion Cactus, Lace Cactus, Old Lady Cactus
Opuntia littoralis	Prickley Pear, Beavertail

All the above take the same cultural requirements: bright window, sandy, well-drained soil, and clay pots. Avoid overwatering and overfeeding.

SOME EASY TO GROW SUCCULENTS

BOTANICAL NAME	COMMON NAME
Agave americana	Century Plant
Aloe vera	Medicine Plant
Ceropegia woodii	Rosary Vine
Crassula argentea	Jade Plant, Paintbrush, Watch Chain Plant
Echeveria species	Hens and Chickens
Euphorbia	(No common name)
Gasteria verrucosa	Deer's-Tongue
Haworthia species	Cushion Aloe
Kalanchoe pinnata	Bryophyllum, Air Plant, Panda Plant
Portulacaria afra	Elephant Bush
Sedum species	Stone Crop, Live-Forever
Sempervivium tectorum calcareum	Houseleek

FERNS FOR THE HOME

The fern family is a large one, and the indoor gardener will find most ferns pleasant companions to have around. Some are not tolerant of indoor conditions, but most of them will do with a little pampering. Florists are using ferns in among pots of poinsettia and in dish gardens. Here are the most common types used for indoor purposes.

ADIANTUM

Adiantum or maidenhair grows both indoors and outdoors; and likes plenty of moisture and plenty of peat or humus. Best temperature is around 72° in summer and a cool 55° in winter. These ferns need a rest period during winter. Repot fern every 3 years, or whenever soil is full of roots. Repotting can be done any time of the year. Scrape off some soil from sides and add a new mixture with plenty of peat moss or humus. Cut off any wire growth. Divide the clump with a sharp knife at repotting time.

Asparagus Fern

Asparagus fern and plumosus are fine houseplants if grown in a shaded spot. Like humusy soil, ample moisture. The *Asparagus plumosus* has flat sprays of fine foliage, and *Asparagus sprengeri* has coarser foliage. Do not allow the plants to become pot-bound. Transplant once or twice a year after well established. Feed liquid plant food (such as Ra-pid-gro) and keep temperature above 65°. Leaves turn yellow from lack of nitrogen or if room temperature is below 50°.

Asplenium

Bird's-nest fern, *A. nidus*, gets its name from the fact that the fronds are formed in a rosette. *Asplenium viviparum* and *Asplenium bulbiferum* (mother's ferns) bear baby ferns on the fronds. These small fronds can be severed (with a section of the mother plant) and placed in pots. New roots will form and the plant will soon make nice growth.

Cyrtomium

Cyrtomium falcatum or holly fern is often placed in potted poinsettia plants by florists as a "filler". This item has tough, leathery dark-green leaves with wavy edges, resembling the foliage of the American holly (ilex), hence the name holly fern.

Davallia

D. fejeensis or so-called rabbit's-foot fern is a handsome fern but not one for a person without a green thumb. Ideal for hanging baskets where it can be grown in peat moss and loam, or sphagnum. It likes ample moisture. Start new plants by dividing the rhizomes.

Nephrolepis

The Boston fern (*N. exaltata bostoniensis*) has many varieties with sword-shaped leaves (fronds) which are divided one or more times into

Boston Fern is easy to grow.

small leaflets (pinnae). Homeowners like the finely divided appearance, but the more finely divided the leaves are, the harder the plant is to grow. The Whitmanii fern is a sport of the Boston fern.

PLATYCERIUM

This includes the handsome and bizarre staghorn fern which takes the same culture as other ferns; semi-shaded window, ample humus in the soil. Many gardeners mount the staghorn fern on slabs of bark with osmunda or sphagnum moss to nourish the roots.

POLYPODIUM

This is the so-called bear's-paw or hare's-paw fern—a good candidate for indoor planters due to the coarseness of its fronds resembling the cut leaf philodendron. Care is same as for the Boston or sword fern.

POLYSTICHUM

Called the tiny tot fern because of its miniature size. Dark leathery fronds grow about 10 to 12 inches tall, sometimes less, making it useful in small planters, bottle gardens and terrariums.

PTERIS

This large group includes *P. cretica*, *P. cretica cristata* and *P. serrulata*, none having a common name. The fronds fork and crest, as do types of the Adiantum fern. Culture is same as for all ferns.

GENERAL DIRECTIONS FOR GROWING FERNS

Sunlight: Ferns need light but not direct sunlight. Too much light is harmful and is the cause of ferns developing sickly, yellowish-green appearance. An east or north window is fine for ferns.

Soil: Ferns need lots of humus. Try a mixture of garden loam, 2 parts leaf mold, 1 part sand and some broken charcoal. Cow manure, rotted woods earth or compost is fine. Feed them a liquid plant food such as 23-21-17 about once a month to maintain green color.

Repotting: One reason ferns do so poorly is that they are seldom re-potted. They should be repotted every 2 or 3 years and divided when necessary. If the pot is full of roots, that's a sign to repot. The job can be done any time of the year. Plants do best in pots just large enough. Avoid too large a pot. Crown should be level with soil. Drainage must be perfect for ferns—a good reason why the soil should contain sand and some charcoal. Put some broken crock or cinders in the bottom of the pot. Ferns should never stand in a saucer or jardeniere of water. This causes yellowing of leaves. Never allow the soil to dry out, it should be kept medium-moist. We find that one of the best ways to water a fern is to immerse the pot in a pail of water for 10 to 15 minutes.

Temperature: Ferns don't like it hot. Give them a cool bright room, 60° to 70°, and keep away from radiators and out of direct sunlight.

OTHER CULTURAL NOTES ABOUT FERNS

When the tips of fronds turn brown, it may be due to warm room, or possibly people brushing against the foliage. Ferns like lots of elbow room; sometimes they send out runners, long strings which never de-velop into fronds or foliage. These take strength from the plant and should be removed at once. Ferns like to be groomed. Reach in and remove dead twigs, etc. If items such as the Boston fern send out long stems with few leaves, don't be discouraged. Remove these, give the plant a liquid feeding and it will throw out young, healthy fronds.

Yellowed leaves are often due to poor drainage, too much light or lack of nitrogen. You can tell poor drainage by the mold on the soil surface. Scratch the surface with tines of a fork, dust a little sulfur in, and be sure to improve the drainage. The new glazed pots are bad for ferns because they do not allow for air drainage or "breathing". The clay pots used by florists are still the best! Too small a pot or low temperature will cause the leaves to yellow.

Diseases and Insects: Be on the lookout for scale and mealybugs. Control: mix up Malathion, 1 teaspoon to a quart of water and spray. Scrub affected parts with this, using old toothbrush. Note: IF YOUR FERN HAS BLACK SPECKS ON THE UNDERSIDE, DON'T WORRY. These are the seed organs which produce the spores, and are not the scale insect as many believe.

There's a nematode disease caused by minute eelworms, causing discoloring on entire leaf. Control: dip whole plant in hot water (110° F. for 10 minutes). Small worms in soil can be killed by dusting DDT on soil and watering it in.

Hardy or Outdoor Ferns

If you have a shady spot where few things will grow, try ferns. They like a soil rich in leaf mold or woods earth, plus sand. Hardy ferns can be planted in spring or fall. If planted late, give them a mulch of leaves to protect from freezing and thawing. This also helps new roots to form. DO NOT PLANT TOO DEEP IN THE GROUND. THE CROWN SHOULD BE LEFT EXPOSED TO THE AIR. Do not plant below the surface. Deep planting is fatal, especially where a long, wet season follows. It causes rot.

Some Good Ferns and Mosses

Arenaria verna, green moss
Asparagus, dark green, nice to cut
Asparagus sprengeri, green sprays, nice to cut
Aspidium taussimense, compact feather-like fern
Asplenium bulbiferum, king and queen, carrot, mother fern
Asplenium nidus avis, glossy leaves
Cyrotomium rochford, holly-like foliage
Helxine solieroli, moss-like green foliage
Nephrolepsis compacta, dwarf variety fern

Polypodium mandaianum, bluish-gray fern
Polystichum aculeatum, graceful
Polystichum coriaceum, bluish fern
Pteris adiantoides, similar to holly fern, low growing
Pteris victoriae, compact variegated silvery foliage
Pteris wilsonia, compact shapely crested fronds
Selaginella brownii, fluffy green mounds moss
Selaginella denticulata, low spreading moss
Selaginella martensii watsoniana, variegated foliage

Miniature Roses

Each year more indoor gardeners are finding that miniature roses make attractive and interesting houseplants. They are the only roses which can be successfully grown in the home, and they need only a little more than average care. Blossoms last for days and the plants are a mass of color for weeks at a time.

Miniature roses growing in jar on patio.

Star Roses

Green Thumb Tips: Indoor rose culture depends upon three factors: sunshine, humidity and moderate temperature (70° or so).

The plants you receive from the nursery are dormant and ready to be planted in pots or other containers. The best container is one made of clay or pottery, with plastic, metal, or china being next best. This pot should be about 4 inches in diameter and about the same depth.

The best soil mixture is 2 parts of good garden or top soil, 2 parts of peat moss or other humus and 1 part of a medium coarse sand. These should be mixed well. A small amount of this mixture should be placed in the bottom of the pot, the miniature rose then placed in the center, and the pot filled with soil. Firm the soil slightly so that it comes to within a half-inch of the top.

Place the pot in a sink and water thoroughly. Soak the soil until all bubbling ceases or water seeps from the bottom of the pot.

For best growing conditions, miniature roses should be placed in a tray that has a half-inch of moist gravel, shells, plastic, or sand in it. Keep this material wet at all times, but do not let water touch the bottom of the pot. This keeps moisture in the air (i.e., maintains humidity in a normally dry house) and promotes the best foliage.

Miniature roses should be kept moist at all times. Under most conditions the roses should be watered every one or two days. Always water from the top of the pot, and apply enough water each time to wet the soil thoroughly.

Place your miniature roses in a window that gets a maximum amount of sunlight; they will not do well with less than three hours daily. An unshaded window in full sun is ideal.

Select a window, if possible, which does not have a radiator or heat outlet under it as excessive heat or dry air is undesirable.

A moderate room temperature of 65° to 70°, away from cold drafts or heat, is the most satisfactory.

When your miniature rose is first potted up, there is no need for fertilizer. About three weeks later, when leaves have started to grow, fertilizer should be added to the soil. Any ready-made soluble fertilizer may be used following instructions on the package. In most cases, dissolve one teaspoonful of soluble fertilizer in a quart of water and wet the soil in the pots thoroughly with the solution. Repeat this procedure every three weeks. Caution: Do not overfeed them.

While roses received from the nursery are free from insects or diseases, they may eventually appear on plants in the home. A good aerosol bomb designed for houseplants, used weekly, is an effective and easy means of keeping them under control. Any spray designed for roses may also be used; follow instructions given on the package.

Excessively high temperatures should be avoided as they cause insects to multiply on the plants.

About six weeks after the miniature roses have been potted up, they will begin to bloom. It is at this time that these amazing little flowers will put on a dazzling show, a real reward for the weeks of waiting. The buds will not open all at once, but slowly one after another for several weeks. As soon as a flower fades, pinch it off in order to promote more blooming. When the first set of flowers has finished, keep watering and feeding and soon the miniature roses will bloom again. They should continue to bloom as long as growing conditions are well maintained.

Remember the three basic needs of your miniature roses are: sunshine, humidity, and moderate temperatures. With these three requirements adequately fulfilled, an indoor garden of miniature roses will bring untold wintertime satisfaction.

In late spring (May north of Washington and St. Louis), your miniature roses should be planted out-of-doors in the garden or a window box.

Incidentally, the flowers may be cut if desired to make dainty, colorful miniature arrangements and boutonnieres.

My thanks to Conard Pyle for his helpful information on miniature roses.

How to Raise Tropical Fruits Indoors

The citrus family: This includes lemons, oranges, grapefruits, tangerines and the like. Many gardeners successfully raise these in the home, for flowers, foliage and fruit. *C. aurantifolia* has small edible limes (golfball size). *C. Limonia ponderosa*, so-called ponderosa lemon, is a houseplant that produces big edible fruit, some weighing over a half-pound.

Citrus mitis (calamondin) or miniature orange has fragrant white flowers, edible fruits, 1 to 1½ inches in diameter. *C. nobilis deliciosa*, the mandarin orange, is another citrus grown indoors. The *C. taitensis* or otaheite (oh-tuh-hee-tee) orange produces golf-ball sized fruit which is attractive, although inedible.

Dwarf limes and pomegranates are also available for indoor growing. Pomegranate (*Punica granatum nana*) is a neat dainty tree with orange-red fruit.

Green Thumb Tips: All citrus prefer a loose, well-drained soil, loam, sand and peat mixed together, fortified with ½ cupful of bone meal to each peck. Soil should be uniformly moist and preferably watered from beneath, although not necessary. A good soaking in sink twice a week is good. Also syringe to wash away dust and to keep insects down. Spring is a good time to give citrus plants a light pruning, cutting out any extra long shoots for symmetry. If plants have not been repotted in past 4 years, do so using above soil formula. When summer comes, set plants outdoors in partially shaded spot, plunging pots up to rim. This summer treatment helps ripen the wood and prepares fruits for late fall and winter display. Bring indoors before frost and grow in sunniest window available.

Citrus plants like cool temperatures from 40° to 50° at night during winter. They also need full sun and an airy location. Temperature and sunlight are important in bringing the plants into flower and fruit. It will take many years for seedlings to bear, and if they do bear, the fruit will be sour, yet decorative.

Propagation: By seeds or cuttings taken in spring or early summer. Take 4-inch cuttings from tips and root in sand. Or you can sow seed in pots of soil any time of year. Plants grown from seed produce nice foliage and blooms but cannot be depended upon for edible fruits. If you do start the plants from seed of a store orange, don't be disappointed if you don't get lots of fruit, since these come from large outdoor trees and should not be expected to bear indoors. In the home they are capricious as to blooming and bearing. Citrus started from seed can be whip-grafted in spring and made to bear. For edible fruit, best results will be obtained by buying grafted or budded plants from nurseries.

Seed sown in a 4-inch pot of soil will produce handsome foliage plants during the winter months.

Trouble with Citrus: Dropping of buds, flowers and small fruits can be due to a lack of light, improper watering (too much or too little) or high room temperature. Failure to flower can be due to lack of summer ripening period, high room temperature or lack of light. Normally citrus are large outdoor trees, taking years to bear, so don't expect the impossible. Grafted types bear and flower indoors. Those started from seed may take years to flower and bear fruit, and even then you cannot count on them to flower or to fruit. Seedlings of all citrus are capricious as to time of blooming. Some are 10 years or older and have had no fruit or flowers. Most citrus need pollination indoors, and you can help this along by taking your cat's tail or camel's hair brush or the tip of your finger and tickling each bloom, spreading pollen from one flower to another.

Black coating on leaves is sooty blotch or mold gathering on secretions from aphids or scale. Wash off with soapy water and syringe plants regularly. Spray with Malathion to check pests. Yellowing of leaves is due to poor drainage, too much water, poor light or insects in the soil.

If your citrus gets too tall you can trim the tips back to size and shape you want them. Trim in spring or early summer. Sometimes you can root the cuttings in sand, although seed and grafting are easier.

Avocado Pears (*Persa americana*)

Most alligator pears we get come from Florida and California. Some also come in from Santo Domingo and Puerto Rico. Judge ripeness this way: If fruit "gives" or feels soft to the touch, it's ready to eat. Pinching or poking will bruise it, cause dark spots. If it feels like a stone, take it home to ripen. Put fruit in brown paper bag and it'll ripen inside bag. Don't put it in refrigerator. Flesh will darken when exposed to air. If you use it in salad, a bit of lemon in the dressing will prevent the flesh from darkening. Store pieces in waxed paper. Try mashing chunks of avocado into hot soup before serving. Adds flavor.

Green Thumb Tips: Keep leaves washed off, if plant gets too tall, cut it back to half so new stems will form at base of old stem. Don't be afraid to trim the plant for symmetry; it's tough and grows fast. If plant gets large, transplant to larger pot or tub and grow in bright room. You may have to use a bamboo stick for support. Feed with Rapid-gro once every 3 or 4 weeks, 1 teaspoon to quart of water.

The plant can pollinate itself, it has perfect flowers (male and female), but it won't fruit indoors. It's even hard to get it to flower, but the foliage is attractive. Spray with Malathion if aphids appear. Hose it in bath tub.

How To Start Seed: There are two ways, in water or in soil. Some have good luck with seed in plain tap water and glass. Water method: Thrust toothpicks in middle of seed (pit) and suspend pit in glass of water. Roots grow out and down from base. Top can be differentiated from bottom of pit easily. Base has a dimple in it, and usually the top is tapered. After you remove the flesh, wash the pit with warm water, NOT COLD WATER. Sometimes the halves have started to split. It's OK, but they shouldn't be entirely separated because there's a vital thread between them and if it's broken, the seed's germinating power may be hurt.

DO NOT PUT ENTIRE PIT IN A GLASS OF WATER as it causes a scum to form, just the base. Place glass in warm spot. Keep water in it at constant level, making sure base of pit is always immersed. Soon you'll see a split and a long tap root coming from base, and a shoot will start from top. If stem grows too fast, cut it back about half, even while seed is still in glass. Sometimes a seed will make several shoots or stems. Don't cut them until you've repotted the rooted seedling. Sometimes shoots will fall off, one by one, leaving a tall shoot. This can be cut back to make a bushy plant.

When a thick set of roots is formed, enough to reach the bottom of glass, you can pot it up, using ⅓ sand, ⅓ loam and ⅓ peat mix.

To me a better method is to start seed in a pot of soil. Set seed in soil so that UPPER HALF OF SEED IS EXPOSED. Water with warm water. Don't keep soil soggy wet. After germination keep in bright window at room temperature.

Troubles: Red spider mites and aphids. Mites cause webs on tips of shoots. Aphids secrete honeydew material which attracts black sooty mold. Control: spray with Malathion, for aphids also syringe plants weekly in bath tub. For red spider mites, spray with Kelthane.

DWARF BANANA

Musa nana cavendishi has same needs as pomegranate, except that it should not be allowed to grow dry. Give sunny window, loose, humusy soil and uniform supply of moisture. Grows well in average home. (See Foliage Plants for more information on dwarf banana.)

COFFEE TREE

Start from seed in sand-peat mixture. Once seedlings are up, transplant to 4-inch pot and grow in a semi-shaded or sunny window. Pinch tip back to make plant bushy. You won't get many berries but the foliage is well worth the effort.

(See chapter on Foliage Plants for more information on coffee tree.)

PYGMY DATE PALM *(Phoenix lonreiri)*

These are harder to start and grow than most tropical plants, since the hard seed coating keeps out moisture. Filing it lightly often helps to hasten germination. The date is a palm of desert regions, and that means it likes lots of heat. Grow in warm room, bright window and use a ⅓ sand, ⅓ loam and ⅓ peat mixture. Yours won't bear in the home because you must have a male and female tree. Male and female flowers are on different trees. Plant outdoors in summer, and keep foliage covered with Malathion to prevent red spider mites or scale insects. Start seeds in loose soil and don't be impatient as it may take 6 months for germination. A temperature of 80° to 85° is necessary for sprouting.

HOW TO GROW FIG TREES INDOORS AND OUTDOORS

You can get fig trees (*Ficus carica*) to bear, even in cold regions, but it takes work. There are three ways to choose from: (1) Grow in ground and give winter protection; (2) in pots, and store in cellar or cool place in winter, and (3) under glass in heated or cool greenhouse. If you grow yours outdoors, give it plenty of winter protection.

In Greenhouse: In a small greenhouse figs can be harvested over a long period. Start new plants from cuttings 10 inches long during dormancy period (winter). Place them in a box of sand and keep in a cool place all winter. They will callous over and during this time get ready for rooting in spring when they are planted out in the garden. They sometimes bear second year. Avoid seed, unless you want plant for foliage effect. Since they fruit on new wood, the plants should be pruned considerably at end of each growing season, which also makes them easier to handle.

In Pots: For planting indoors in pots, the greenhouse plants are set into 4-inch pots and when roots fill these pots, shift to 6-inch pots. The dormant, field-grown plants are set in 8-inch pots or small tubs. Cramping roots a little will keep the plants smaller and hasten production of flowers and fruit. You can buy dwarf fig trees from nurseries. These are grown in tubs so plants can be taken inside and stored for winter. Plants will winter safely in ordinary cellar. Or you can wrap and bury the top in ground for winter protection. The common fig matures fruit without pollination, thus differing from the dried fig of commerce which needs a Capri fig tree and fig wasp for pollination. So-called Smyrna-type figs need special pollination for fruit formation.

Outdoor Culture: The best way to grow the figs outdoors is in the bush form, as it is much simpler to give the tree protection in winter. Shrubs are root-hardy but still need winter protection. If tops happen to winterkill despite protection, they are then cut back nearly to the ground in spring. Some gardeners do not use containers but simply grow them in ground during summer, take them up with balls of soil about roots before frost and carry them into the cellar for the fruit to ripen.

Winter Treatment: Trick #1: In fall, cut some of the longest branches back a bit. Take some snow fence and wrap this around the bush tightly, tack heavy insulation on this and tie the whole bush with rope, tightly, packing straw and leaves in between the branches first. Straw is also packed around the roots. Some folks pack straw on top of the entire bush, covering the whole thing with canvas. Tar paper is wrapped around the outside of the snow fence and on top of the bush. Tie the whole works up tightly with a good wire or rope. In spring, after danger of frost is over, unwrap, removing the straw and leaves. Soon new leaves will start to come out. You may have a couple of bare branches killed by the winter, but these can be cut off.

Trick #2: Train the plant so its branches grow close to the ground. Some do this; others don't. Dig a large hole alongside the tree, large enough so that the tree can be bent or pushed into the trench and buried. Place a rock over the tree. Cover with leaves, straw, hay, etc., and mound with a foot or more of soil. In spring, uncover the tree, set upright and pack soil around it.

Propagation: You can purchase dwarf fig plants from various nurseries which sell rooted plants. Some folks take a shoot, stick it into the ground and it eventually roots for them. Keep it watered until roots start. Or you can get a plant from your friend who has one by layering. Bend a branch over in early spring so that a portion 2 years old may be fastened down and covered with soil. Keep this moist and roots will form by summer. The new plant may be detached and planted.

Troubles: Figs are relatively free of insects and diseases. Scale and aphids are apt to be troublesome. Spraying with Malathion and syringing the foliage regularly while the bush is growing outside will help to keep these pests (and red spider mites) down.

Figs pollinate themselves so you don't have to worry about another one nearby for cross-pollination.

Failure to bear is due to bad weather, age of plant or lack of light.

Dwarf Kumquat

There are two varieties which can be grown. The dwarf (*Fortunella margarita*) seldom bears flowers or fruit. When it does flower, blooms are white and fragrant, followed by orange-yellow fruit about 1-inch across. Grown mostly for foliage.

The dwarf kumquat, *Fortunella hindsii* is a free-fruiting variety which is almost always covered with fruit. It has small ½ inch, nearly round, orange-colored fruits with almost no juice. It is highly ornamental.

The care for all kumquats is similar to that of citrus.

Mango (*Mangifera indica*)

Here's an item to add to your collection of tropical fruits which can be raised indoors. It may not bear because the mango is a tropical tree that is sometimes 100 feet in height. Start the seed in a pot of sand and peat moss. Do not overwater. After the seed has germinated, then you can add a bit more water. If you apply too much before germination starts, rotting instead of rooting sets in.

Olive Trees (*Olea europaea*)

You can plant olive "pits" (seeds) in a pot of loose soil and get good foliage plants. Use those of the black olive, since they are ripe. Put two or three seeds in a 5-inch pot. These take up to 3 months for germination as the seed coat is a hard shell. After they start to grow, transplant to another pot. Give lots of light, ample moisture and a warm room. Keep foliage cleaned off by syringing from time to time. In summer, place plant outdoors in tubs. The *Olea europae* manzanillo bears edible fruit and is an excellent decorative tree.

PINEAPPLES (*Ananas comosus*)

Usually, the pineapple will not fruit in the home, but it makes a fine bromeliad or foliage plant. Many gardeners get their plant to fruit by this trick: Place a plastic sheet over the plant (mature one) so no air will reach it for 4 or 5 days. An apple is enclosed inside the tent, first, to gas the plant. Apples give off gas fumes (ethylene) which will force the pineapple to flower and form edible fruit. The plastic bag confines the fumes. After four days, remove the plastic tent, and you'll see new leaves starting from the center of the plant. Finally, you'll see rows of pineapple fruit appearing on the bottom of the new leaves. The fruit that follows is golden yellow and will grow about six inches above the old plant, on a stalk about ¼ inch thick.

Green Thumb Tips: Plant needs full sun and ample water. Make sure soil is well drained. If heavy, add peat moss or broken charcoal. If sandy or light, add only peat moss. A good mixture is ⅓ sand, ⅓ loam and ⅓ peat. You can bake it in oven, 200° for ½ hour before using it. Let it cool before you put the top in. The top will root fast in a good soil mixture.

Now that the top is potted, you simply wait for the "red bud," which consists of more than a hundred very tiny flowers, beginning at the bottom of cluster, to open into blue-velvet blooms. Each lasts but a day and each remaining flower brace develops into one segment of the fruit.

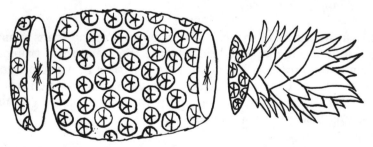

To start a pineapple indoors, first cut the top off and place in soup bowl with small amount of water in the bottom. Rooting will take place within a few weeks.

Propagation: To start a pineapple plant, first slice off the top with 1 or 2 inches of fruit attached. Scoop out the meaty part being careful not to injure the tough little stem in the center. Now air-dry the top until it's partially dry. Next, line the bottom of a clay pot with chipped rock, gravel or sand, for drainage, and over this a thin layer of sphagnum moss. Now you place the top in the pot and add just enough soil to cover the skin. Place it in a draft-free, sunny spot. Groom it by nipping off any damaged leaves. Water it sparingly from the bottom each day. Grow in full sun and pinch back from time to time to induce bushiness.

How to Freeze Pineapples: Peel and cut into desired shapes. Pack into freezer cartons. Cover with cold syrup made of equal measures of sugar and water. Dissolve sugar in tap water by stirring. Then chill. It's not necessary to heat the syrup. Seal cartons and freeze at 0° F. Will keep 8 to 12 months.

Serving Mixed Fruits On the Half Shell: Cut pineapple in half lengthwise. With grapefruit or paring knife, cut around entire half, ¼-inch from outer peel. Cut pineapple into chunks and remove from shell. Chop pineapple, add other fruits and pile into shells. Place on small serving plate and garnish. For seafood or chicken salads, line shell with salad greens of your choice. Add some fresh pineapple to your favorite salad and pile into shell. Garnish with radish roses, carissa or cherries. Serve each person a half shell.

Whole Pineapple For Fruit Tray: Wash pineapple. With sharp knife, cut around each section or "square" of pineapple. Be sure to cut deeply enough to reach core. Leave row of uncut squares or sections at top and at bottom. Guests pull them out in sections, as they serve themselves. Place on fruit tray and surround with other fruits and cheese. Serve as dessert or as party refreshment.

Shredded Fresh Pineapple and Cream: 2 cups fresh, shredded pineapple, 1 tbsp. fresh lemon juice and ½ cup sugar; 1 cup heavy cream, whipped, ¼ teas. ground nutmeg. Combine pineapple and sugar. Fold in whipped cream and nutmeg. Chill and serve as dessert. Yield: 3½ cups.

Pineapple Sour Cream Salad: 1½ cups mandarin oranges, 1½ cups diced fresh pineapple, 1½ cups diced marshmallows, 1 cup shredded coconut; dash salt, ½ pint sour cream. Combine first four ingredients and blend in sour cream.

How to Judge for Ripeness of Pineapples in Stores: For tangy flavor, eat fruit when the entire shell is green. For full sweetness, allow fruit to remain at room temperature until lower ¼ to ½ of pineapple shell turns orange. IMPORTANT: DO NOT OVERRIPEN. The ripening process may be slowed by refrigerating at temperatures from 45° to 60°. (Thanks to Knapp-Sherriff Koell, Inc., Donna, Texas, for recipes.)

POMEGRANATE *(Punica granatum)*

Grown for its flowers and foliage, as well as small edible fruit.

Green Thumb Tips: Likes sunny window, 72°, ⅓ sand, peat and loam mixture. Keep soil uniformly moist. Place plant outdoors in summer and water regularly. Trim back any extra long shoots, bring in before frost. Goes through a semi-rest period in winter and sheds leaves.

Propagation: Seeds sown in sand-peat or by rooting the cuttings.

Troubles: Aphids and red spider mites, syringe plant regularly, spray with Kelthane.

Sweet Potato Vine

This makes a fine houseplant. All you do is select a good medium-sized sweet potato, put a toothpick in each side and allow it to rest on rim of glass container (about 8 inches deep). The lower end of the potato is constantly covered with water. Plant will send out many roots, often filling the glass container. Train the vine to climb up around the window frames. Grows in sun or shade, in room temperature of 60° to 70°. Some gardeners have better luck by putting the sweet potato in the dark for two weeks to encourage root development. Note: Sometimes sweet potatoes have been treated with a sprout inhibitor, making it difficult to get them to start. You can often offset this by placing the tuber in a warm room for several days to break the dormancy. If a lot of leafy shoots develop, pinch out a few, leaving two or three for climbing. Don't forget that carrots, horseradish, beet tops are also decorative in the window. Cut the tops back, leaving some of the fleshy root, and arrange in flower bowls, containing pebbles. Fill bowls with water, place tops in but do not allow them to become submerged. Soon you'll see a mass of graceful greenery coming along. Some gardeners pot these up in sandy soil.

Tiny Gardens for Tiny Tots Indoors

Children love the excitement of watching seeds and flowers grow. There are countless types of miniature gardens that can be made with the simplest of household articles. Your child can watch these from day to day. The seed also makes fine classroom projects. Here are a few ideas.

Coal Gardens: Also called depression plants, these were the rage in the '30's of Depression years when people didn't have money to buy flowers. Take pieces of coal, place them in a shallow glass bowl (never use metal). Combine about 4 or 5 tablespoons of water, 4 tablespoons of laundry bluing, and 4 tablespoons of ammonia. Pour this over the pieces of coal, making sure you wet all pieces with the solution. For extra color, you can add a few drops of food coloring as well as a few drops of bluing on the coal. The children will be amazed at the chemical effect. The coal garden will grow and grow. After two days or so, add 2 more tablespoons of water and 2 tablespoons of ammonia. Add these to the edge of bowl, not over the crystal effect that has been produced. This will start the garden "growing" again, and when it gets to the exact size you want, stop adding extra fluid. Your garden will stop growing completely when the ammonia water solution evaporates.

You can mess the garden up or knock it down and start all over again. Just leave the powder in the bowl and add more of the original mixture to it. It's sometimes prettier! Occasionally the garden grows too fast and grows over the side of the bowl. When it does wipe it off with a sponge. Don't let any of the crystals get on furniture, as it may mar the finish. By the way, some use chunks of broken brick (egg-size), porous types not the slick ones, instead of coal; others use pieces of synthetic foam rubber, or cellulose sponge. They like sponge because it can be cut in any shape. Be sure to wet the brick, and, if sponge is used, wet it and wring out well.

Ball of Green: Here's one kids like. Dampen a large coarse sponge and hang it from a cord in a sunny window. Sprinkle the moist sponge with clover, redtop, grass, flax or mustard seeds. Keep the sponge damp at all times. Seeds will sprout and cover the sponge with a solid coating of greenery.

Pixie Pie Plate: Cut a piece of flannel to fit inside a large pie plate. Cover this with water and sprinkle on small seeds. Place the plate in a sunny window and keep it damp. The garden will grow before your eyes, almost!

Hanging Blooms: Using a soft cord or fiber plant binders, attach paper-white narcissus bulbs to a large sponge covered with sphagnum moss, found in woods or florist's shop. Hang the ball in a sunny window and keep it moist with warm water. Bulbs will sprout and later bloom just as though planted in a bowl.

Garden in a Glass: Line the inside of a water glass with blotting paper. Add just enough water to the bottom of the glass so that the blotting paper gets damp enough to cling to the sides. Place a variety of small seeds between the dampened blotting paper and the glass. Seeds will soon sprout and the children will be able to see the roots fill the bowl of the glass, and the greenery shoot out the top. Enough water must be kept in the bottom of the glass to keep the blotting paper moist all the time. Leftover vegetable seeds, grass seed or even flower seed can be used.

Green Pastures: Pack moist earth or sawdust into a wide shallow cake pan. Sow the material with grass seed and place the pan in a sunny window, keeping the sawdust, earth or peat, moist. When the surface is covered with green, let the children place miniature animals in the "pasture".

Carrots & Pineapples: Your children will be fascinated if you cut off tops of carrots or pineapples and root them in a mixture of sand and peat. They'll make new plants. Also show them how to take cuttings ("slips") from your houseplants, root them in water or sand, and make new plants for friends.

Venus Flytrap: This is a carnivorous plant (eats bugs), can be started in sand and peat from seed, or you can buy the plants. Grow it in glass bowl as it likes lots of humidity. Children like to see the "jaws" close when an insect touches them or when a child tickles the jaws with his finger.

Herb Gardening: Growing herbs in the window offers children a great chance to experiment and grow useful plants for cooking. If you have a sunny bay window, it's ideal for starting seed. Get some clay pots or a wooden box. Use a soil mixture of ⅓ sand, ⅓ loam and ⅓ peat, and add some vermiculite or perlite to loosen it further. These are obtainable from garden stores. Sow seeds in pots and cover lightly with loose peat or sphagnum. Seed is sprinkled on top of loose soil, not buried. You can scatter a little perlite or vermiculite on this. Water it well, cover with a pane of glass to keep the moisture in, or place the pot in a polyethylene bag and forget the glass. One drying out can be fatal. After they see the seed has started to germinate, you can tell them to remove the glass plate, and keep the pots in a bright window. When seedlings are 2 inches high, these can be transplanted to clay pots. Later when weather is warm, these can be set in garden or grown in window. They'll get a lot of pleasure picking off sprigs of parsley, chives, basil, etc. when you are cooking, so don't hesitate to tell them they did a good job growing these for you.

Here are some herbs to try: Anise, catnip (cats love a sprig of it), chives, mints, parsley, sage, to name a few.

Terrariums: A goldfish bowl, brandy snifter, candy jar, or any glass receptacle is ideal for making a terrarium for growing plants indoors. Sprinkle some woods soil in the bottom, plus a few bits of charcoal; then take your children to the woods, meadows or swamps to gather tiny plants. Try anything you can find—mosses, small flowering plants, evergreen seedlings, tiny moss-coated pieces of wood. Be on the lookout for tiny evergreen seedlings, odd bits of bark, lichens, anything you think will make the indoor planting more attractive. Try to create natural scenes, copied directly from the woods. If the moss is used, don't forget that you see it through the glass, therefore, it must be placed face down in the container in some places. Get some white sand and spread a little in it to give the appearance of a small lake or stream. A piece of broken mirror is wonderful for creating a lake effect. Pieces of rock can be added to suggest steps or cliffs.

CAUTION: Do not let your children water the "bottle garden" too much. Try once a week, dependent on room temperature. In schools this is usually high, so perhaps twice a week is necessary. If you keep a plate of glass over the top, there is less watering. If you do use a glass covering, be sure to leave it partly off; the ventilation is important. If you do not ventilate, moisture will collect on the inside and visibility will be at a minimum.

Growing Cactus Plants: These offer the youngsters a lot of enjoyment, since cactus plants are easy to grow and come in odd shapes. Buy seed from any seed house. They list many of the bizarre types which will fascinate kids. Start seed in a sandy mixture, and make sure they do not water cacti too heavily. This causes them to rot. Grow in a bright window, and any warm temperature is fine.

Tropical Fruits: Have your children save seeds from grapefruits, lemons, or oranges. Plant these in a pot of soil and watch them grow into handsome foliage plants. Some will even flower and bear fruit (sour). Another trick is to start the seed ("pit") of an avocado; these are called alligator pears. If you plant the seed in a pot of porous soil, it will sprout in 3 or 4 weeks and grow into a handsome foliage plant. Do not overwater. Do not try to grow the seed of alligator pear in glass of water. Soil is better.

Cut the top off a pineapple plant, set it in a soil that's fairly rich and you'll have a bizarre plant. In 9 months it will bloom, In 3 years it will fruit.

Take a medium-sized sweet potato and keep it in a glass of water. Keep the lower end of the potato constantly covered with water. Plant will send out many roots, often filling the glass container. Train the vine to climb up around the window frame. Grows in sun or shade, room temperature of 60° to 70°.

Olive Trees: Plant olive seeds (use those of black olives, as they're ripe) and see how the kids like these! It'll take some time for the hard shell to split and seed to germinate, so tell kids to be patient.

Starting Seeds: Kids like to start seeds of tomatoes, peppers, melons, beans, and others. Fill egg shell halves with soil and start seed in these, or you can use peat pots (from garden stores). Seeds germinate in these, and you start them indoors 2 or 3 weeks ahead of outdoor planting time. When plants are 3 inches tall, set the pot and all outdoors.

Growing Acorns: If you want to have an interesting indoor plant why not grow a couple of little oak trees. You just take a tip from squirrels and plant the acorns in the ground this fall. Use a clay pot and place some wet moss or a mixture of sand and peat moss in it. Then plant the acorns in this and set the pots in a cold frame or you can place them on a window sill. Acorns don't need cold winter weather for germination. Keep the pots well watered and by the time spring rolls around or even earlier (February), the acorns you grew indoors will have sprouted into novel miniature oak trees with green, waxy leaves. Of course, if you leave the acorns outdoors during the winter, you don't get growth until spring. With a bit of imagination this tiny oak will look like the beginning of a Ming tree and provide interest all winter long.

When spring comes plant the seedling in your front lawn or back yard in memory of someone in your family. Our oak trees are threatened with a serious disease, and we need more of them to meet the threat. This is one way to do it and have fun doing it.

Starting Plants from Your Shopping Bag Groceries
(A) Carrots make a fine "fern" plant. Cut top off and place in dish of pebbles and water. (B) Sweet potato is an excellent vine for trailing or climbing indoors. (C) Onion bulb (or garlic clove) can be started in glass of water. Pieces can be eaten during winter months. (D) Avocado pit (seed) can be started in glass of water. Thrust toothpicks in sides to keep it out of water. (E) If you've had poor luck starting avocado seed in water, bury seed in pot of loose soil. (F) Seeds of grapefruit, orange, lemon and other citrus can be started in a pot of loose soil. Plants may not bear edible fruit but you'll like the foliage effect.

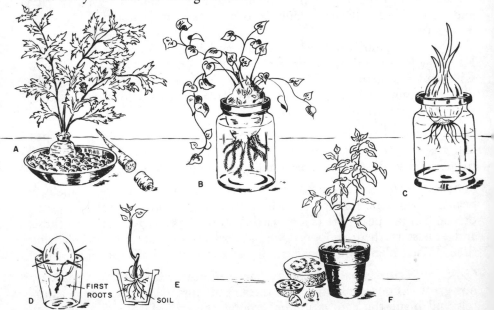

Lima Beans: Plant a few lima bean seeds in a pot of soil. Place in a bright window. Soon you'll have a plant with nice green leaves, blossoms and even pods with beans in them. Everyone will ask you what the plant is.

Window Sill Tomatoes: These are novelties more people should grow. Sow seed of the Tom Thumb type, in sand-peat mix and after the plants are about an inch tall, place each seedling in a 4-inch pot. This is important; if you leave the seedlings close together, they won't bloom or bear fruit, and the plants will be spindly. The fruit will ripen and tastes great in salads. We find the plants have a tendency to grow too tall, but train them to a stake and keep in the brightest window you have. Once in a while the bottom leaves turn yellow, just pull them off. . Aphids (plant lice) cause black, sticky mold to form on the leaves; check this by washing the plant under a shower in the bath tub. These tiny tomatoes are a great novelty.

Dancing Snow Balls: For entertaining children try making dancing snow balls. I use a small brandy snifter and fill it half-full of water, and then add several moth balls and some citric acid. The acid coats the ball with bubbles and makes them rise and fall. When the action stops, add more of the citric acid. The acid is in crystal form and can be obtained in drug stores. This always seems to amuse grownups as well as children. Add a little cake coloring for extra effect. CAUTION: moth balls are poisonous—caution children.

CHAPTER V

New Ways To
Use Old Plants

HANGING BASKETS

Homeowners who run out of space are going "vertical"—that is, they are using hanging baskets with cascading plants. Hanging baskets are nothing new. In fact, they are old-fashioned but are making a comeback. Plants in a hanging basket form drooping sprays which give the baskets their grace. Without drooping, graceful sprays, the hanging baskets look rather naked and colorless.

Soil: A good soil mixture consists of ⅓ peat, ⅓ loam, and ⅓ sand. This will grow all types of plants in a hanging basket. Feed them every 3 weeks using a liquid plant food such as Ra-pid-gro.

Watering & Repotting: Hanging baskets are exposed to air on all sides, thus they dry out faster than ordinary flower pots. Some must be watered almost daily. An indoor hanging basket should be repotted every second or third year. Old plants can be removed and new ones started if necessary. Sometimes you have to cut back a long shoot or two, and these can be used for starting new plants. Cut off any dead leaves and twigs you may see from time to time. Outdoor hanging baskets usually need to be repotted every year.

Types of Baskets: These usually come in plastic, redwood or wire. We line ours with plastic sheets, then place some sphagnum moss on top of this. A tiny hole is punched in the bottom for drainage. The plastic keeps the water from dripping out and also prevents the plants from drying too quickly.

Fuchsia

Hanging Basket Begonia

Sterns Nursery

Weeping Lantana

Type of Plants to Grow: The kind of plants you use in hanging baskets depends on your own taste and whether you want to grow them indoors or outdoors. An all-fern basket is an attractive item, and can include Boston fern and asparagus fern or sprengeri, both types used by florists. And don't forget the handsome ivy geraniums. I particularly like the sunset ivy (L'Elegante) which has a variegated green and white leaf, which tints pink when grown dry or in bright sun. Flowers are single white, tinted with a touch of lavender. This variety is sometimes called Mme. Margot. Here is a list of some good plants for hanging baskets. There are many others that can be used. Don't be afraid to try new plants not mentioned in the list. Almost all plants will trail. Your selection of plants depends upon whether your basket will be growing in the sun or shade. (See following chart)

SOME GOOD PLANTS FOR HANGING BASKETS

PLANT	COMMON NAME	SUN OR SHADE	GREEN THUMB TIPS
Adiantum cuneatum	Maidenhair Fern	Sun or semi-shade.	Humusy soil, ample moisture.
Asparagus plumosus	Asparagus Fern	Sun.	Ample moisture; dry soil causes shedding.
Begonia	Tuberous and other species	Semi-shade.	Uniform supply of moisture, humusy soil.
Browallia speciosa	Browallia	Sun or semi-shade.	Red spider mites, spray with Kelthane. Likes well-drained soil, ample moisture.
Campanula, Isophylla and others	Basket Bellflowers Falling Stars Italian Bellflower	Semi-shade.	Uniform moisture, good drainage, fed every 3 or 4 weeks. Dry leaves due to spider mites or dry soil.
Ceropegia woodii	Rosary Vine	Filtered light.	Humusy soil; allow plant to get moderately dry before watering.
Chlorophytum comosum	Spider Plant, Airplane Plant	Filtered light.	Will tolerate dry heated room; good drainage; use ⅓ each sand, peat and loam.
Chrysanthemum	Chrysanthemum, trained to cascade.	Full sun.	Good soil mixture, uniform supply moisture. Red spider mites and aphids, spray with Malathion and Kelthane.
Cissus discolor and others	Kangaroo Vine, Grape Ivy.	Sun or shade. Filtered shade is best.	50° or so. Let grow on dry side before watering.

SOME GOOD PLANTS FOR HANGING BASKETS (Continued)

Plant	Common Name	Sun or Shade	Green Thumb Tips
Coleus pumilus or *C. rehneltianus*	Trailing Queen (All will trail or weep)	Semi-shade.	Humusy soil, well drained; keep flower spike pinched out; remove dead leaves. Pinch tip out and root in water.
Columnea gloriosa, or *C. mirta*	Columnea	Filtered sun.	Same as African violet and take about same care. Humusy soil.
Cymbalaria muralis	Kenilworth Ivy	Filtered sun.	Uniform supply of moisture, cool room is good.
Episcia cupreata	Flame Violets	Diffused light.	Warm room, soil rich in humus, soil evenly moist.
Fittonia verschaffeltii and *F. argyroneura*	Mosaic Plant	Semi-shade.	Soil should be humusy, well drained. Keep evenly moist.
Fuchsia	Fuchsia, Lady, all trailing kinds	Filtered or bright light.	Humusy soil, cool room 50°. Soil evenly moist but not soggy. Bud drop due to dry soil and dry air.
Hedera helix	English Ivy	Sun or shade.	Cannot tolerate wet feet, don't let soil become soggy. For scale and aphids, spray with Malathion. Red spider, use Kelthane.
Helxine soleirolii	Baby Tears	Semi-shade.	Avoid bright sun, do not let dry out, mist foliage often with warm water.

SOME GOOD PLANTS FOR HANGING BASKETS (Continued)

PLANT	COMMON NAME	SUN OR SHADE	GREEN THUMB TIPS
Hoya carnosa	Wax or Parlor Plant	Bright or full sun.	Takes 2 or 3 years to flower, but foliage is handsome.
Kalanchoe uniflora	Prostrate Kalanchoe, "Coral Bells"	Bright window.	Likes loose, well-drained soil.
Lantana montevidensis	Trailing Lantana	Sunny window.	Keep soil moist until winter when plant can be cut back to about a foot.
Lobelia erinus pendula	Trailing Lobelia	Sun or shade.	Prefers well-drained soil.
Nephrolepis exaltata bostoniensis	Boston Fern	Semi-shade.	Likes humusy soil, avoid direct light, feed liquid plant food once every 4 weeks. Repot when plant is potbound.
Pelargonium peltatum	Ivy Geranium	Sun for best colors.	Well-drained soil, cool window, feed every 3 or 4 weeks.
Petunia hybrida pendula	Balcony Petunias	Full sun.	Ample water and feed every 3 weeks. Snip off seed heads before they form.
Philodendron oxycardium (cordatum)	Heartleaf Philodendron	Semi-shade.	Humusy soil, uniform supply of moisture. Syringe foliage from time to time, avoid wet feet.
Saintpaulia, many varieties	African Violet	Bright window, out of direct light.	Humusy soil, well drained. 72° or warmer. Avoid temperatures below 65°.

SOME GOOD PLANTS FOR HANGING BASKETS (Continued)

PLANT	COMMON NAME	SUN OR SHADE	GREEN THUMB TIPS
Schlumbergera bridgesii	Christmas Cactus	Bright window.	Grow in cool window in fall. Apt to get plant lice (aphids), spray with Malathion in bathtub.
Tropaeolum majus	Nasturtium	Full sun.	Same as above.
Verbena peruviana	Peruvian Flame Verbena	Bright window.	No special care. Leaves are apt to get brown due to dry soil.
Vinca major variegata	Periwinkle	Sunny window.	Lots of moisture. Red spider mites cause leaves to yellow. Use Kelthane.
Zebrina pendula, similar to Tradescantia	Both called Wandering Jew	Sun or shade.	Good colors in bright window. Apt to get too lanky, trim them back anytime to length you want.

GROW YOUR VINES ON TOTEM POLES

Moss sticks are "totem poles" used for growing house ivies such as philodendrons, grape ivy, sweet potato vines, to name a few. You've all seen these vines clinging to moss sticks in florist shops and there is no reason why you can't make them for yourself or for friends as gifts.

All you need is some dried sphagnum moss, an item you can get in the woods or from your florist or garden supply store. One pound of dried sphagnum will make an average-sized stick. If you happen to live near a sawmill, chances are you can pick up some slabs of wood with bark attached. This gives your moss stick a rustic effect, although the bark isn't absolutely necessary for that professional look.

An ordinary stick, 1 by 1 inch or 1 by 2 inches is wide enough. One end can be sharpened to drive into the pot. The length of the moss stick will depend on how tall you want the vine to climb. All you do is wrap the moss on the stick and fasten with fine wire.

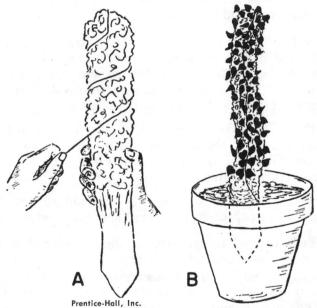

A   B

Prentice-Hall, Inc.

Totem poles made from a slab of wood covered with florist's sphagnum moss, are useful for supporting philodendrons and other vines. (A) How to wrap copper wire around the moss. (B) Vines growing luxuriantly in the moss.

Don't use string around the moss as it rots and is not satisfactory. Some folks use chicken wire but it's not quite stiff enough and you have to use more moss to cover it. The vines can be pinned to the moss by means of hairpins or twist-ems. If the pot is large enough, you can have a vine on each side of the totem pole, and you can use all of one variety or a combination of vines.

Wrapping The Wire: Be sure to wrap the wire snugly around the moss so it'll be nice and neat when you get thru. After the stick is wrapped, you can take a pair of shears and snip off any loose ends of moss that might be left on. After the moss stick is wrapped, select a pot at least 6 inches across. When the moss is wet it's quite heavy so you need a good sized pot to anchor it. Insert stick in center of pot and plant one or two vines on each side, or you can use only one vine.

How to Water: You can add water slowly over the top of the stick. Moss will absorb lots of water and furnish the plant with humidity too. Any excess water will run down into the pot. Do not allow the soil to be soggy at any time. Leaving pots in jardinieres or pans of water is a poor practice since it shuts off oxygen to the roots. This causes leaves to turn yellow and drop. A clay florist's pot gives best growth since it allows for better root and air circulation.

Feeding The Vines: You can feed the vines by mixing up a solution of liquid plant food such as Ra-pid-gro, 1 level teaspoon to 2 quarts of water. This can be sprayed on the foliage and moss. Any that rolls off will collect on the soil surface and be absorbed. The vines' roots will penetrate the moss and be perfectly content.

Keeping Foliage Shiny: Wash the foliage under sink or in the bathtub. Dust collects and clogs the pores in leaves. Do not swab the leaves with olive oil. Glycerine is much better. Or a little milk and water makes a nice bathing solution.

Soil Mixture: A good soil mixture for all vines and houseplants is made of 1 part each of rotted leaves, peat, sand and good garden soil.

Troubles: Yellowing of foliage may be due to poor drainage (over-watering), poor soil, unsuitable container, or too much fertilizer. Dying of foliage from base upwards may be due to lack of light, high temperature or gas injury. Dead areas on edges of leaves is result of too much fertilizer or improper watering. Dead spots on leaf is from too much sun, dry soil, disease or insects.

Pinching: If vine is growing out of bounds pinch the tip back.

HOW TO MAKE TERRARIUMS AND BOTTLE GARDENS

What's a terrarium? It's simply a transparent container, such as a goldfish bowl, brandy snifter, candy jar, or any glass receptacle which can be used to grow tiny plants indoors. These plants are found

in meadows, swamps or woods in fall or early winter. It's an easy way
to bring the outdoors indoors.

If you've never made yourself a terrarium, you're missing out on
a real treat. These small plants are so arranged as to suggest a bit of
natural landscape and they give you the feeling of having a breath
of outdoors in your own living room. A terrarium makes you feel
restful; so friends, if you want a respite from the hustle and bustle of
this fast moving world, start making yourself a terrarium so you can
enjoy it in the winter.

Here are a few types of containers you can use to grow outdoor
plants: For large-scale materials, use aquariums, fish globes or wine car-
boys. For smaller plant materials use glass jars, old-fashioned candy jars,
fishbowls, aquariums, large goblets, bottles or brandy snifters.

The secret of growing plants in a terrarium is to control the heat,
the light and humidity just as nature would outdoors. The discovery
of the terrarium is credited to a natural scientist, who while strolling thru
the woods one day found a bottle containing some soil supporting lush
green growth of fern and other plants.

The first step in making a terrarium is to select with care your glass
container. Then sprinkle some woods' soil in the bottom with a few
bits of charcoal to keep the soil sweet. Plan on taking a trip to the
woods to collect small ferns, small flowering plants, mosses and tiny
moss-coated pieces of wood. Try anything you find, you don't have
to know the name of the plants! Be on the lookout for tiny evergreen
seedling, odd bits of bark, lichens, sticks, etc. that might make your
outdoor picture more attractive indoors. Small seedling evergreens
can be dug up with roots and planted in leaf mold, where they'll stay
alive all winter. Then they can be planted outdoors in spring.

Small ferns can be planted with crowns just above the soil. Whatever materials you use in your woodland terrarium, make sure that
each plant is in scale with the others. Try to create natural scenes,
copied directly from the woods. If moss is used, don't forget that you
see it thru the glass, therefore it must be placed face down in the container in some places. If you can get some white sand, spread a little
in, to give the appearance of a small lake or stream. A piece of broken
mirror is wonderful for creating a lake effect. Pieces of rock can be
added to suggest steps or cliffs.

How To Water The Terrarium: Terrariums and "bottle gardens" must
have water added from time to time or the plants will dry out. Just
how often to water cannot be said, but depends on the room temperature. If you keep a glass plate over the top, you'll need less watering,
since water will not be lost by evaporation. If you do use a glass
covering be sure to leave it partly off for ventilation, otherwise
moisture will collect on the inside and visibility will be impaired.

In a nutshell, you should have good luck if you water the terrarium the following way: After plants have been inserted, wet down the entire planting using a bulb sprayer. Add water until it seeps through the soil on the bottom. Wipe off the inside of the glass and put a glass cover over the top.

Do not let water stand in bottom of the terrarium. If you over-water, remove the cover for several hours and allow the excess water to evaporate. Plants need very little extra water in a terrarium. Moisture condenses on the sides of the glass and drips back into the soil where it is reused by the plants. Water should be added as soon as plants appear dry.

Feeding Your Terrarium: If you use woods soil and lots of humus, don't bother to feed the plants in your terrarium. It may cause them to grow out of bounds, and, in the confined area you want to keep the plants as dwarf as possible.

You can have a lot of fun making up a terrarium. Don't be afraid to experiment with seeds, nuts (acorns are great for starting in a ter-rarium) and other items.

Bottle Gardens: A vinegar jug, wine bottle or fruit jar make a first-rate bottle garden. Don't let the narrow mouth discourage you. After you add some loose soil material scatter seed of African violets, grass seed, corn, almost anything. Try all kinds of seeds, and after you find some-thing that works well, stick with it. The fascinating part of starting a bottle or terrarium is experimenting with the plants, trying out those growing in your woods, swamps or backyard. Long tweezers can be used to insert plants. Some like the high humidity of a closed container, some don't do as well.

GROWING PLANTS IN TUBS OR BOXES

With the increased use of patios and outdoor "living rooms," tubbed plants are being used more and more as a flexible, inexpensive way to concentrate color where you want it. These plants in pots or tubs can be moved from one place to another and can highlight your terrace, porch, house entrance, balcony or what have you. By using foliage plants and blooming items in tubs, pots or boxes, you can rearrange them or move them just as you would furniture in your living room. The wooden tubs can be made, or purchased from a florist. Some gardeners grow decorative plants in 5-gallon paint cans or even in nail kegs. These containers are ideal for tuberous begonias, fancy-leaved caladiums, geraniums, fuchsias and many vines to decorate the porch or terrace. Shade is no problem with these items. Even sun-loving plants can be used on the shady terrace by rotating them every week.

If you're handy with a saw, you can make your own plant tubs.

Nail kegs make a good container for growing plants. You can also use paint cans or similar containers. Put holes in bottom for drainage.

There's no trick to it, and you'll be surprised to see what effect the tubs can create.

Your paint dealer has discarded paint cans and you can get nail kegs from the lumber yard. There's no set way to use these tubbed or boxed items. Your own terrace, lawn or porch will dictate how you use these. Your florist or garden store handles green tubs and these can be painted any color you want.

Some items to dry include tuberous or fancy-leaved begonias, fancy-leaved caladiums, fuchsias, geraniums and philodendron. These can be moved back and forth, from a shady spot to a sunny spot every week. Use plenty of humus in the bottom to hold moisture.

TUBBED EVERGREENS

You can use tubbed evergreens such as yew, euonymous, hardy box-wood, etc., to accent the opening to a doorway or a terrace. Also clipped privet, hydrangeas, floribunda roses, etc. are useful. For the winter it's a good idea to set the tubs in the ground and mulch with leaves or straw, as they may winterkill if left on an open terrace (they actually desiccate or dry out due to winds, and lack of moisture in the confined tubs). These pots can be used to soften up bare steps, also. Feed them once or twice a year and be sure to give them ample water, especially during the summer, as they have very little moisture and soil to live on. You can also resort to vines such as German ivy, vinca, English ivy, and don't forget to use plenty of coleus for colored effect. Spikes (dracena) are extremely useful in tubs or boxes.

Window Boxes

A porch or window box brings the glory of the garden right up to your door. Window boxes help to soften a home's architectural features, and make it gay and cheery. Plants, such as coleus, fuchsia, begonia, vinca and tradescantia, can be brought inside before frost and planted indoors in boxes, planters or hanging baskets for use in the home or office. The only care plants in window boxes need is regular watering and a little plant food.

How to make a porch or window box: Window or porch boxes are made of metal or wood. They should be 8 inches deep (inside measurement); the length would depend upon space available. If made of wood, brass or galvanized screws are used to resist rusting. To prevent decay the inside is painted with Cuprinol or any safe wood preservative found in garden stores. Metal containers are usually provided with false drainage bottoms. Otherwise broken pieces of pots or pebbles are placed in the bottom layer for drainage. A hole every 6 inches is needed for drainage in a wooden box.

Window boxes usually take a lot of water, sometimes require daily watering. A self-watering window box can be made using simple carpenter tools. The length of the box is determined by the width of the window for which it is to be used. Use 1-inch by 8-inch boards. The width at the top of the box should be 8 inches and the bottom tapered to 6 inches wide. The end pieces, the sides and the bottom are cut and fastened together with galvanized or brass screws. The false bottom board, located 2 inches from the bottom of the box, is held in place with small wooden cleats. It should fit tightly to prevent soil from seeping into the reservoir. The bottom edge of the side boards are planed to provide a flat surface to which a bottom board is fastened with screws. Before assembling, all joints except those of the false bottom should be caulked with a strip of caulking compound. When completely assembled the inner surfaces of the box are painted with horticultural asphalt paint to preserve the wood and make it waterproof. Horticultural asphalt is safe to use because it does not contain creosote, which is toxic to plants.

Holes ⅜ to ½ inch in diameter are drilled every 8 inches along the center line of the false bottom to receive the wicks. A larger hole, ¾ inch in diameter, is drilled to receive a ¾ inch galvanized iron pipe, 8 inches long, through which water is poured to fill the reservoir.

Wick material should be cut into 4- or 5-inch lengths and inserted through the holes to the bottom of the reservoir. Glass wicks can be purchased from a garden store or florist. Twisted lengths of burlap may also be used for the same purpose but are not as permanent as glass wicks.

Boxes can be fastened to the house by means of metal or wooden brackets. The color of the box should be a subdued dull color like dark green rather than a bright color. The color of the flowers, foliage and vines should harmonize with the color of the house.

PLANTS SUGGESTED FOR PLANTER USE

Outdoor Annuals, Not Hardy For Year Round Use

The following plant combinations have been chosen for pleasing combinations of color, growth habits and leaf texture.

Taller plants are listed first, which you can use for the center or back of planters, window boxes, tubs or cemetery urns. Others are low growing, which you may group around the center plants.

FOR FULL SUN:

- French marigolds and ageratum (blue bedder)
- Scarlet sage (*Salvia splendens*), St. John's fire and dwarf snapdragon (*Antirrinum*)
- Zinnia (scarlet), French marigold (*Tagetes*, yellow), creeping zinnia (*Sanvitallia procumbens flore-pleno*, yellow)
- Bedding-type snapdragon (*Antirrinum*), dwarf celosia (*Plumosa*), verbena (scarlet) with variegated periwinkle (*Vinca major variegata*)
- Annual phlox (red, pink, and white), ageratum (blue); sweet alyssum (white)
- Geranium (white), balcony petunias (dark purple)
- Petunia (pink), balcony petunias, white and crimson (pink)
- Heliotrope (blue), French marigold (*Tagetes*, yellow with maroon), dwarf nasturtium (*Tropaeolum*, scarlet flowers)
- *Lantana camara* (orange), verbena (purple), variegated periwinkle (*Vinca major variegata*)
- Geranium (salmon-pink), balcony petunia (deep blue)
- French marigold (yellow), African marigold (deep orange), ageratum (blue)
- Scarlet sage (*Salvia splendens*, red), dwarf celosia plumosa (gold), portulaca (golden yellow and scarlet)
- Petunia "comanche" (scarlet), verbena (dark purple), verbena (blue or white)
- Rainbow pinks (*Dianthus chinensis beddewiggii*, dark scarlet), marigold (*Tagetes tenuifolia, T. signata*, orange), ageratum (blue)

- Petunia (white, striped red), dwarf morning glory (*Convolvulus tricolor*, deep blue with white throat), variegated-leaved (ivy) geranium (*Pelargonium peltatum*)

For Light Shade:

- *Begonia semperflorens* (red, pink and white), hanging lobelia (*Lobelia*, blue with white eye)
- Geranium (dark scarlet), geranium (salmon), geranium, variegated foliage, with variegated periwinkle
- *Torenia fournieri compacta* (deep blue with white), cupflower (Nierembergia), purple robe (purple), sweet alyssum (white)
- Geranium (leaves variegated), dwarf geraniums

For Northern Exposure:

- Fuchsia (red and blue) or "Tom Thumb," hanging basket fuchsias such as trailing queen or cascade
- *Coleus blumei*, Golden Bedder (foliage golden yellow), *Begonia semperflorens* (red foliage, scarlet flowers)
- *Coleus blumei* (dark red foliage, margined orange), coleus trailing queen (small-leaved, green and red variegated)
- Tuberous begonias (red, white, salmon and yellow), hanging tuberous begonias (scarlet), small-leaved periwinkle (*Vinca minor*)
- Coleus, *Impatiens sultanii* (scarlet)

Soil Mixture: A common mistake is to make soil too rich for porch boxes, and as a result you get all "bush" and no blooms. A good mixture is ½ garden loam, ¼ peat moss or finely sifted humus, and ¼ sand. To this, add an ounce of high-grade plant food, like 5-10-5, in each bushel. Soil should be changed once a year for best growth. This soil mixture can be conveniently sterilized before use by the formaldehyde method as outlined under greenhouse soils. To fill the box, a ½- to ¾-inch layer of sand is placed over the false bottom and the wicks are spread out. The soil mixture is next added to within 1 to 2 inches of the top.

Location: Most porch boxes are exposed to a relentless midsummer sun, hence need plants which will tolerate sun. Select plants according to exposure from the list "Plants Suggested for Planter Use".

Planting: Plants should not be crowded. If the box has a surface area of 4 square feet for instance, the right proportion would be five erect plants, such as geraniums, and three vines, such as vinca or tradescantia. The wider the box, the more plants can be grown. The more soil there is, the less liable the plants are to become dry in hot summer weather. Plants can be set directly into the soil or set potted plants into the box.

Watering and Feeding: Window and porch boxes are exposed to sun and wind, and thus should be looked at for water every day. If weather is rainy and cool, water is applied less frequently. If plants such as petunias, etc. are allowed to go dry, they quickly turn brown, go to seed and the box becomes unsightly. Water is the most important item in maintaining a porch box. When plants have been sufficiently established, one or two applications of Ra-pid-gro, a water-soluble fertilizer, a month apart, should be sufficient to carry them through the summer months.

Summer Care: The growing tips of the plants should be nipped off now and then to keep them from becoming too tall. This makes them bushy and more attractive. Faded blossoms should be removed before they go to seed. Seed pods are a drain on the plants and make them unsightly.

As a final word, be on the lookout for red spider, the most offensive pest for window boxes. Frequent syringing with a garden hose will help control this pest, or they can be sprayed with Kelthane, an effective mite killer. Malathion is a good all-round insecticide to use for leaf-chewing pests.

Winter Care: In winter, porch or window boxes need not be bare. Instead of storing them, they can be filled with evergreen trimmings. The kind of greens used makes little difference, although some kinds are better than others.

Norway spruce is showy for a little while, but the needles drop or become yellowish. Colorado blue spruce is good, but balsam is one of the best for color and persistence of needles.

Australian pine, red pine, Swiss mountain pine (mugo pine) are all good candidates for the window box outdoors. It's better to use one kind, rather than branches of 2 or 3 different varieties. In arrangements, have the taller branches in the center with the lower ones in front and on the ends. Sharpen the ends of the branches to a point and insert them into the soil. Water them and the earth will freeze the soil, holding the branches in place all winter. We like to string Christmas tree lights on ours, and they're showy when the snow falls on them.

As an added feature, cones (both natural and colored) can be wired to the branches. A few branches of red ruscus from your florist makes attractive and decorative material. Also the foliage of evergreens (or laurel branches) can be spray-painted for color effect.

Window boxes can be used for tulips, hyacinths and other bulbs in spring before the regular season of bedding plants arrives. Bulbs, planted in the fall in the boxes, which are stored in cool cellar or cold frame and brought into a warm window in the spring, will bloom indoors or may be moved outdoors.

Cemetery Urns: A common mistake in fixing urns and pots is to put stones in the bottom for drainage. Instead of encouraging water to drain away, organic material like peat moss, sphagnum or even a layer of perlite is placed in the bottom to absorb and hold the moisture. Water is usually at a premium, especially during the hot, dry months. Sometimes in wet periods water may accumulate in the pots or urns, but can be drained off by tipping the pot on its side.

When the plants don't do well, it's usually because of a lack of water. The same soil mixture as recommended for window boxes is satisfactory for urns and tubs. For plants used in urns and tubs refer to the list of plants suggested for planter use.

Don't crowd too many plants in a cemetery urn. These plants need room for expansion, so leave space between the plants.

BONSAI AND MING PLANTS

Bonsai is the Japanese art of dwarfing plants by various means. Though the practice is correctly known as Bonsai, a popularized term today is the "Living Ming Tree." To many, the word "ming" is used to refer mainly to the dwarf trees made of dead material (such as grape stumps, pine stumps, etc.) which you often see in florist shops. The dwarf Japanese trees you see growing in pots are another thing and are referred to as dwarf potted trees or Bonsai. The dead replicas of living potted Japanese dwarf trees seen in flower shops are also known as cypress and Peruvian cypress.

The dwarf potted trees are manipulated to give the appearance of old age. Some of the specimens you see in Japanese books are at least 100 years old, and some may be even 300 years of age. The gnarled trunk, the twisted branches and the evenly spaced foliage gives a feeling much admired by the Japanese.

Subjects to Use: Usually items that have small needles and small leaves are best to use. Here are some that are available in this country and which you might start with: Hinoki false cypress (*Chamaecyparis obtusa*), Japanese black pine (*Pinus thunbergi*), Japanese white pine (*Pinus parviflora*), Japanese maple (*Acer palmatum*), flowering cherry (*Prunus subhirtella*), sargent juniper (*Juniperus chinensis sargentii*) and other low-spreading junipers. Larch, daphne, flowering peach, flowering quince, apricot, crab apples and many others can be used. Anything which has a trunk and branches that are easy to bend can be used.

These young trees are taken up from the soil in autumn and potted, a small pot being preferred to accustom the plant to smaller space for root growth and to check the growth of foliage. Ordinarily, the shallower the pot you use, the better the result.

I'm not a Bonsai expert but those who practice it shorten the trunk
in height and lower the branches by means of wires fastened to the
trunk. By wiring branches you can get them to grow in any shape
you want within a year or so. When you do this year after year the
tree is improved in form and you carefully snip out the tip buds,
shortening and cutting out undesired shoots. Quite often pines, maples,
daphnes, larch and others are bent almost completely upside down by
the wire winding method. Usually, heavy copper wire is used. The soil
in the pot should be drier than usual when wiring is done, in order that
the trunks and branches can be worked more easily. In winter, these
potted plants must be protected from freezing winds and sun. Place
them in a cold frame until early spring when you can start dwarfing
again.

Seeds: It's possible to raise dwarf trees from seeds. Sow the seeds
in pots of sand and peat moss. When seedlings are an inch or two
long, pinch them back, leaving only one or two leaves on any one
branch. Tree dwarfing is an art that is more suited to the Japanese
way of life than it is the American. Most of us do not have the
patience to carry on this distinctive form of Japanese art, and it's not
likely that many Americans will seriously go into the tree-dwarfing business. If you are interested, you can get an excellent book on the
subject by writing to the Brooklyn Botanic Garden, Brooklyn, N.Y.

MINIATURE POTTED TREES

Dwarf trees may be started from seed, but this is a slow process,
and many of the evergreens in particular are difficult to grow from
seed. It is best to start with small plants (these will be from 3 to 10
years of age). Poorly shaped stunted plants may be the best subjects
with which to work.

The Japanese often select small plants that have been naturally
dwarfed by growing in rocky crevices near the timberline of some
mountain. Great care is taken in the transplanting of these plants.
They are not potted at once, but rather are grown in special planting
beds for two years. Dwarf potted trees are trained to give the appearance of great age.

Planting In A Container: The selected tree or shrub should be grown
in a comparatively small pot so that the root system will be restricted.
The soil mixture should contain good garden soil and sand. Charcoal
and crushed stone should be placed at the bottom of the container
which should be provided with a drainage hole.

The selection of a flower pot requires as much thought as one ex-
ercises in selecting the correct frame for a painting. Our standard
flower pot is hardly fitting and certainly a decorated flower pot would

not be in character. The standard azalea-type pot (three-quarters the depth of the standard pot) might be used if a more suitable one is not available.

Care Of The Plants: Repotting should be done every 3 to 5 years in the case of evergreens, and every 2 to 3 years for non-evergreens. Transplanting should be done in the spring before active growth starts. At this time, roots are straightened out and pruned. Some new soil is added to the container. A small amount of organic or other mild fertilizer should be applied every year.

During the summer, plants must have daily attention to be sure that they do not dry out. On very warm days, the potted plants should be kept in partial shade. It is good practice to sprinkle the tops of the plants. Do not overwater in late spring or early summer, since this is the period of active growth and growth is to be kept at a minimum. Someone once said that "Bonsai is a symbol of a life of austerity."

Pruning And Training: Pruning of dwarf trees requires considerable skill. Pinching back is a common practice. This is accomplished by cutting back the new soft growth as it finishes the growing or elongation process and before it has time to harden or mature. One-half to three-quarters of the new growth should be pinched out. Some branches should be pruned back flush with the main stem. This is done to give an open effect which permits the line of trunk and main stems to show through and add to the character of the plant.

Branches may be twisted to give a windswept appearance. Wind a copper wire around a branch in a spiral manner. A branch may thus be bent and trained to some desired angle. The wire should be removed in about six months. A network of bamboo splints may be used to train a set of branches to a desired horizontal plane.

At the time of transplanting older specimens, the plant may be set higher in the pot than would normally be done. This results in exposing some of the roots. If these flair out from the trunk, they add to the aged appearance found in trees growing in difficult sites. Moss growing on the surface of the soil is very much in keeping with desired effects.

Winter Care: Dwarf potted trees require special treatment during the winter in some areas. The drying effect from freezing and excessive cold to which a potted plant is subject would soon kill these plants if they were left out during the winter. The potted plants may be placed in cold frames or pits which are covered with glass and in severe weather furthur protected with mats. The plants should be watered occasionally. A simplified practice that an amateur might follow with younger specimens would be to remove the plants from the pots and set them out in the nursery row or vegetable garden in late fall. It would be desirable to mulch the plant. The plants should be repotted in early spring and the process of dwarfing and training continued.

CHAPTER VI

Gardening under
Glass and Lights

Gardeners who are handy with a hammer and saw can build themselves a small lean-to greenhouse attached to their home. This makes a true winter garden and you can step from a warm house into a warm greenhouse without sloshing through snow or mud. Besides this, electricity, water and drains are usually handy for connecting to the greenhouse. If you heat with hot water, the house heating plant can be extended for heating the greenhouse. The best location for the greenhouse is on the south or east side of your home so the plants will receive as much sun as possible. It should be located away from trees and buildings so that light from the south, west or east is not blocked off. It is recommended you buy or build the largest greenhouse you can afford because you'll find your family of growing plants will increase rapidly.

PLASTIC GREENHOUSES AND HOTBEDS

When greenhouse construction is considered, the use of plastic as a substitute for glass should be investigated.

By and large, many of the commercial growers find the plastic houses quite satisfactory and practical. Many home gardeners are completely satisfied with plastic houses. Plastic is not as durable as glass, but a plastic house can be built for a third the cost of a glass house.

Flexible sheet plastics are used for covering the frame of the greenhouse. The cheapest plastic on the market is polyethylene, costing from 2 cents to 18 cents per square foot. The estimated life of polyethylene is three months during the summer and nine months during the winter. The breakdown of polyethylene and many other plastics is caused by the ultraviolet rays of the sun. The more expensive the plastic, the longer it lasts. Sheet plastics may be obtained in any thickness and width. The thickness normally used for covering greenhouses varies from 2 mils (.002 inches) to 15 mils (0.15 inches). The thicker the plastic, the more expensive per square foot. The width of a plastic sheet varies from 2 feet to 40 feet. Plastics may also be obtained in comparatively thick ($\frac{1}{16}$ to $\frac{1}{8}$ inch) rigid panels. The cost per square foot of this material is greater than for flexible sheet plastic, but the rigid panels last much longer. Rigid plastic panels are not as transparent as sheet plastic. This would not be a problem in the summer, but the light intensity is naturally lower in the winter months and only those plants that require low light intensity, such as African violets, orchids and some foliage plants, can be grown successfully. Because promising new plastics are coming on the market every day, it is best to check with your county agricultural agent about the type best suited for your needs.

The main problem with polyethylene is its susceptibility to ultraviolet light which causes it to break down. You can now buy an ultraviolet-resistant polyethylene which lasts longer. Commercial growers use the sheets in two layers with an air space of one inch between the layers. The two layers cut down on condensation of moisture and plants don't need watering as frequently. Also, it's easier to hold a uniform temperature in a house with two layers of film.

A large number of plastic houses have been designed. Three major types are: conventional, sash and quonset.

The conventional plastic greenhouse is built with the same general design as the rectangular-shaped glass greenhouse. Sheet plastic is rolled on and stapled to the roof and sash bars. When the plastic has been applied, wood lath is tacked over the bars. If the plastic house is to be used during the winter months and a snow load is expected, roof bars should be no farther than 20 inches apart.

Ventilation of the conventional plastic house is similar to a glass house except the vent mechanism is simpler. Exhaust fans can be substituted for ventilators, but must be large enough to remove all the air in the house once each minute in summer, and once every ten minutes during the winter.

The sash greenhouse is the same shape as the conventional type except for the roof, which is made up of panels or sashes. The panels may range in size up to 4 feet by 15 feet and are constructed to slide in channels on the roof. The panels are covered with sheet plastics and thus easy to handle. Ventilation is achieved by sliding the panels up and down. The important and outstanding advantages of this house is that the panels can be removed and stored in a dark room when the greenhouse is not in use. This greatly increases the life of the plastic.

Quonset greenhouses are patterned after the quonset huts of World War II and designed for plastics. The half-circle frames are made of either wood or metal (aluminum). They are covered with one piece of plastic. This type of house is constructed up to 20 feet wide. The greatest advantage is the ease of erection. Ventilation is only by exhaust fans at the ends of the house.

The details of framing need not be elaborate, but must be sufficient. A simply designed greenhouse, using 2 x 4's and 2 x 2's, can be erected without highly skilled labor.

Soils and Soil Treatment

A soil mixture for the small greenhouse may consist of one part garden soil, one part peat moss and one part sand or perlite. Perlite holds large quantities of air and moisture, and is usually better adapted to heavy soils than sands. Twenty per cent superphosphate should be added to the soil mixture at the rate of 4 ounces to the bushel. The above mixture is also recommended for starting seeds. (See Soils section for more information.)

In a small greenhouse, the soil should be changed every two years unless there is equipment to steam-sterilize. Every three weeks apply a liquid plant food (23-19-17) to potted and benched crops, at the rate of 1 teaspoon in 2 quarts of water, after the crop has started. Liquid feeding is easy because the food is applied with a hose attachment as the plants are watered.

The most discouraging part of growing plants in the small greenhouse is getting the seeds to germinate and grow. When seedlings die after germination, but before they are transplanted, the cause is damping off disease. There are several methods to avoid damping off; these include soil sterilization, starting seeds in sterile media such as perlite, vermiculite or a sand-peat mixture, and using liquid soil drenches. (See Starting Seeds under Plant Propagation.)

Soil Mixture for Indoor Sowing: Seeds do not need rich soil. The main thing is to have a loose, well-drained mixture. A good formula is 2 parts loam, 1 part peat moss and 1 part coarse sand. Heavy soil just won't do. Fill your seed box half-full of this mixture and the balance with screened and moistened leaf mold, fine grade peat moss or sphagnum. Level it off with a stick (don't pack it down) and sow the seed in rows or "broadcast". If you've had poor luck with your soil mixture try the new Cornell instant "peat-lite" mixture.

Here's the recipe for a peck:

Vermiculite #4, 4 quarts; Peat moss, 4 quarts
(Vermiculite and peat moss should be sifted through an ⅛-inch mesh screen)

Starting seeds is an easy job. First mark off the rows with a stick. Drop seeds in rows and cover lightly with vermiculite, milled sphagnum moss, or sifted peat moss.

To these add 1 ounce 20 percent superphosphate (powdered); also add 1 tablespoon of 33 percent ammonium nitrate, or 4 tablespoons of 5-10-5 commercial fertilizer. Moisten this mixture well before using. We water the young plants with an extra feeding of liquid plant food (23-19-17), about a month after growth has started. These mixes can now be purchased through the larger seed companies, or you can buy the ingredients and make your own.

In preparation of the peat-lite media, thorough mixing of the components is most important. For larger amounts, a cement mixer may be used.

The amounts of materials have been calculated for 1 cubic yard batches. Two basic mixes have been produced for florists. You can mix any size batch you wish. The formula for peat-lite mix A is as follows:

Peat-lite Mix A for 1 Cubic Yard:

Shredded German or Canadian sphagnum peat moss	11 bushels
Vermiculite (horticultural grade)	11 bushels
Ground limestone, preferably dolomitic	5 pounds
(never use hydrated lime)	

Superphosphate 20 percent, preferably powdered	1 pound
5-10-5 fertilizer	2 ½ pounds

All of the materials should be mixed thoroughly. If the peat moss is dry, additional water should be added to avoid dust problems during the mixing. The amount of 5-10-5 is variable. If 12 pounds of 5-10-5 is added, this amount is sufficient to carry plants in a rapid growing condition for 5 to 6 weeks during the period of April 15 to June 1. At other times of the year, increased or decreased frequencies of watering will reduce this period or stretch it out. Only growing plants should be planted in the media with the 12 pound rate of fertilizer added.

If only 2 pounds of 5-10-5 are used, then a regular fertilizing program should begin immediately upon potting of the plants. A completely soluble fertilizer such as 20-20-20 may be applied.

Peat-lite Mix B for 1 Cubic Yard:

For Mix B Cornell recommends horticultural perlite for the vermiculite. The amount of 5-10-5 should be increased to 16 pounds per cubic yard. The same conditions apply for Mix B as for Mix A if the entire amount of 16 pounds is added or if only the 2 pound rate is used. Mix B may be trickier to use than Mix A because of higher soluble salts and the need for much more careful attention to watering practices. Mix A is probably the best bet for first-time users, according to the Cornell specialists.

Treating Soil for Hotbeds and Greenhouses: While commercial growers steam-treat their soils, it's hardly practical for the small greenhouse operator. A recommended treatment is the use of formaldehyde to control soil fungi. The disadvantages of this method are that the soil cannot be planted for 10 to 14 days after treatment and that the soil must be diluted with large volumes of water. It does not control nematodes or insects.

The treatment is as follows:

1. In the bench or the ground the soil is worked up thoroughly to a depth of 6 inches.

2. A solution is made of 1 part commercial formalin to 50 parts of water.

3. The solution is applied with a watering can at the rate of 2 qts. to 1 square foot of bed.

4. The bed is covered with moist sacks, canvas or several layers of newspaper. It is kept moist for 2 to 3 days.

5. It is uncovered at the end of 3 days and must be aired for 10 to 14 days or until no odor exists.

Seed flats or pots of soil are treated in the same manner. Treating the soil and flat together prevents contamination of sterilized soil from dirty fungus-infected flats or pots.

Heat sterilization of soil mixtures is very satisfactory and easily accomplished when only small quantities are needed. Heat the soil to 180° F. for 30 minutes.

The author has had good luck using a drench known as Pano-drench for treating seed flats. Two teaspoons of Pano-drench to 3 gallons of water applied at the rate of 1½ to 2 pints per square foot of soil is recommended. When soil is treated in the seed flat before sowing the seed, a couple of days are allowed for soil to dry out for easier planting. Pano-drench will not harm plants when used as recommended. The solution can also be applied as a post-emergence drench. The seedling stems should be wet one-half inch above the soil level. If "damping off" has started, the infected area should be well saturated by the drench.

Pano-drench is useful for treatment of cuttings. Dip the cuttings deep enough into the solution so one-half inch of the treated stem will be above soil level after planting.

Another good drench can be made by mixing 2 ounces each of Captan, Terraclor and Ferbam in 12 gallons of water. Pour this on bare bench soil to help eliminate fungi prior to planting.

Watering: It should be remembered that plants vary in their ability to tolerate either a dry or wet soil. Kalanchoes and other succulents do best in relatively dry soils, while hydrangeas, gardenias, geraniums, etc. do best with a constant supply of soil moisture. Most plants are not harmed by wetting the foliage, but there are some exceptions. Mum plants may develop mildew or black spots on the foliage if moisture is left on overnight. Plants such as African violet, calceolaria, gloxinia and others with thick, hairy foliage are injured if water is splashed on the foliage. On African violets, cold water (water lower than room temperature) will cause white or yellowish spots or rings.

In the greenhouse or home, morning or early afternoon are the best times to water the plants, since foliage has a chance to dry before evening, thus reducing the dangers of disease.

When a plant is repotted the soil should be watered immediately. Water should not be withheld for several days following repotting because water is needed to encourage root formation. Plants in small pots dry out faster than those in larger pots due to a smaller volume of soil, so they may need watering a second time during the day.

Insects and Disease Control: Most greenhouse pests can be licked by using smoke generator bombs, effective against the spider mite, aphids and white flies. Malathion sprays will banish scale, mealybugs and aphids. Sanitation is the best way to keep diseases from flaring up among your plants. For more information see chart on Insect Control.

Gardeners interested in greenhouse gardening should subscribe to

Under Glass magazine, published bi-monthly by the Lord and Burnham Company, Irvington, New York, or *Grower Talks* by George J. Ball Co., West Chicago, Illinois. These firms will tell the best ways to keep insects and diseases at a minimum in your little greenhouse.

PLANTS UNDER LIGHTS

Growing plants under artificial light is a hobby that pays off in better plants and more of them. You can grow the plants in attics or in basements where natural light is lacking. African violets, because of their low light need, can be made to flower freely in a dark room with the aid of artificial lights. Fluorescent lights give off less heat than ordinary incandescent bulbs and are now used extensively. Plants do well under fluorescent lights alone, but will benefit more from a mixture of fluorescent and incandescent lights. The bluish light of daylight and white fluorescent tubes produces stockier plants. And the reds and yellows of incandescent bulbs produce strong root systems.

A good system for lighting most plants is a 3½ foot unit consisting of two 40-watt fluorescent tubes arranged side by side with a single 40-watt incandescent bulb at one end. For larger plants or where more light is needed, use two or more units of this type. Place the unit about 18 inches above the plants.

Put a thermometer at the height of the plants and if the temperature gets too high, reduce the amount of light. Maintain a 60° to 65° daylight temperature, with 50° to 55° at night. It's best to keep the lights on from 12 to 16 hours a day and give the plants a rest period, although no ill effects will result from 24-hour lighting of most plants. Artificial lighting can be used for just about every houseplant, except those needing high light intensity. Cacti and geraniums will do a lot better in full sunlight.

Bench: A bench 30 inches high can be erected with a frame of 1-inch by 6-inch boards to form the sides for the tabletop or bed. Redwood lumber or pine treated with Cuprinol will be adequate. The bench frame should be made of 2 x 4 lumber for stability. The table or bottom of the bench can be made from ¼-inch tempered Masonite or better still Transite, which is an asbestos and cement board commonly used for greenhouse benches. The bottom should be cross-braced every 16 inches with 2 x 4 lumber. For pot culture a 3- to 4-inch layer of sand is placed on the bottom for drainage.

Watering: Plants may require more watering because of the low humidity in the basement or attic. A 4-inch layer of sand kept moist will help maintain the humidity. If high humidity happens to be a problem, an electric fan located nearby will keep the air in motion and help prevent disease.

Soils: The same type of soils and mixtures as suggested under greenhouse gardening can be used for the poor man's greenhouse. Sterilization of these soils is important and can be accomplished by the heat method or by use of formaldehyde. However, perlite, perlite-and-peatmoss mixture, sphagnum moss or vermiculite can be used without sterilization.

Disease and insects should be no problem provided good sanitation and culture is practiced. If trouble occurs, however, treat as in a greenhouse.

The lights: To start plants it would be advisable to use a 4-foot, 2 or 3 tube, 40-watt industrial fixture with a reflector. For convenience and efficiency a poultry-type clock switch should be placed in the circuit. If the temperature is abnormally low, i.e., lower than 50° at times, provision should also be made for a heating cable to provide bottom heat. Probably a separate circuit will have to be provided for the heating cable. Follow the instructions given for installation of heating cable under hotbeds.

Daylight or cool-white fluorescent tubes are preferred for plant growth. Intensity is another factor to be considered because each plant has its own requirements. To provide maximum flexibility, the fixture should be hung on a pulley arrangement. Raising the fixture lowers the light intensity at plant level, while lowering the fixture increases the intensity. For starting seeds of vegetable and flower plants, it's advisable to lower the fixture to within 6 inches of the seedling plants. Spring bulbs are forced at low intensities thus calling for a smaller fixture.

The accompanying chart shows appropriate temperatures, daily light periods and location of fluorescent fixtures above the plants. These recommendations are general and may have to be adjusted from experience to suit conditions.

Since the amount of light required by a plant is based on the duration of that light, it may be necessary to give a longer light period to compensate for too low an intensity. Twenty-four hour lighting of plants is not harmful except where the length of day affects short-day plants for flowering.

LIGHT AND TEMPERATURE CHART *

PLANT	DURATION	TEMPERATURE	HEIGHT ABOVE PLANTS
African Violets	12–18 hours	60°–65°	10–12 inches
Begonias	12 hours	60°–65°	8–10 inches
Cineraria	15 hours	40°–50°	6–8 inches
Cyclamen	15 hours	50°–60°	6–8 inches

Plant	Duration	Temperature	Height above Plants
Geraniums	15 hours	55°–60°	6–8 inches
Gloxinia	15 hours	55°–60°	10–12 inches
House Plants	12–18 hours	60°–65°	12–24 inches
Tulips	12 hours	50°–60°	18–24 inches

CUTTINGS AND SEEDLINGS

Alyssum	15 hours	65°–70°	6–8 inches
Chrysanthemums	15 hours	55°–65°	6–8 inches
Dahlia	15 hours	60°–70°	6–8 inches
Marigold	15 hours	60°–70°	6–8 inches
Petunia	15 hours	60°–70°	6–8 inches
Stock	15 hours	55°–65°	6–8 inches
Tomatoes	15 hours	65°–76°	6–8 inches
Zinnia	15 hours	65°–70°	6–8 inches

* University of Wisconsin

HOW TO MAKE COLD FRAMES AND HOTBEDS

Cold frames and hotbeds are similar in construction with the principal difference in heat and insulation.

A cold frame utilizes the sun's heat, with no artificial heat supplied. The soil is heated during the day and gives off the heat at night to keep the plants warm. The frame may be banked with materials like straw, sawdust or leaves to insulate it from the cold outside air. Mats of straw, paper or cloth may be placed over the sash at night to conserve the heat.

Cold frames are used to "harden" plants which have been started in the greenhouse or hotbed before transplanting to the garden. The process of hardening matures succulent tissues. This reduces injury from sudden temperature drop and from conditions which cause rapid drying after transplanting.

Early lettuce and radishes, as well as bulbs and perennials, are forced in a cold frame a few weeks before normal season. Cold frames are also used for azaleas, heather, hydrangeas and other tender plants. These plants may be set directly in the soil of a cold frame or in pots or flats. Chrysanthemum, stock plants and biennials are also placed in a cold frame for winter protection. Cyclamen, azaleas and some houseplants may be grown in a cold frame during the summer. Partial shade should be given to these plants in the summer by using lath sash or roll of snow fence in place of the glass sash.

Since cold frames are movable, they can be erected or set over beds of pansies, violets, primroses, etc. in very early spring to bring these plants into bloom ahead of normal season. Just set the frame over the plants which are to be forced and bank the outside with leaves or straw to keep out the cold. Rhubarb can also be forced a couple of weeks earlier in the same manner.

Spring flowering bulbs, planted in flats or pots of soil, are placed in the cold frame in the fall and removed after proper storage time to the house or greenhouse for forcing. Leave them in cold storage until the first week in January, then remove. To do this, pot up the bulbs and place in the frame in the fall. Cover the pots with 6 to 8 inches of peat moss or sawdust for insulation. Additional protection is provided to keep the temperature from fluctuating by banking the sides and covering the glass as previously described.

Cold frames are built of wood 2 inches thick for rigidity, but wood 1 inch thick may be substituted. Cypress, chestnut or redwood are the best now available. Heartwood grades are best because they are most resistant to decay. However, there are corrosive effects from compounds contained in redwood. For this reason, it is suggested that aluminum or hot dipped galvanized nails, screws or bolts be used to fasten the wood.

Wood preserving materials containing zinc or copper are best for treating wood to be used in frame construction. Wood that has been treated for decay resistance with pentachlorophenol, mercury or creosote compounds must not be used in plant-growing structures. Toxic fumes from these compounds will injure or kill plants.

Materials needed for construction of a two-sash cold frame are:

> 1 piece of wood 2" x 8" x 6'
> 1 piece of wood 2" x 14" x 6'
> 1 piece of wood 2" x 2" x 6'
> 2 pieces of wood 2" x 6" x 5'11"
> 2 pieces of wood 1" x 3" x 5'11"
> 2 pieces of wood 2" x 8" tapered to 2" x 5'11"
> (This may be made from one 2" x 10" x 6')
> 2 L-irons 2" x 2" x 6"
> 2 L-irons 2" x 2" x 12"
> 24 round-head bolts, ⅜" x 3", with washers
> 30 number 8 nails

Hotbeds or heated frames are similar in construction to cold frames except for the addition of an 8-inch board below ground. The walls are sometimes insulated and are usually higher than those of cold frames so that tall-growing plants may be placed in them.

Artificial heat is supplied by electricity (i.e., light bulbs or electric cable), steam or hot water.

Heated frames or hotbeds are used for bulbs, azaleas, hydrangeas and chrysanthemums. They are ideal for starting vegetable and annual flowering plants from seed. Summer propagation of cuttings from woody plants and ground covers like pachysandra is also accomplished in a hotbed.

An electric lead-covered cable is the most often-used method for heating hotbeds. The lead covering is necessary to resist soil corrosion. This heating cable is operated by a thermostat which controls the hotbed automatically, saves electricity and assures constant temperature.

Heating cable is purchased in 60- to 120-foot lengths, with the 60-foot length being used on a 110-volt power supply and the 120 feet of cable on a 220-volt power supply. Each 60-foot length of cable will heat 36 square feet of frame space. Both heating cable and thermostats can be purchased from garden supply houses.

To install the cable in a frame, put a 12-inch layer of fine gravel or cinders below the hotbed to provide both insulation and drainage. Next, add a 1-inch layer of sand or soil which acts as a bed for laying out the electric cable. Loop the cable back and forth across the bed, 3 inches from the sides, with the lines 6 inches apart. On top of the cable place hardware cloth, ¼-inch mesh, to act as a heat conductor and for keeping uniform temperatures. Soil or coarse sand is then placed on the hardware cloth to a depth of 4 to 6 inches.

For less-expensive heating use electric light bulbs. Use eight 25-watt bulbs for heating a 3- by 6-foot frame mounted on a strip of wood spanning the bed just beneath the center of the sash. Porcelain sockets and waterproof electric cable must be used for the installation.

The standard sash for covering cold frames and hotbeds is 3 feet wide by 6 feet long with three rows of 10-inch glass lapped to allow rainwater to run lengthwise. Construction can be made simpler by using plastics.

CARE OF HOTBEDS AND COLD FRAMES

Seeds started in a cold frame or hotbed are sown directly in the earth of the frame or in flats or pots. If the seed is sown directly, the soil is prepared by spading and raking to provide a finely pulverized bed. A 4-inch layer of fine peat moss added before spading is beneficial.

For sowing in pots or flats, 3 to 4 inches of the soil is removed and replaced with cinders. This provides drainage for the bed and prevents earthworms from entering the pots or flats.

Cuttings may be started in the frames during the summer months by removing the soil and inserting plain sand, or a mixture of sand and peat moss, or perlite alone.

Ventilation of the cold frames during the spring months is important. The temperature inside the frames should not rise above 70° during the periods of sunshine. Wooden blocks are used to raise or lower the sash on the side opposite the direction of the wind. The sashes are closed before sundown to conserve heat. If the night temperature is expected to fall below 40° F., insulating mats are used to cover the sash.

U.S. Department of Agriculture

If you're handy with a saw and hammer you can make a simple homemade cold frame for less than $50. U.S. Department of Agriculture has complete instructions free of charge.

Watering must be done in the morning so that the plants will dry off before closing the frame for the night. Care must be taken to avoid getting the soil too wet during periods of low temperature and cloudy days. Such conditions favor damping-off fungus, which quickly kills young seedlings.

Window Greenhouses: Homeowners who do not want a regular greenhouse for growing and starting their plants can install a window greenhouse. Today, it's a lot more than a sunny place for needy houseplants. It's a real greenhouse, right at your window tips, with its own environment of controlled temperature, ventilation and humidity. The modern window greenhouse is built of aluminum, in slip-together panels for quick assembly. All the necessary climate controls are available with the unit and it comes in enough sizes to accommodate just about any standard window size.

One of the nice things about a window greenhouse is that it lends itself to almost any architectural design and setting; also all plants are easily accessible from the window opening. The price is within reach of all, and you'll be surprised to see how many plants you can start in this "house greenhouse". Even a small one has about 5 shelves to accommodate up to 100 or so potted plants.

Lord and Burnham

Window sill makes a fine spot for a tiny greenhouse.

WINDOW SILL GREENHOUSE

You can convert your picture window into a greenhouse at a cost of only a few cents. Follow the steps outlined below and you can root some of your favorite shrubs and houseplants without even stepping outside.

TRICKS FOR STARTING SEEDS AND PLANTS
BY INDOOR LIGHTS

With the advent of fluorescent lighting, you can now have year-round blooming plants. It also means you may now grow plants superior to those grown in the greenhouse, or at least just as good! Fluorescent lights for starting and growing plants is one of the biggest things to hit the indoor gardening industry, because it means you can grow plants

Window Sill Greenhouse

U.S. Department of Agriculture

(1) Mix peat moss and sand together, two parts peat and one part sand. (2) Sprinkle moisture on peat. (3) Place mixture in plastic bag. (4) Insert cuttings of favorite plants and syringe lightly. (5) Seal end of bag and place in northern window where it will get plenty of light but no direct sunlight.

in your own home, without spending a lot of money. Due to the many questions sent me concerning this new phase of horticulture, I hope the following will help you:

Q. What are some sources of light we can use for growing plants indoors?

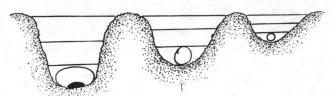

SOW SEED AT DEPTH 3X DIAMETER
OF SEED

SCATTER FINE SEED
ON TOP OF SOIL
PRESS DOWN
LIGHTLY

THIN OUT SEEDLINGS TO GIVE
PLANTS ROOM TO DEVELOP

OR

SOW IN FLATS INDOORS FOR
EARLY PLANTING OUTDOORS

SPACE SEEDS WHILE SOWING IN ROWS OR IN HILLS

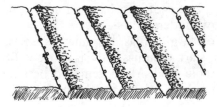

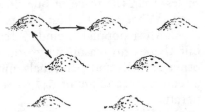

Prentice-Hall, Inc.

Starting plants from seed is the simplest and most common form of plant propagation. Start out with good seed, use a good soil mixture (see text) and you'll have all the plants you and your friends can use.

A. There are various sources of light: Natural light (greenhouse or window), warm-white fluorescent, cool white, Gro-Lux, combination natural-white fluorescent and daylight fluorescent, Plant-Gro (Westinghouse) and combination warm-white and cool-white fluorescent.

Q. How about incandescent (bulbs) light, are they OK?

A. Some people use these to supplement natural light. You can place up to 30 young plants under one 150-watt bulb. Best distance between bulb and leaves is 14 inches. If less, heat will cook leaves. Keep light on seed (65° to 70°) to hasten germination. Leave on for 14 hours or so per day.

Q. How about fluorescent lights?

A. There are several kinds of fluorescent light tubes. Many gardeners use either daylight tubes or a half-and-half combination of daylight and deluxe warm types. The lights are burned for 16 hours a day, usually going on at 6 A.M. or 7 A.M. and off at 10 P.M. or 11 P.M. A timer to turn lights off and on automatically costs about $10.00. If lights are allowed to burn continuously for several days, some plants may be burned. Fluorescent lights will not burn foliage unless they come in contact with the leaves.

Q. Do you have to switch plants back and forth to natural light?

A. No. Plants will grow under artificial lights indefinitely. No need to move them from natural to artificial light. Plants brought into bloom under lights can be used around the house for decorative effect, then returned to the lights for a few days recuperation.

Q. How much light is needed?

A. Some need little light. The houseplants most easily grown under artificial light do best under intensities of 400 to 700 footcandles. A minimum of two 40-watt fluorescent tubes should be used.

Q. How about the cost?

A. Less than you think. Power cost to operate a 20-watt tube for 15 hours each day for a week is about 4 cents. A fixture with two 40-watt tubes will cost about 25 cents a week. Thus for an operating cost of less than the price of one flowering plant, you can have a lot of fun.

Q. What are the best plants to grow under lights?

A. Most popular include African violets, gloxinias, begonias, episcias, but there's no reason why you cannot start petunias, salvias, dozens of other annuals and perennials and vegetable seed. Most items do best in a temperature range of 65° to 80° with a drop of 10° for the night temperature.

Q. What about the new Gro-Lux? How do these lights work?

A. Gardeners like them. The Gro-Lux lamp differs from standard fluorescent tubes for lighting because it produces more red and blue light energy (twice as much total effective light energy as the warm-white light) and gives more energy for plants, improves germination of seeds. You can use them in standard fixtures. Many gardeners tell us that Gro-Lux increases number and size of blooms and produces a bigger root system. You can buy them in 2-, 4-, 6-, 8-foot lengths, from $2 to $5.

Q. What other factors are needed for growth besides light?

A. Right temperature—daytime 70° to 75°; nighttime 60° to 65°.

Cool night temperature is fine because it aids in assimilation of food the plant made during the day. Also, good ventilation prevents disease. Proper humidity (between 50 percent and 60 percent) for normal growth. Avoid overcrowding and overwatering (just enough to soak soil). Best time to water is in morning so leaves can dry before night. Use lukewarm water.

Q. Do all plants need light for flowering? What determines it?

A. Plants fall into 3 groups: short-day plants, long-day plants, and indeterminate types: Short day, 10 to 13 hours. (Christmas begonia, poinsettia, and mums); long-day, 14 to 18 hours (China asters, calceolaria, dahlias and many annuals for spring flowering); indeterminate will flower at all seasons, whether they receive 12, 14 or 16 or 18 hours of light. Roses, carnations and a great majority of houseplants such as African violets, gloxinias, coleus, geraniums fall into this group.

SELF-WATERING POTS

In the home, potted plants are often "orphans" when it comes to getting the proper amount of watering. They get either too much or too little. Homeowners who want to go away for a few days neglect their plants completely or keep them standing in bathtubs until they get back. At least many do this, although it is not necessary now that we have a new method called "wick culture," which is nothing more than allowing plants to water themselves automatically.

For potted plants, little material is needed for wick culture. A container is needed to act as a reservoir, and this can be a glass baking dish, or a cake pan.

Your porch or window flower box can water the plants automatically. Pieces of wick extending through a false bottom, into the reservoir, automatically take up water and keep plants supplied constantly.

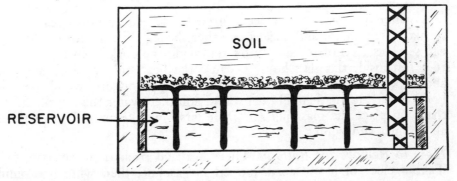

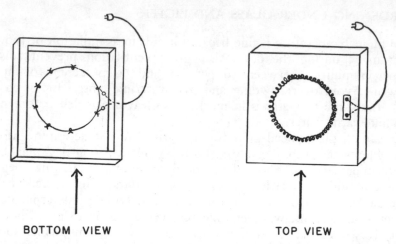

BOTTOM VIEW   TOP VIEW

A simple homemade gadget for removing the bottom of a glass jug. The coil heats up, warming the glass. Then dip the jug into a pail of cold water. Presto! The bottom drops out and you have a miniature greenhouse for rooting roses and other shrubs. Be sure to place a piece of tape along the sharp edge to prevent cutting your finger.
NOTE: Do not let children play with this. Always be careful about getting a shock. Do not touch any wire, terminal or coil.

The wick can be made of burlap, oil lamp wick or cheesecloth, but fiberglass wick material is best because it never rots. You can buy the material at most leading seed stores. For potted plants, a wick 4 inches long is enough. You push the wick thru the hole in the empty pot, leaving about 2 inches inside. The ends are fluffed or unraveled and spread uniformly in the bottom of the pot. Dirt is put on top, then the plant is potted up in the normal manner. Add water to the reservoir when necessary. Water flows up the glass wick and waters the plant automatically.

GLASS JUGS MAKE SMALL GREENHOUSE

A gallon jug makes a perfect "greenhouse" for rooting roses, forsythia, spirea, privet and dozens of other shrubs. The mouth of the jug can serve as a ventilator simply by removing the cork from it. Cuttings root fast inside the glass house because the heat and humidity are just about perfect. You can take cuttings from immature wood (called greenwood), insert them in the ground and then water them well. After that you place the glass jug (or fruit jars) over them and leave them all summer and winter.

How to Remove the Bottom? There are two tricks you can try: (1) Take a piece of heavy cord, dipped in gasoline, then wind it around the bottom of the jug. Ignite it and after it burns a few seconds quickly dip jug into a pail of ice water. The bottom will usually drop off. If there is a jagged edge left, better cover the raw edge with Scotch tape, masking tape, plastic tape or anything to prevent your getting cut. (2) This consists of using electricity. You can make a homemade jug cutter in the following manner. First, make a small wooden frame and nail a piece of asbestos fiberboard on it. This material comes from your lumber yard. Next, cut a circle in the board so it will just about hold the bottom of the jug. Now, get a steel spring from your hardware store to be used as a heating filament.

Each end of the element is fastened to a bolt, and a piece of electric cord it run to each terminal. When you plug the cord the steel filament or element heats up.

CUTTINGS IN SAND   GLASS JAR

You can start your own houseplants, roses and other shrubs by (1) inserting cuttings into sand or ground and (2) covering with glass fruit jar.

To Operate: Place the glass jug on the element. Turn on the electricity (that is, plug the cord in). Leave glass jug on the heat element; in just a few seconds the glass will crack all the way around the base of the jug.

It is not necessary to dip the jug in cold water, but it is a good idea to wrap the cut edge with tape of some sort; either adhesive, plastic or polyethylene film so you won't cut yourself on the sharp edges.

To water the cuttings you can either pour water down the mouth, or pour it down the outside of the jug. Glass fruit jars also make fine greenhouses. Leave cuttings under the glass jar all winter, without any cover.

QUESTIONS AND ANSWERS FOR
THE HOME GREENHOUSE GARDENER

Each year my wife and I receive hundreds of questions from gardeners who are interested in the home greenhouse. I picked out the most common questions and present them here.

Q. Do you have to be rich to own a small backyard greenhouse?

A. No, there are greenhouses you can put up by yourself. The cost will fit the pocketbook and be an excellent investment for health, fun and profit.

Q. Where can I get simple instructions on small do-it-yourself greenhouses?

A. Your best bet is to send for catalogs from greenhouse firms, of which there are many. Write to Lord & Burnham Co., Irvington, New York; Hill Greenhouse Corp., Medina, New York, or look in horticultural magazines for information on greenhouse gardening. Many seed firms have catalogs which list information on seed sowing, temperatures, etc., all free for the asking. George J. Ball Co. Inc., West Chicago, Illinois, has an excellent booklet *Grower Talks* which will help you. There are many good books on the subject: Chabot's *Greenhouse Gardening;* Noble & Merkel, *Gardening in a Small Greenhouse;* Posts, *Florist Crop Production* (mainly for commercial growers) and my own book, *The Green Thumb Garden Handbook*, published by Prentice-Hall, Inc. All contain helpful information on plants under glass.

Q. What temperature should be maintained in a greenhouse?

A. Depends, but usually a minimum night temperature of 50° to 55° is ideal for a large variety of commonly grown plants. Daytime temperature can be around 70° to 80°.

Q. What plants are easiest to grow in the greenhouse?

A. I'd try geraniums, coleus, begonias, chrysanthemums, snapdragons, and a few calla lilies for a starter. In spring, you can grow all kinds of bedding items such as petunias, zinnias, snaps, phlox, verbena, celosia, portulaca and countless other items. With a minimum amount of heating, you can grow just about any plant you want. Experiment with vegetables, too. You're in for a real experience once you get started on vegetables, annuals and perennials.

Q. How much ventilation is needed in a small greenhouse?

A. On warm days in winter, open vent slightly; open wide in summer. Cool air is needed to give plants stiffer stems.

Q. Do you have to shade the roof in summer to keep out sun?

A. Yes, it keeps it cooler indoors and prevents foliage from burning on extra hot days. Use a specially-prepared shading compound, or mix some lime with water.

Q. Is a cold frame or hotbed handy to have too?

A. Yes, a cold frame or hotbed can be used for an overflow of plants from the greenhouse, or you can start plants indoors and harden them off in the cold frame.

Q. What do they mean when they say to "harden off" plants raised indoors?

A. It simply means placing the plants outdoors or in a cold frame so they can toughen up at night (without benefit of heat). Such plants stand the shock of outdoor planting better.

Q. What are some plant diseases encountered in a small greenhouse?

A. Bacterial disease (difficult to cure), keep leaf surface dry and sterilize soil. Rot, use bichloride of mercury tablets or Captan; blight, use Zineb, Ferbam or Nabam. Mildew, use sulfur, copper or Karathane (Mildex); rust, red pustules, use Zineb, sulfur; sooty mold use Ferbam or sulfur. Leaf spots, use disease-free plants, cut diseased leaves out and burn, dust with Ferbam or Captan. Virus diseases, cause stunted, distorted markings, so use healthy plant; no known cure.

Q. Please name some plants for the tropical greenhouse.

A. Try philodendron, night-blooming cereus, aroids (philodendrons, anthurium, dieffenbachias, caladiums, syngoniums and pothos). Most of these plants like a humusy soil, plenty of humidity. Calla lilies are not lilies, but aroids. They like a soil that's well drained. In June, dry off the plants, allow tubers to rest until August, then repot and water. Gesneriads (African violets, gloxinias, episcias, achimenes) are plants which need a light potting mixture.

Q. If I want to root cuttings of plants, what materials are best?

A. Try sand (pure mason's sand), perlite, vermiculite or a mixture of sand and these materials, or sand-peat mixture. Stick cuttings in and keep moist. You can dip the cuttings of hard-to-root items in a rooting powder. You won't gain anything on cuttings easy to root. Have fun, get more out of life! Build yourself a small greenhouse!

CHAPTER VII

Decorating for

the Holidays

HOMEMADE CHRISTMAS DECORATIONS

One of the nicest things about Christmas is the planning and making of festive decorations for the home. They are as much a part of the celebration as the tree and the gaily wrapped packages.

Decorations add much to the spirit of the season, but, when overdone, may ruin the effect. A few boughs arranged nicely in a vase or jar give a more pleasing effect than greens suspended from every lighting fixture and picture frame.

There is no reason why you can't make some extra cash at holiday time by making Christmas decorations to sell. It will take work gathering the greens but often you're rewarded by the finished product and the extra cash that comes in.

Evergreens: There are many kinds you can use. If you have some growing in front of your home, winter's a good time to prune them and use the clippings. Pine, cedar, fir, juniper, yew and arborvitae are good. Needles of hemlock and spruce drop soon after being brought indoors, but both are good for outdoor work. Pines, especially white pine and red pine, are good for both indoor and outdoor use because they keep their needles longer. Balsam is a good keeper and very fragrant. You can prune your evergreens at Christmas time without injury to them.

Wreaths: You can make a frame out of boughs or #9 wire. For a wreath 14 inches in diameter, wire on sprays of greenery that are from 4 to 6 inches long. For trimmings, you can use cones, teasel, burrs, milkweed, dried grasses, seed pods, sumac fruits, sleigh bells, turkey bells and colored berries, such as bittersweet, bayberry, mountain ash, rose hips, winterberry.

Keep in mind that pleasing effects are obtained when more than one type of evergreen is used. A wreath of only white pine can be monotonous, but interest can be created by combining materials of different textures.

If you want to give your wreaths and garlands a different touch, try using fruits on them. Fruits such as pears, grapes, cranberries, tangerines, limes and crab apples may be used successfully. These fruits will not stand extremely low temperatures, but will last satisfactorily under ordinary conditions if you dip them in clear lacquer, white shellac, or clear varnish. After they have dried, arrange them on the wreath or festoon.

Decorations look best if they are in good proportion to the space in which they are used. A small wreath in front of a large window fails to give the desired effect. Color is also important. For example, in a room where orange and brown are the predominant colors, large bows of bright red ribbon may clash. A bow of gold ribbon or a trim of bittersweet and cones may give a better effect.

How to Make Snow: Artificial frost or snow effects for outdoor decorations can be obtained by applying to the finished piece a creamy paste of casein glue, plaster of paris or even white paint. For indoor use, a thick starch paste, a creamy paste of whitewash or a saturated solution of Epsom salts may be used. When the water evaporates, the crystals remain and give a frosty effect. A heavy lather, made by beating soap suds very stiff and dry, may also be used. It will last for the entire holiday season if whipped dry. Perhaps the simplest method is to apply liquid white shoe polish. You can also use "snow" or white paint in pushbutton aerosol spray cans.

A glitter or powdery artificial snow may be made to adhere to the decorations if the evergreens are first sprinkled or sprayed with a solution made by dissolving 1 tablespoonful of powdered glue in 2 quarts of water. The glitter or powder is sprinkled on the greens before the glue dries.

Sprays: Sprays can be wired to a coat hanger.

Evergreen Roping: You can gather your own material for making festoons, garlands or Christmas roping. All you need is a foundation cord or heavy wire, such as clothesline wire, and some evergreen boughs. Pine and hemlock are fine for this job.

Tie one end of the cord to a door knob and start binding pieces of evergreen to it. Twine or fine wire are good for wrapping around the foundation cord. A string of lights can be fastened to the rope of greens.

Almost any kind of evergreen can be used. Among the narrow leaf evergreens, pine, cedar, fir, juniper, yew and arborvitae are the best. Pine, particularly white pine, is excellent for both indoor and outdoor use because it remains in good condition for a long time. Needles of hemlock and spruce drop soon after being brought indoors; both are fine for outdoor use or for decorations to be used in the home for one or two days.

Table Decorations: Don't make them too tall. Remember you have to look over them when seated. Make them in good proportion to the table. One interesting arrangement for a table consists of a few sprays

Place a small candle inside a bowl. Decorate base of bowl with pine cones, silver balls and evergreens for a striking effect.

of huckleberry, pine or balsam, informally arranged in a low bowl and brightened with colorful berries and a few pine cones wired to twigs. Fresh flowers are also pleasing arranged with some evergreen foliage.

The "Kissing Ring": Instead of just tacking a spray of mistletoe in a doorway, try making a kissing ring. You can do it by winding an embroidery hoop with white crepe paper and striping it with colored Scotch tape.

Christmas Bells: If you've got some of those small two-inch clay flower pots lying around, here is a new use for them. Wrap them with florist's plant foil, or aluminum kitchen foil, tip them upside down, and they make a fine Christmas bell. A small glass ball suspended from a wire makes a fine clapper for the bell. This is one way to use those flower pots which have accumulated in the cellar.

To Color Cones: You can color cones silver, gold, bronze and other colors simply by dipping them in diluted solutions of paints. When you dilute the paints, use turpentine for flat effects, linseed oil or varnish if you want them glossy. You can buy spray paints which work nicely, or you can apply paint with brush.

Treating Cones for Fireplaces: With a small outlay of time and money you can treat pine cones to burn in all colors of the rainbow. First, you get a supply of pine or spruce cones, or use small blocks of well-dried wood; then decide what colors you want, when burned: Barium nitrate (blue); copper sulfate (bluish); strontium nitrate (red); calcium chloride (orange); copper chloride (green); lithium chloride or potassium permanganate (purple).

These materials can be bought in a drugstore. The simplest and best method for treating is to dip cones into a solution of chemical and water. Use a wooden tub or pail, or an earthen crock, as the chemicals may destroy metal. You can use a metal bucket if you plan to throw it away afterward. Dissolve the chemical in water, 1 pound to 1 gallon of water. Place the cones in a cloth mesh bag (onion sack is good) and immerse in the solution. Since many of the chemicals will stain hands, use rubber gloves. Potassium permanganate, in particular, leaves dark brownish stains which remain a long time.

Remove cones after soaking in solution for 10 to 15 minutes. Let them drain over container for a few minutes, then spread on newspapers to dry overnight. When dry, they are ready for use in the fireplace.

There are many chemicals you can use, but be sure to select those that are harmless or noninflammable. Treatment of cones with resin or turpentine has been suggested, but this mixture is volatile and very flammable, and consequently dangerous.

Another method for treating the cones is to dip them in a solution of ordinary glue, two tablespoonfuls to a gallon of water, draining off the excess solution and dusting the powdered chemicals over the cones so they will adhere to the moist gluey surface. The cones are then dried. Here are the chemicals to use and the colors: red, strontium chloride; green, barium chloride; bluish green, copper sulphate; orange, calcium chloride; lavender, potassium chloride; yellow, sodium chloride (common salt). Sodium and calcium colors will obscure those from other metals. Nitrates and chlorates are not recommended since they can be dangerous. You can buy commercial forms of these chemicals from your local drugstore and some can be obtained from your fertilizer supplier.

Christmas Logs: If you want a crackling, snapping fire cheerily blazing in the fireplace, you'll find oak is one of the best fireplace woods. It burns slowly, gives off a lot of heat and will not throw off sparks. Beech is another dandy because of its heat and pleasant aroma. Ash gives off smoke if wet; if seasoned too long, it's short-lived in the fireplace.

Logs from apple, plum, pear and cherry trees are good since they release a lot of heat and the burning wood gives off a delightful fragrance. Most evergreens, such as pine, fir, spruce and other resin-containing species, also give off a nice aroma, but these throw off sparks.

Willow, poplar, elm are among the poorest of fireplace woods.

How to Keep Christmas Greens Green

You can get more fun and enjoyment from your Christmas greens if you follow a few green thumb tricks. A dried out Christmas tree is a fire hazard. Freshly cut trees are quite fire resistant. You can make them fairly resistant by cutting about two inches off the butt and placing the tree in water. A tree 8 feet high will take up a quart or more of water in 24 hours. That's why the container holding the tree should be large enough to hold a day's supply. Refill it every day and your tree will be flame resistant for about a week or longer in the house.

To further reduce the flammability of a Christmas tree, spray a 25 percent solution of water glass on it. The chemical name for water glass is sodium silicate. This process also helps the tree retain its needles somewhat better. All the pines have relatively long needles and retain them well as long as the tree is kept. Sodium silicate is used 9 parts to 1 part of water.

Red, Scotch and Austrian pines are naturally fire-resistant to a degree. Hemlock, pretty outdoors, makes a poor tree indoors as it sheds its needles quickly. Other short-needled species include fir and spruce, and these also shed foliage quickly.

Whatever, you do, do NOT try to flameproof your Christmas tree by using a dangerous suggestion passed on every year. Never use ammonium sulfate in a solution, as this will cause some trees to become more flammable than before.

Several plant waxes are on the market and these can be sprayed on the needles. Even with waxes, the species you use for Christmas trees determines the keeping qualities to a large degree.

Tests at Cornell were conducted to show how Christmas trees may be made to last longer indoors. Eight kinds of conifers were cut and kept dry at a room temperature of 80° F. The periods in which they remained green without dropping their leaves were as follows: hemlock, four days; spruce, 5 days; balsam fir, 10 days; Scotch pine, 15 days; red pine, 20 days; Douglas fir (*Pseudotsuga taxifolia*), 30 days. The same kinds were also kept standing in the same room but with its butt in a pail of water weighted with gravel. All of the Christmas trees in this second set remained in good condition for 30 days. This shows that moisture is the important feature, even with evergreens that dry quickly.

So, to boil this all down: You can use almost any Christmas tree available, so long as the tree is kept in a pail of water, weighted with gravel or coal to keep the tree erect. To me, keeping the tree standing in water is the most practical, satisfactory and convenient method for reducing fire hazard and preventing the needles from discoloring or falling. Additional protection against fire can be provided by using fire-resistant coatings or wax sprays.

Spud Centerpiece

Potatoes are not only a wholesome food, but they make a fine holder for an evergreen centerpiece.

Take a good-sized potato, slice off a portion of the bottom so it will rest flat. Then trim off some evergreen branches from your shrubs, cut off small twigs, sharpen the ends and thrust them into the potato from

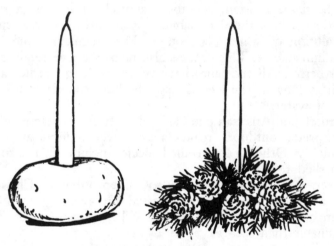

all sides until you have completed a centerpiece. Scoop out a hole in the top of the potato and set a candle in the center.

Since a potato contains over 75 percent water, it will keep the evergreen twigs fresh for several days. Most evergreens will work satisfactorily except hemlock, which sometimes loses its needles very quickly indoors.

Fun With Homemade Candles

Candles add a lot of glow and warmth to a room. They do something to us all. Everyone admires the soft flickering light candles give off. You can use candles any time of the year, not just Christmas. Here are a few tips on how to use and make candles.

Square Candles: Use an empty cardboard milk carton for a form, or you can make your own form. Four pieces of cardboard are cut in a tapering shape and taped together. Then after the form is made, put a short length of wick on the underside of top. For wax, you can melt old

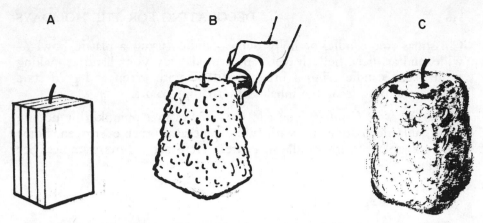

To make a "block" candle, heat and press several blocks of paraffin together as in (A) with string for wick. Then pour melted wax down sides for rippled effect (B). For frosty effect whip up melted wax and pour it over entire block (C).

candles, or use ordinary household wax or paraffin, used for sealing jelly jars.

Wicks: Use a piece of heavy white cord or you can buy wicks. Be sure to grease the forms or molds before pouring wax. When the wax has almost set, place the molds into cold water. This will hasten the setting and make removal of the candle simple.

Forms to Use: You can make any size or shape you wish. Some forms can be muffin pans, gelatin molds, cookie cutters, tin cans, rubber balls cut in half. If you want flat candles, use the common muffin pan. These flat ones can be used for floating in water. A paper cup makes a good mold. Have fun experimenting! Try making a star candle (using a star-shaped dessert mold) or tall candle (using cardboard tube with end covered with aluminum), square candle (using milk container) or

You can make yourself a striking centerpiece with star candles floating in water.

Christmas tree candle, or holly berry candle (using a plastic bowl 6″ wide, and artificial holly leaves. You can also try your hand at making a hurricane candle using a brandy snifter, with green and gold stars around the outside of the inhaler, alternating colors.

Centerpieces of Candles: You can use candles in a pumpkin or potato; for a table decoration use with white pine and other evergreen. Some use an eggplant, with candle in center. Here are a few examples. See drawings.

Candles can be used in a variety of ways. Try these two simple Christmas centerpieces.

Equipment Needed: All you need is a large double boiler, fork, egg beater, paring knife, spoon, scissors, plastic bowls, a variety of other dessert dishes and containers for molds and wax crayons for color. You can get wicks from 5 & 10 cent stores or use the wicks from inexpensive tapered candles. If you want to make your own wick, soak heavy string or cord overnight in a solution of 1 tablespoon of salt, 2 tablespoons of borax, 1 cup of water. Dry, then dip in melted wax to stiffen.

For Frosty Effect: If you want to make your candles look frosty or snowy, it's easy. Melt wax in a double boiler and mix to a froth by beating. Then while in a foamy state, dab the froth on each candle with a spoon or knife. After each candle is dry, you tie a big red ribbon bow for Christmas effect, if you wish. Some people like color in their wax candles. Melt pieces of ordinary school crayons and mix with wax.

Scented Candles: Scents can be added to candles. If you have some oil of wintergreen, oil of cedar or oil of rose, these can be added to the paraffin while still in the molten stage.

Helpful Hints: Cover working surfaces with paper for easy cleanup. Melt wax in double boiler; NEVER over direct heat. Heat forks and utensils to melt off wax, wipe with paper towels, wash in hot, soapy water. To clean pans, reheat, pour off excess wax, wipe with paper towel. Repeat until all wax is gone. WARNING: Never pour melted wax down a kitchen drain!

For best results: 1. Grease all molds well and chill in a refrigerator. Chilling makes wax candle easy to remove from molds. 2. Allow melted wax to cool slightly before pouring into molds. 3. If possible leave newly molded candles in refrigerator overnight to insure hardening. Candles removed too soon will sag and lose shape. 4. Tap metal or plastic containers gently to loosen wax before removing from mold. Molds you can cut of cardboard should be sealed with masking or adhesive tape, then wrapped in newspapers to insure against wax leaking. Tie newspapers with several turns of cord which will strengthen cardboard mold and give support.

Candlewax Stain: Many homeowners use candles in centerpieces and sometimes the wax drips on the table linen. To remove the wax gently scrape the hardened wax from the surface of the cloth with a dull knife. Then sponge the stain with cleaning fluid as you would to remove any grease spot. This is easier and usually more satisfactory than the familiar method of using a blotter and pressing with a warm iron. If any traces of color are left, they can usually be removed by sponging with a cloth dipped in a mixture of two parts water to one part rubbing alcohol. Caution: Whenever cleaning fluid is used (even a small amount), it should be used out of doors, or in a well-ventilated room.

DECORATING WITH GOURDS

Ornamental gourds are ideal additions to floral arrangements in the home. You can also mix them with real fruits and vegetables. Start your own plants in pots indoors and move them to the garden when all danger of frost is over, or you can start them in the ground.

Keep the gourds watered regularly in summer and dusted with Sevin or Methoxyclor to keep out the borers. They must be allowed to mature before picking or they will rot. Don't use the fingernail test for maturity, as the scratch on the shell of an unripe gourd destroys its future use. Leave gourds on the vines until frost threatens; harvest in the afternoon of the first clear day that portends frost.

Cut stems with a sharp knife, leaving a few inches of stem attached to avoid bruising. The stem usually drops off as the gourd dries. Wash gourds in warm soapy water with household disinfectant added. Dry each one in a warm place (takes about 10 days) and paint with shellac, varnish or floor wax for glossy effect. We clean ours with a soft brush, then rub on a good floor wax. This finish is more attractive and natural than the varnish or shellac which some gardeners apply. Remember that the gourds should be dry when wax or polish is applied, since sealed-in moisture will hasten rot.

Uses for Gourds: You can use gourds in floral arrangements, low baskets and cornucopias. You can even make them into ideal containers for both dried and fresh plants. Make a narrow slit in the long side of the gourd, scoop out the seed and flesh. A small saw is ideal for this operation. If you use fresh flowers or plants, a small receptacle for water is inserted into the opening.

CHAPTER VIII

Extra Indoor

Green Thumb Fun

ARRANGING FLOWERS IN THE HOME

Everyone can arrange flowers. Some people do a better job at it than others. It takes practice and a genuine interest in the subject to produce a bouquet that registers "pleasing" to the eye, heart and soul. This chapter deals with arrangements you can make right in your own home, using flowers you grow or buy. It has nothing to do with "Japanese" arrangements or the so-called "modern" arrangements, which we hear so much about. These modern arrangements belong in a class by themselves. While many modern arrangements are pleasing, they take practice and it takes an experienced arranger to put up a bouquet that doesn't make one feel like standing on his head to get the best vantage point.

Some gardeners worry too much about the right way to arrange flowers. Garden flowers picked and placed in a container, with no attention to size or colors, produce what we call a "bow-kay" or a nosegay. And really, what's wrong with an old-fashioned nosegay or bouquet of flowers arranged in a vase? I don't mean you should jam them together. Leave a little space between each flower, for a touch of filler (such as baby's breath) or a piece of greenery (such as peony foliage or evergreen twigs). Amateur arrangers have been bogged down under a lot of rules which stifle them.

It's not necessary for an arrangement to be one-and-one-half times the height or width of a container. Arrangements do not need to contain an uneven number of flowers. If another flower is needed to achieve balance or fill in a gaping hole, it should be used. And here's another crazy rule that can be broken: dark colors need not be put at the bottom of an arrangement, nor light colors at the top. That's pure bunk.

It was once considered a cardinal sin to use both dried plant materials and fresh items in the same arrangement. Today, florists use many attractive combinations. Likewise, formerly it was bad to use exotic or foreign flowers along with native ones. Mix them together and you get a striking effect.

Don't let a lot of rules frustrate you when it comes to arrangements. Flowers are pleasing and beautiful. Arrange them with a little common sense and you'll enjoy them more.

Containers

The type of container you use can "make or break" an arrangement. Choose the right container for the flowers you have. For example, if you are arranging glads or other large flowers, you wouldn't want a narrow-necked tall slender container. The vase for these should be broad and wide-necked; otherwise the arrangement will give the illusion

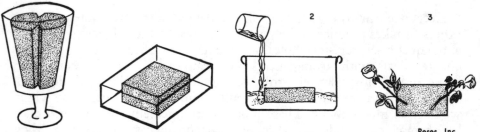

Roses, Inc.

Homeowners who arrange their own flowers indoors find that the new foam materials are ideal for holding flowers in place. They must be used correctly to insure the longest possible vase life for roses and other flowers. Roses, Inc. makes the following suggestions for using the foam materials: (1) Place the foam material in a glass or container, allowing enough room for fresh water to be added. (2) Saturate the foam well before using. (3) Make sure the cut end of the flower stem is in solid contact with the foam block. DO NOT PULL STEM PARTIALLY OUT AFTER IT HAS BEEN INSERTED into the block. This will leave an air pocket at the end of the stem. Do not push stems through the foam block unless they go into water. Add water daily to each vase arrangement to replace water used by the flowers.

of being several feet long. For small flowers, use a small container which can be a teapot, custard cup, cereal bowl or a regular small vase. Copper and brass containers harmonize well with zinnias, calendulas, pom poms, etc. in shades of gold, yellow and orange. Be sure the color of your vase harmonizes with the color of your flowers.

No law says you cannot mix different sized flowers, but let the larger flower guide you in selecting the size of the container. For table centerpieces, the low bowls are the most practical. Vegetable tureens, soup bowls and fancy baking dishes often lend themselves very well to the low table arrangement.

Stuffing a Container: Here is something most folks forget to do. If you are using a container of sufficient depth, you can use evergreen twigs, stuffed in your vase, to keep the flowers from swaying from one position to another. This is one of the best "stuffing materials" we know of. Vermiculite and shredded styrofoam can also be used.

For the low shallow bowls, you can use needlepoint holders or crumpled chicken wire secured with modeling clay. There is also a very handy material called "oasis" which is available at most florist shops.

A word about these foam materials. The foam materials which florists use in arrangements are easy to handle, light in weight and prevent spilling of water. However, many home owners find that foam materials do not work out well. They must be used correctly to insure longest possible vase life for flowers.

Here are tricks to help you:

(1) Leave room in the container for fresh water to be added.

(2) Saturate the foam in a good preservative solution before using. Be sure it is fully saturated.

(3) Be sure that the cut end of the stem is in solid contact with the foam. Do not pull the stem partially out after it has been inserted. This will leave an air pocket at the end of the stem. The cut end of the stem must be in firm contact with the foam brick.

(4) Do not push stems through the foam unless they go into water or cut flower preservative solution.

(5) Add water daily to your vase to make up for evaporation and water used by the plant. Some cut flowers are heavy drinkers (roses for example) and it is important that there be plenty of reserve water available.

TYPES OF ARRANGEMENTS

In striving to do a good job, don't be too fancy. Let your own hands and your soul be your guide. Be simple. The simplest things in life are often the most effective. To us, the simplest arrangement is the formal or symmetrical one shown in the illustration.

Formal arrangement simply means if you drew a line down through the center of the arrangement, one half of it would look almost like

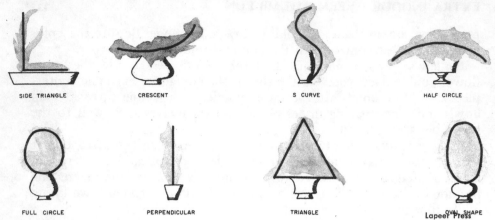

SIDE TRIANGLE   CRESCENT   S CURVE   HALF CIRCLE

FULL CIRCLE   PERPENDICULAR   TRIANGLE   OVAL SHAPE
Lapeer Press

Arrange your flowers according to these distinct patterns and your arrangements will have that professional touch. Study and follow these diagrams which illustrate 8 basic forms approved by leading floral designers.

the other half. That's the simplest type to make and most appropriate for any occasion.

Modernistic Arrangements: If you're one who wants to try your hand at making fancy arrangements like those you see in florist shops, don't hesitate to give it a whirl. Remember, not all florists went to a design school. They mastered the art of floral arrangement by practice and work.

Study these diagrams which illustrate eight basic forms approved by leading flower arrangers. Arrange flowers according to their shapes and you will give your arrangements a professional air. You'll be able to arrange flowers for your church, P.T.A. and fairs.

SCALE

One of the most important principles to keep in mind is scale. That simply means this: You wouldn't get a good effect using a tiny flower such as a forget-me-not with a large flower such as a dahlia or calla lily. Likewise, feathery foliage wouldn't look well with large flowers such as mums or glads. In other words, you want the flower, foliage and container to be in scale with each other.

In most cases, spiky flowers look well when mixed with round flowers such as glads with dahlias; or snapdragons with carnations. When using both, form the outline with the spiky blooms, as they give greater height and breadth to the arrangement.

BALANCE

Another term you hear a lot about is balance, or placing the flowers in such a way that they appear stable and not about to tip over. All this comes with experience and practice. Now that you've had a few pointers on arranging flowers, let's start making a bouquet.

Step 1: You'll have more fun and enjoyment from your arrangements if you use fresh flowers which are "hardened" off. Cut the blooms with a sharp knife in the evening or early morning. Then toughen up the flowers or harden them by putting them in warm water and allowing them to set overnight in a cool place, or if this isn't possible, allow an hour or so for this treatment. These hardened flowers take up a lot of water, and won't wilt after you arrange them.

Step 2: Select a suitable container, one that is in scale and harmony (color) with the flowers. Then go out and clip off some evergreen twigs and stuff the container; the stuffing will hold the stems in place. If you use a shallow dish, you can use a frog, chicken wire, etc. (see Stuffing). Also be sure the container is thoroughly clean.

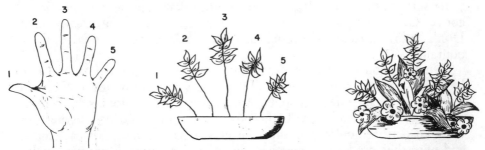

Beginners who want to arrange flowers should start out by holding the right hand out in front of the body, palm facing in, and fingers outstretched. That's the way a pleasing bouquet (formal or symmetrical) should have its outline. The flowers all rise from a single point (middle finger) and spread out in a symmetrical fashion. Place a tall flower in the center, then on each side place another flower slightly lower. Then beside these, insert two more still slightly lower. In other words, graduate the flowers so that none stands in front of another. They go up and down the container like a pair of steps. Don't make the flowers all the same length!

Step 3: Hold your right hand before you, palm facing you with fingers outstretched. That's the outline for a pleasing bouquet of formal or symmetrical design. The flowers all rise from the base, spreading out in a symmetrical fashion.

Step 4: Now decide what height you want your bouquet. Take one of the taller flowers, hold it in front of your vase, at the center point and measure with your eye before breaking the stem. After breaking the stem at the correct height, insert the center flower. Then on each side, place another flower slightly shorter. Then beside these two, insert two more, somewhat lower (they may be almost horizontal). They go up and down the outline like steps.

A common mistake is to make all flowers the same length, that's why so many homemade arrangements look all "chomped" together without a pleasing effect. Don't forget, each time you insert a flower you should give a "quick measure" with your eye before breaking the stem. The rule about flowers being one and a half times the height of the vase doesn't always hold true.

Some flowers can be fully opened, and some can be in bud stage— all add interest. Don't be afraid to leave blank spaces between flowers. Don't crowd your flowers. It's a strange fact that many times a few flowers can be more striking than a lot of flowers massed together.

Step 5: Don't be afraid to use green in your bouquet. Green is nature's peacemaker. This can be woods fern, twigs of evergreen or foliage from your shrubs. Put a touch of green in the blank spaces we mentioned above. Green is to a bouquet what a necktie is to a well-dressed man. Don't be afraid to allow a touch of green to hang over the edge of the container.

Whether you use flowers from florists or use your own, don't overlook those with crooked stems. They are very handy for use on the sides of the arrangement. Also, two different types of blooms often make a bouquet more pleasing. Whether you use all one color or whether you use two or three colors, be sure the colors harmonize with each other and with the vase. And remember, don't be discouraged; practice makes perfect.

LANGUAGE OF FLOWERS

In grandmother's day flowers in the form of bouquets were collected to express one's most intimate feelings. Certain leaves represented days of the week. Sunday was distinguished by a simple olive leaf.

Flowers had definite meanings, and a mixture of them created messages that were easily read. For example, "a red-striped tulip leans from a clump of yellow-brown to caress the tips of white jasmine flowers," a declaration of love from humility to amiability. My thanks to the Society of American Florists for their help in presenting this information. You may find some of their meanings amusing:

Aster	Afterthought. (It begins to bloom when other flowers are scarce.)
Camellia, red	You're a flame in my heart.
white	You're adorable; or adorable you.
pink	Longing for you.
Carnation, dark crimson red	I'm carrying the torch for you.
striped	Sorry I can't be with you; or wish I could be with you.
white	Sweet and lovely.
pink	I'll never forget you.
yellow	You have disappointed me.
Chrysanthemum	You're a wonderful friend.
Coreopsis	Always cheerful.
Daffodil	The sun is always shining when I'm with you; or you're the only one.
Daisies	I'll never tell.
Forget-me-not	Forget me not.
Gardenia	You're lovely.
Gladiolus	Give me a break, I'm really sincere.
Iris	Your friendship means so much to me.
Jonquil	Desire for affection returned.
Lilac, purple	First emotions of love.
white	Youthful innocence.
Lily, white	It's heavenly to be with you.
yellow	I'm walking on air!
Lily of the valley	You've made my life complete, or return of happiness.
Mistletoe	Give me a kiss.
Narcissus	Stay as sweet as you are.
Orange blossoms	Your purity equals your loveliness.
Orchid	Beautiful lady; or lady, you are beautiful.
Pansies	I'm thinking of you.
Petunia	Your presence soothes me.
Poppy, red	Consolation.
white	Oblivion.
yellow	Wealth, success.

(Poppy is the floral sign of consolation, probably because Ceres created it to assuage her grief while in search of her daughter Proserpine.)

Ranunculus	You are radiant with charms.
Rose, Christmas	Tranquilize my anxiety.
red	I love you.
white	You're heavenly; or you're innocent.
tea rose	I'll remember always.
pink	Please believe me; or you're beautiful or young.
yellow	Try to care; or I'm jealous.
dark crimson	Mourning.
full-blown placed over two buds	Secrecy.

white	I'm worthy of you.
white and red together	Unity.
rose garland	Reward of merit.
Spider flower	Elope with me.
Stephanotis	Will you accompany me to the East?
Stock	You'll always be beautiful to me.
Sweet peas	Thank you for a lovely time.
Tulip, red	I love you, believe me.
yellow	There's no sunshine in your smile.
variegated	Your eyes haunt me day and night.
Violets, blue	I'll be true, always.
white	Let's take a chance on happiness.
Zinnia, mixed	In memory of absent friends.
white	Goodness.
magenta	Lasting affection.
scarlet	Constancy.
yellow	Daily remembrance.

SYMBOLS OF WEDDING ANNIVERSARIES

First, paper; second, cotton; third, leather; fourth, books; fifth, wooden; sixth, iron, sugar and candy; seventh, copper and woolens; eight, bronze and rubber; ninth, willow and pottery; tenth, tin and aluminum; eleventh, steel; twelfth, silk and linen; thirteenth, lace; fourteenth, ivory; fifteenth, crystal; twentieth, china; twenty-fifth, silver; thirtieth, pearl; thirty-fifth, coral; fortieth, ruby; forty-fifth, sapphire; fiftieth, golden; fifty-fifth, emerald; seventy-fifth, diamond.

FLOWERS AND BIRTHSTONES
(With Each Month's Sentiment)

MONTH	FLOWER OF MONTH	MONTHLY SENTIMENT	BIRTHSTONE
January	Carnation	Constancy	Garnet
February	Violet	Sincerity	Amethyst
March	Jonquil	Wisdom	Aquamarine or Bloodstone
April	Sweet Pea	Innocence	Diamond
May	Lily of the Valley	Love	Emerald
June	Rose	Wealth	Pearl or Moonstone
July	Larkspur	Freedom	Ruby
August	Gladiolus	Friendship	Peridot or Sardonyx
September	Aster	Virtue	Sapphire
October	Calendula	Hope	Opal or Tourmaline
November	Chrysanthemum	Fidelity	Topaz
December	Poinsettia	Success	Turquoise or Lapis

INDOOR FUN WITH CUT FLOWERS

Appreciation of flowers is associated with a high culture in society and I am heartened to see more Americans are buying and growing more plants and flowers. All the artificial flowers in the world could not equal the supreme beauty of a single rose bud unfolding its petals. That's all it takes to cheer up a drab room—a single blossom and a sprig of green. They're even more meaningful if they were grown in your backyard or window.

Who buys flowers? While flowers are appreciated the world over, it is interesting to compare flower consumption in our own country with that of European nations.

Each person in Copenhagen buys 21 chrysanthemums, 1 gladiolus, 13 carnations, 13 roses and many other cut flowers each year. In the United States, each person buys 0.4 of one chrysanthemum, 1.8 gladiolus, 1.6 carnations and 2.4 roses.

In the same city of Copenhagen, 24 plants are purchased by each family annually whereas in the United States, 4 families out of 5 buy only one plant a year.

Cut flowers are plants without roots. That means the only food they have is the sugar stored in the leaves and stems. This sugar is produced during the daylight hours. That means, do not cut flowers in the morning as recommended in past; cut them in the early evening or late afternoon.

After flowers are cut, place in hot water (100°), not cold water. They take up hot water faster and easier than cold water because a liquid becomes thinner when it's heated; thus, the hot water flows more easily up the stems. It also expands the cells.

A good cut-flower preservative is: 4 teaspoons of cane sugar, 2 tablespoons of white distilled vinegar mixed with 1 quart of water (100°) Vinegar makes the water acid and prevents spoilage due to fungi and bacteria. Sugar serves as food but cannot be used alone.

Here are a few green thumb tips to help you keep your cut flowers longer:

Calceolaria: Pocketbook plant should not be confined to small room or placed next to cut flowers. Plant gives off gas and can gas itself to death if left wrapped. Gas is harmless to man.

Chrysanthemums: Woody-stemmed plants, such as mums and peonies, should be pounded at end, or split at least 3 inches from cut end. Mums often wilt; however, they can be freshened by cutting a few inches off the stem and pounding the end with hammer. Works like magic. If a petal or two falls off a big mum, melt a few drops of wax from candle into the hole it leaves so as to seal the remaining petals in place.

Daffodils: Thick-petaled items such as hyacinths, tulips, daffodils, etc. can be restored when wilted by being completely covered with cold water. Violets keep very well out of water if wrapped in wax paper and placed in refrigerator. Lily of the valley likes same treatment. NEVER PUT CARNATIONS & SNAPDRAGONS IN REFRIGERATOR with other flowers or fruit. Water lilies often close when cut. Prevent this by pouring a few drops of paraffin into the heart.

Dahlias: Flowers which have milky juices in stems, such as dahlias, heliotropes, poinsettias, poppies, hollyhocks, etc., should have stems seared, either place stems into a flame or put them into 1½ inches of boiling water for 1 minute. After searing, place flowers in cool water. Dahlias will not open in water if cut immature.

Dutch Iris: If Dutch Iris wilts, don't toss it out. It can be freshened by standing stems in water which is tingling to the touch (110°), then setting in a cool place to be revived.

Easter and Holiday Flowers: If you get a corsage of gardenias or camellias, place in icebox dish in refrigerator. Be sure there is no fruit inside, since fruit gives off ethylene gas which shortens life of cut flowers and blooms. Orchids can be ruined by the tiniest amount of gas liberated by vegetables or fruit. As little as 1 part in 500,000,000 is harmful.

Gladiolus: Best cut when first floret is open. Arrange in cool water.

Iris: If iris wilts, don't toss out. They can be freshened by dipping stems into hot water tingling to touch. Remove after few minutes and arrange in cool water.

Lilac: Lilacs, mock orange, rhododendrons, spireas, delphiniums, etc. should have the bark cleaned off at least an inch or more of the stem end. Then split ends or pound them.

Pansies: Pick daily and keep pansy bed well watered in summer. Long stringy shoots should be cut back half to encourage tender growth.

Peonies: Can be cut as petals are opening. Give the same pounding and warm water treatment as mums. In the case of both these items, a fine mist of water sprayed on the wilted blooms while they are standing in the warm water will hasten their revival.

Roses: Cut before the buds open. If blooms start to wilt in a vase, remove, cut off half-inch from stem end, and place in hot water (110°). Can be revived by cutting inch off stem end and plunging stems in boiling water for 3 or 4 seconds, then place in cool water. Or with a sharp knife, cut about an inch off the bottom of each stem. Remove any leaves that would be below the surface of the water in the final arrangement. Place them in tall, clean container in a cool place to harden for an hour before arranging. Use warm water, about 100° F., to hasten the flow of water up the stem. Use warm water and a floral preservative when you arrange your roses. If you use floral foam as a holder, be sure that it is thoroughly soaked and add water daily to replace that which is absorbed by the flowers.

Sweet Peas: Cut them daily. Vines will produce seed and cease to flower if flowers are not picked. Keep blooms cool.

Tulips: If you want to keep tulips from opening wide, drop some candle wax on underside of blooms. Tulip stems will stiffen if immersed in solution of calcium nitrate, 2 ounces in 5 gallons of water. Dipping the tulip flowers in beaten egg white keeps them from opening wide.

OTHER TIPS ON CUT FLOWERS

A few drops of gelatin dropped into heart of poppy flower will prolong life several days. Few drops of formaldehyde in zinnia water prevents water fouling. Charcoal, salt, ammonia, camphor, when added in small amounts, help keep flowers longer. Boric acid, ½ teaspoon to 2 quarts of water, increases life of carnations 3 to 7 days. Aspirin is of no value.

Remove leaves from stems to prevent fouling of water, especially with such items as asters, or zinnias. Copper vases sometimes keep flowers longer due to action of copper. Rinse containers well with household bleach solution. All flowers like a cool air temperature so the longer you can keep them in a refrigerator or cool room the better.

Keep in mind that cut flowers detest coal gas or artificial gas, even in tiny amounts. Flowers should not be kept in drafts, or near open window or door, or electric fan. Bright sunlight is bad for them. In winter, keep them away from radiator. The cooler the room in summer or winter, the longer your flowers will live.

How to Revive Wilted Cut Flowers: Many flowers wilt after cutting because air is blocked in the stems. This air-block can be removed by cutting the stems an inch or two longer than you want them, setting them into warm water immediately after cutting.

We use water that is tingling to the touch (about 110° to 120°) for reviving most wilted blooms. Merely cut an inch off the bottom of the stem and then stand the flowers in the warm water. Put them in a cool place and you will be surprised to find that within half an hour they will have revived. Roses and Dutch iris are especially responsive to this treatment. These two items have a tendency to wilt for no apparent reason, although the blooms are fresh. So don't blame your florist if the roses you received suddenly flopped. It doesn't mean they are stale. Quite often cut flowers will droop their heads. The stem ends seal over and the blossoms cannot draw up water. Recutting the stem, then removing to a cool place and standing in warm water will usually correct this. Sprinkling the blooms with warm water at the same time also helps a great deal.

Are cut flowers harmful to sick people? Some people believe cut flowers and plants are harmful to patients in the home and in hospitals, and also that blooming plants should be removed from the room at night. Aside from possible allergies, there is no truth to the idea that these plants will rob the patient of oxygen. The nurse entering the room to remove the flowers uses more oxygen than the room filled with plants would use during the entire night. Likewise, the plants or cut flowers in the home have no harmful effect on the air we breathe. In fact, plants are actually beneficial because they remove the carbon dioxide and give off moisture and oxygen.

DRIED ARRANGEMENTS FOR INDOOR BEAUTY

Nature is very generous. Along the roads, in the fields, woods and swamps are many materials which can be gathered and processed for winter bouquets.

WHAT TO GATHER

There's no law which says you should gather certain types of materials for your arrangements. Gather anything which is pleasing to your eye. These can be cultivated flowers and vegetables, including seeds, pods, vines, grains, certain weeds in the meadow, grasses, ferns, wild flowers etc. Don't overlook cattails, bittersweet, strawflowers, cockscomb, statice, sensitive fern, tassels, teasel, spirea, pepper grass, curled dock, mustard, goldenrod, globe amaranth, love-in-a-mist, milkweed, lily capsules, lunaria, hydrangea PG, rue, pearly everlasting, squirrel-tail grass, broom grass, fountain grass, pampas, winged euonymus, staghorn sumac, lilac seed heads, silverbell and many more. Try anything that happens to catch your eye.

TYPE OF CONTAINER

Avoid large flashy containers; select one in harmony with the down-to-earth materials you are using. Simple shapes and dull earthy colors are best. Wooden salad bowls, slabs of wood, board, and shelf fungus are good bases or holders. If you have brass, copper, bronze, pewter or lead containers, use them. A hollowed out pumpkin is also good. A potato, fastened down with clay serves as a good flower holder.

How to Preserve Your Gathered Materials for Arrangement

Drying: Pick materials on hot, dry days, so no moisture is on them. They dry best in hot weather. Dry flowers by hanging upside down in a garage, which is better than a basement. Attics are good places to dry flowers. Moisture doesn't harm the flowers to be dried, if it is absorbed through the stems. The trouble comes when flower heads are moist on the outside. Many flowers can be dried by the upside-down method. Foliages are best treated with glycerine; cones, pods, branches, grains and grasses can be stored in a box without the upside-down treatment.

Sand or borax treatment: Take fine, dry sand (never damp) and pour it in a box about 3 or 4 inches deep. Put flower heads in upside down, and pour more sand in gently until the flower heads are covered. Store in a cool dry place for 2 to 3 weeks, then take them out, pour off the sand and carefully wipe the flowers, using a soft brush or a piece of cleansing tissue.

Often, borax is used in the same manner as sand. However, we prefer a mixture of sand and borax, or sand and corn meal rather than using either sand or borax alone. Sand works slowly, whereas borax is fast acting. The borax alone may make the flowers too brittle if they are not watched carefully and removed at the right time. We like a drying mixture of two-thirds borax and one-third sand. Round or daisy-like flowers can be placed face down, spike flowers can be laid on their sides on a layer of the mixture and then the borax-sand is gently sifted around and over the flowers until all the floral parts are covered. Experience will tell you how long to leave each variety. Heavy-textured flowers may take 3 weeks to dry, while thin-textured flowers may take only a few days. Remember, the way the flower stems are curved when you put them in a box is the way they will dry permanently.

Silica Gel: Cut flowers, corsages and wedding bouquets can be dried in silica gel, an extremely absorbent material which does not change the colors or forms of flowers. White petals stay white, reds stay red, and greens stay green. Available now is a special mixture of a fine white powder and a certain amount of blue crystals known as Tel-Tale silica gel. The blue crystals change color when the mixture has absorbed too much water and you'll know that the silica gel must be dried out to restore its effectiveness. You can use it over and over again. Just heat it in your home oven.

Take a fruitcake tin and pour the silica gel in to a depth of 2 inches. Place shortened flowers (cut the stems off leaving 2 inches) face up into the material. Then add more of the mixture over the blossoms until they are thoroughly covered. The tin is then sealed with masking tape and put aside for a week. When the drying period is up, open the sealed can and pour out the powder until the flowers are uncovered. They will be dry and ready to display after you add some wire stems to the heads. Use floral tape or a small piece of freezer or masking tape to cover the wire stem.

You can use the silica gel over and over again. It pulls water from flowers quickly and evenly from all parts of the blossoms at the same rate. Thus there is no shriveling, no change of color or form.

Flour for Flowers: Did you know that you can preserve the colors of most of your favorite garden flowers by treating them with ordinary all-purpose flour? Many indoor gardeners preserve gladiolus blooms, callas, roses, lilies and many others by covering the blossoms with the flour for 2 to 4 weeks, depending on the size of the blossoms. After that period the blooms are carefully removed and the flour is dusted off them.

Glycerine Treatment: Glycerine is used mainly for foliages. Remove dust from leaves, pound lower ends of stems with hammer to split bark and loosen wood. Stand material in jar containing solution of ⅔ water, ⅓ glycerine, so it reaches 3 or 4 inches up stems. Allow a week or so for solution to be absorbed. Leaves and low growing plants may be laid in the solution so they are covered: ivy, lily of the valley, etc. Glycerine will change the foliage to a darker color and it will last indefinitely. Save your glycerine solution; it can be used over again until it is all gone.

Pressing: Press leaves and flowers between pages of a book or several thicknesses of newspapers weighted down with bricks. Takes 2 or 3 weeks for complete drying.

Skeletonizing: If you want to skeletonize branches and leaves, soak and boil them in soda solution for 30 minutes, using a teaspoon of baking soda to a quart of water. Let the leaves cool in the solution and then spread them out on a piece of newspaper. Scrape off the fleshy part of the leaf on both sides. Then mix 2 tablespoons of bleaching solution and allow the leaves to stay in the bleach for 1 hour. This makes them white. Place between sheets of absorbent paper to dry. To tint: spray with aerosol spray paints or dip in cake coloring, school inks or tinting materials.

OTHER HELPFUL TIPS

Use materials of varying length. Put a "bend" in some of the stems before drying. Paint or color some of the materials, such as cattails, pods, cones, etc., using water or oil paints, dyes, etc. Aerosol paints are handy or you can pour a thin film of paint in a bucket of water and then plunge the materials quickly in and out of the bucket. Paint sticks as materials pass thru the thin layer of paint. Some can be dipped in shellac to preserve the natural color. Some items can be dipped in cold water glue and shaken in a bag with various colored powders.

Here are a few items my wife and I have found useful for dried arrangements, and we hope they help you.

Amaranth (Gomphrena, Joseph's coat): A useful everlasting. May be cut when fully mature and air-dried.

Asparagus: Cut the red berries as soon as mature, dip in shellac and alcohol. Drip dry.

Aster: Single and double varieties shatter when dry. Glue petals to calyx before drying in borax.

Astilbe (in variety): Use Borax.

Azalea: Borax.

Baby's Breath: Air dry.

Balloon Flower (Platycodon): Wire flowers before drying in borax, 6 days.

Barberry: Glycerine.

Bayberry: Dip in shellac and alcohol. Drip dry.

Beech: Use glycerine. Remove in 36 hours while still green; green will gradually darken to purple or bronze when exposed to light.

Bells of Ireland: Molucella is an interesting annual well adapted to drying for winter bouquets. The green shells are so closely spaced around the stem, there's little room for leaves. Two ways to dry: (1) Air-drying, by hanging upside down in a garage. Cut stalks after the insignificant white flowers (called clappers) have shed and the green bracts ("bells") have started to fade. Some gardeners snip off all leaves for a better display of the bells. Others take the trouble to secure the bells to the stalk by adding a speck of glue before drying. (2) Use borax-sand treatment. To dry the young green stalks with bells and white flowers (clappers) in place, mix up a batch of material, 2/3 household borax and 1/3 washed sand. Place some in a shoe box, add the stalks, sprinkle on the sand-borax mixture and allow it to work for 4 or 5 days. This will work fine for drying hundreds of other flowers.

Bittersweet: Apply shellac and alcohol to prevent fruit from dropping.

Brown-Eyed Susan: Use borax mixture. Use some black or brown shoe polish to brighten up the centers.

Butterfly Weed (Asclepias): Air dry or borax mixture.

Canna: Green or reddish leaves in glycerine; 5 to 7 days.

Cattail: Cut and dry at whatever color stage you prefer. Cutting should not be delayed after they have attained their ultimate dark-brown shade. Spray with hair spray. I cut my cattails in June and they don't shed. Dropping of flowers can be checked by a shellac and alcohol dip. Drip dry.

Chinese Lantern: Air dry, or protect with coating of shellac and alcohol.

Christmas Rose (Helleborus): Wire flowers before drying in mixture of borax, 5 days.

Chrysanthemums: Some dry well, others don't. I prefer borax method. Apply glue to backs of the flowers where the petals join the calyx; 7 to 15 days.

Clematis: For the large-flower varieties, glue sepals to calyx and wire. Use borax; 4 days. One of the most beautiful dried flowers.

Cockscomb: Cut as soon as mature or they may shatter. Cut crested types when they reach the stage you like, but before they begin to set seeds. Remove foliage. Air dry.

Corn: Gather when mature, pull back husks before drying. Air dry tassels.

Daffodil: Cut stem off below seed vessel, wire and use borax.

Dahlia: Good for dried arrangements. Miniatures are best. Borax. Bits of cotton should be wedged between the dense overlapping petals to reduce flattened effect.

Daisy: Gloriosa, treat same as black-eyed Susan. Borax.

Delphinium: Borax, 6 days.

Deutzia: Glue the florets before drying to avoid shattering. Borax.

Dogwood: Bracts dry well if left on branches. Or dry separately, with 22-gauge wire stems. Borax, 4 days. Dip dogwood berries in alcohol-shellac mixture. Dogwood foliage is pressed or treated with glycerine mixture.

Euonymus: All respond to glycerine.

Euphorbia (Snow on the Mountain): Responds to borax.

Ferns: Several ways to handle ferns, try glycerine.

Feverfew: (Same as mums).

Floss flower, Forget-me-not, forsythia, galax, gas plant: All borax.

Gerbera, Gladiolus: Borax.

Globe Thistle, Goldenglow, Goldenrod: Air dry.

Gourds: Varnish.

Hollyhock: Use perforated box or arrange with faces down and stems. Borax, 5 or 6 days.

Honesty: After the seed pods mature, hang until dry. Rub off the outer coverings to expose the luminous discs. Can be sprayed with aluminum paint, ideal for Christmas decorations.

Hydrangea: Borax.

Ilex: Borax.

Iris: Not too good. Try the blue or white Siberian iris. Borax, 7 days.

Ivy: Glycerine.

Larkspur: See Delphinium.

Lavender: To most gardeners, the name lavender means freshness, fragrace and loveliness. In fact, the word comes from the Latin word *lavo,* which means to wash. In ancient times it was used to perfume water for cleansing the body. Today, the United States imports over a quarter of a million pounds of oil of lavender for making toilet water. The most aromatic parts of the plant are the fresh flowers and the young foliage. Uses: sachets, potpourris, nosegays and to make linens flower-fresh. Gather when almost one-half the flowers on a spike are open, if you want to use them in fresh arrangements. They'll last about 10 days. For drying, cut the stalks when they are about ¾ of the way open, tie in bunches and hang upside down in an attic or warm garage. Or you can press the flowers and foliage between pages in a book.

If your lavender bush is full of old wood, it should be cut back so that the new growth can take over. It's the flowers and tender leaves you want, so cut out any old wood. Usually winter injury will cause the twigs to die back but you can rejuvenate the plant by a good cutting job.

Lilac: Borax; ideal with 4 to 6 days drying.

Lily of the valley: Odor lingers for months after dehydration. Borax.
Magnolia: Glycerine.
Maidenhair Fern: May be pressed. Also use glycerine.
Marigold: Borax.
Milkweed Pods: Air dry. Split open and remove the silky filling to reveal their yellow coloring. Spray paint for effect.
Orchids: Borax.
Periwinkle, Queen Anne's lace: Ideal for borax.
Redbud, rose campion (Lychnis): Borax.
Rose of Sharon (Hibiscus): Borax, 7 days.
Rubber plant: Glycerine.
Salvia (blue salvia): Cut when fully matured. Air dry.
Red Salvia: Borax.
Snapdragon: Borax.
Snow on the mountain: Borax mixture, 6 days.
Spirea: Borax.
Stock: Borax.
Strawflower: Cut when flowers are ⅔ to ¾ open. Provide wire stems and air dry.
Sumac: Cut fruit when young and green or later as soon as they turn red. Air dry. Brilliant red leaves are pressed.
Tansy: Air dry.
Ti leaves: Glycerine.
Tithonia, Violet: Borax.
Waterlily: Borax.
Yarrow: Air dry.
Zinnia: Borax.

Try all the flowers you have available. They all work and you can have a lot of fun making them up for dried arrangements.

The Missouri Botanical Garden has performed an excellent service by listing some of "Winter's Pleasant Ornaments" in one of its recent bulletins. It lists some good items for dried arrangements and while the list is not complete, it will help you get started on this project. Here are the plants they recommend for hanging (followed by H) or drying upright (followed by a U):

ANNUALS

Baby's breath: Gypsophila, white or pink (H)
Bachelor Button or *Cornflower: Centaurea cyanus,* blue, red, white (H)
Celosia, Cockscomb: Crested and plumed in crimson and yellow (H)
Globe Amaranth: Gomphrena globosa, clover-like blossoms which dry like everlasting. Purple, pink, white and lavender. (H)
Grasses, Ornamental: (H)
Honesty: Lunaria biennia or money plant; flat, silver seed pods. (H)
Job's Tears: Coix lacryma-jobi, foliage-like ornamental grass. (H)
Larkspur: Delphinium; white, pink, blue, lavender. (H) or (U)

Salvia: Farinacea or mealy sage; a true blue flower, ideal for drying. (H) for straight stem. Very graceful. (U).

Strawflower: Helichrysum monostrosum; pink, rose, salmon, white. Pick before flower opens. (H)

Sunflower: Helianthus; golden yellow, six inches across. (H)

PERENNIALS

Artemisia: Silvery king; feathery gray spikes. (H) or (U)

Chinese lantern: Physalis franchetii; lantern-shaped orange-red fruits. (H)

Delphinium: Blue. (H)

Dusty Miller: Coneraria maritima; silver-gray foliage. (H) or (U)

Globe thistle: Echinops ritro; large globes of blue flowers. Can be picked when the globes are green, or immediately after they turn blue. Otherwise they tend to shatter. (H) or (U)

Lamb's-Ears: Stachys lanata; silver-gray foliage. (H) or (U)

Lavender: Lavandula; for flower spikes. (H)

Onions, ornamental: Allium; pale pink, blue, white or violet. (U)

Poppy, Oriental: Papaver orientale; pick the seed pods when dry. (U)

Sea Lavender or *Statice: Limonium;* a delicate lacy, many-branched plant, (U)

Yarrow: Achillea; clusters of yellow, white or rose pink. (U)

TREES, SHRUBS

Bamboo: Polygonum cuspidatum; for line arrangements. Cut in fall. (H) or (U)

Beauty-Bush: Kolkwitzia amabilis; pink cascade of blossoms in June. Seed pods later. (H) or (U)

Beech: Fagus sylvatica; tree, glycerine or press methods. Can be used for years by freshening up each season.

Dogwood: Cornus; tree. Glycerine or pressed, green in summer or as they turn red in fall.

Hydrangea: H. domotoi; large globe-shaped clusters of flowers, white in early summer, turning pink around September. Sometimes beige or brown. (U)

Magnolia: M. grandiflora; glycerine method.

Okra: Pick the seeds which have turned striped beige and brown in fall.

BOUNTY OF THE WILD

Boneset: Eupatorium perfoliatum; flat clusters of small white flowers. Pick before buds open. Dries a lovely green in June. (U)

Cattail: Typha latifolia; pick when pencil-size in June. Then they will not shatter. They grow in marshy, swampy ground. (U)

Dock: Rumex; long spikes are green in June, rosy-beige in summer and chocolate-brown in fall. (U)

Ferns: All kinds. Press.

Goldenrod: Solidago; all varieties from the earliest in July till frost in the fall. Pick in bud stage. Opens into bloom when drying. If picked when the bloom is too far gone it is apt to shatter. (U)

Pick quantities of goldenrod, the stems are useful too for blossoms that have stems too frail to hold them.

Grains of millet, rye, wheat, oats and barley: Green or dried in the fields.

Heather: Rose or lavender (H) or (U)

Joe-Pye-Weed: Eupatorium purpureum; pick before clusters of buds open in order for it to retain the rosy-purple hue. (U)

Milkweed: Asclepias syriaca; dry the spikes with the pods on, remove all leaves, open the pods and remove the silky seeds. The open pods will dry a pale yellow inside, if exposed.

Mullein: Verbascum thapsus; pick the velvety gray-green leaves early when they are in rosettes. Later pick the tall spikes when they are green; late summer, tan; fall, brown. (U)

Pearly Everlasting: Anaphalis margaritacea; produces clusters of tiny white blossoms on gray-green stems.

Queen Anne's Lace or *Wild Carrot (Daucus carota):* The fields are white with their large lacy flower heads in late June. Cut some of the curled green flower buds too. (U)

Sumac: Rhus; pick green early in summer, or red in fall. (U)

Teasel: Dipsacus fullonum; prickly cone-shaped heads. (U)

Thistle, Canada: Cirsium arvense; small lavender flowers. (H) or (U)

Bull Thistle: C. lanceolatum; large lavender flowers. They bloom much of the summer, dry beautifully with their leaves intact. Wear gloves to pick them. (H) or (U)

There are scores of others for your experimentation, just as there are different materials for use in drying. The best way to learn about them is to try drying them yourself.

How to Paint Cones, Seeds and Flowers for Indoor Arrangements

Dried arrangement enthusiasts are constantly seeking ways to paint evergreens, milkweed pods, certain weeds, teasels and other items gathered in the fields and meadows for winter bouquets. Tinting or painting them is easy and we'd like to pass along our hints for coloring your gathered materials.

The kind of paint you use to color cones, weeds, pods, etc. makes no difference. You can dig up all your odds and ends and mix up some interesting color combinations. Or you can buy paint in aerosol form, all you do is push a button and a spray of paint comes out. These work fine; you can buy them in 5 and 10 cent stores, or possibly at your florist. Or you can go to a paint store and buy small tubes of primary colors in oil. These can be true colors so you can lighten or darken them as you wish. If you want to lighten your color, add some white lead, or if you want to darken it add some lampblack. If you use the sprayer on your vacuum cleaner, mix the paint very thin, using turpentine or a good paint thinner.

You may not want to spray the paint on, just use a paint brush or resort to dipping. Spraying should be done in a well-ventilated room to avoid fumes. If you use dried flowers, keep them out of direct sun since too much light is apt to fade the colors.

Here's a little trick many gardeners use to dip their cones, pods, weeds, etc. First, fill a basin with water, and, over the water, pour a thin film of the paint color you want, aluminum, gold, red, or whatever. This

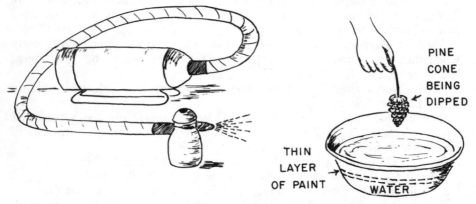

PINE CONE BEING DIPPED

THIN LAYER OF PAINT

WATER

Attachment on your vacuum sweeper makes a good sprayer for applying paints to cones. Or, you can dip cones, pods, weeds, etc. into a basin with water in the bottom. Over the water pour a thin film of the paint color you want. That saves on paint and the water helps to spread the paints more evenly.

serves 2 purposes: You don't need much paint, and the water helps to spread the paint more evenly. All you do is dip the flowers, cones, etc. thru the film of paint. Then dry the materials after dipping.

How to Use Dyes: Certain dyes such as cake coloring, tints, etc., can be used to impart colors to dried flowers. Add dye to hot water and get the blend or color you want. Then, you simply dip the dried flowers in the hot bath for 8 to 10 seconds. Practice will tell you how long, it depends on the color you want to impart. This system is known as the flower-bath method or the dye bath. You can get some fine shades of colors with such items as strawflowers. With practice, and by trial and error, you'll find which flowers will dye and which won't. Some flowers take hot water dyes readily, and then you'll find that hot water will ruin the florets of others. We find it's a good idea to place dried flowers to be dyed in a refrigerator or some place where the atmosphere is humid the night before you dye them. This helps to close the flower heads. Then when you move them to a warm dry room, some of the outer petals start to unfold. That's the time to dip the flowers in a dye bath. You will have a bicolor effect, because some of the inner petals will not come in contact with the color. Then move them to a warmer room; the warmer temperature will open the flower heads.

Hand Painting: If you're painting pods, cones, etc., you may have to give them a second coat for best effect. Some decorative materials are dark, some light. You'll have to use your own judgment. After the weeds, dried seed pods, etc. are painted you can put them on a paper to dry, or if they are too "gooey", you can tie them to string suspended in air. Items you can collect include cattails (get them before they burst open), teasels, chinese lanterns, milkweed pods, goldenrod, etc. There are many garden flowers you can use. The list is long, and you can tell which flowers will color best simply by practicing and experimenting. You'll be surprised to see what nice floral arrangements you can make with your painted items.

If you paint leaves, be sure to cover both sides. It's a good idea to let one side dry before you start to paint the other. Usually a single heavy coat is sufficient, but if you want a porcelain-like finish, apply more than one coat. Always give pods at least 2 coats for best effect. Pine cones can be dipped, then tinted on ends with paint brush. Incidentally, if you want to arrange your materials in a centerpiece you can use modeling clay (the kind children use in school) for a base, in the bottom of the container. Just stick the ends in the clay and they stay in place. Or, if you don't use clay, you can use chicken wire in the bottom of the container. In making your decorative arrangements, don't be too fancy with the materials. Your materials don't have to be chumped in a lump in a vase, but arranged just as you would a cut-flower bouquet. Keep materials in proportion to containers used. Tall spikes take a tall container, shallow containers take lower items.

FLOWERS FOR THE HOSPITAL OR SICKROOM

Quite often homeowners want to arrange a vase of flowers to send to a friend in a hospital or at home. Everyone wants flowers when they're down in the dumps or ill, but there are a few precautions to take.

Here are a few suggestions from volunteers at the University of Rochester Medical Center as a guide for sending flowers to the sick:

Don't send overly large plants or bouquets, most hospital rooms don't have space for massed arrangements or huge potted plants, no matter how beautiful.

Do consider a little terrarium that will stay fresh and green for weeks with no care, a nosegay or a pretty planter.

Don't send a box of cut flowers. A vase must be found and someone has to take time to put them in water. An arrangement by the florist is more likely to please everyone. (Florists cooperate by sending flowers only in containers.)

If you want to send a bouquet, do choose long-lasting flowers. Chrysanthemums are excellent; carnations, daisies and roses do well, too. Longest-lasting flower is the orchid. Most flowers growing in your garden will do.

For sick youngsters (or even well ones), don't send berried plants. Youngsters might be tempted to sample them, and, unfortunately, some berries are toxic.

Finally, avoid flowers that have an overly strong fragrance or that shed a lot of pollen. Both of these qualities are apt to be very irritating to someone who is confined to bed in a hospital room.

What's an ideal floral gift for patients? "Just about perfect" is a small bouquet of sweetheart roses or tiny yellow daisies arranged in a clear glass apothecary jar, complete with glass cover. It needs no water (the covered container maintains the correct humidity) and lasts for a week to ten days.

HOW TO BUY FLOWERS FROM YOUR FLORIST

If you're planning to buy cut flowers from a florist, here are a few tips worth remembering. First, buy flowers that are in season. They are usually much cheaper.

Secondly, don't overlook short-stemmed flowers. Florists charge a premium price for most long-stemmed items and for the largest blooms. This means that for less money you can usually buy shorter-stemmed flowers with smaller blooms and get more for your money. Here again we are referring to flowers which are in season. In other words, if you want roses, but feel the long-stemmed ones are too expensive, settle for the short-stemmed ones. They're a lot less expensive and may be even better suited for the occasion. A bouquet for a centerpiece isn't expensive if you're willing to take shorter stems and seasonal items.

Good quality flowers are fresh, hard and undamaged. A fresh flower is not too far open, and, of course, is not wilted or faded. Some flowers just naturally keep better than others. We all know for example, that chrysanthemums keep better than roses, or sweet peas.

ARRANGING FLOWERS FOR A HOUSE OF WORSHIP

THE ROLE OF FLOWERS

Plants and flowers are an aid to worship. In a house of worship their role is secondary and for that reason it isn't necessary to bank the inside of a church with flowers until it resembles a greenhouse. A few flowers put worshippers in a better frame of mind, and flowers should be used as often as possible. In summer there is no reason why any house of worship should be devoid of flowers. Parishioners should make it a point to supply flowers regularly.

The problem of arranging flowers for church differs from that of arranging a bouquet for the home, or for a flower show where a small size is important. Arrangements for places of worship should be made large, in some instances well over three feet tall, because they are usually viewed from a distance and in a somewhat subdued light. However, these large arrangements require the same rules of design which we discussed in the Flower Arrangement chapter.

Sprayed Foliages: You can get an excellent effect in dark churches by spraying the foliage of small needle evergreens and large leaf evergreens such as laurel, rhododendron, euonymous, etc. with spray paints. Gold, silver, white, yellow and light pink shades of spray paint, which can be bought in aerosol cans, make excellent means of making colorful decorations when flowers and plants are hard to get.

Containers: It isn't necessary to have bronze, brass, pewter, etc. for containers. Use whatever you happen to have. Baskets or papier-mâché containers such as those used by florists make fine receptacles. Places of worship often have their own containers for flowers, and these often harmonize with the general architecture and design.

Number of Arrangements: This depends upon the design of the church, but if it is symmetrical, usually a pair of urns or vases gives a most effective display. If it is not symmetrical, one large vase may be sufficient. This, of course, does not take into account special occasions such as holidays, etc. when a more elaborate display is required.

For arrangements in a pair of urns or vases, try to have flowers of adequate height, such as chrysanthemums, glads, stocks, snapdragons or other tall flowers. Stuff the containers with evergreen or shredded Styrofoam, then arrange the flowers using plenty of green, both between the blooms and for backing the flowers. Begin by selecting two straight stalks cut to the same height. Place one of these stalks in each vase and commence to build your arrangement around the tall flower in the center. And of course, make the arrangement to be viewed from the front only.

Color of Flowers: If you happen to be on a committee to arrange flowers in your house of worship, don't let anyone talk you into believing that only white flowers should decorate the church. There is no law which says that only white flowers are acceptable. Use flowers that are available. Don't drive your florist crazy by always insisting on all white flowers. Certain times of the year they may be more scarce and hence higher priced.

If churches or any house of worship can have stained glass windows, mosaics, they certainly can be decorated with colored flowers. When Christ said, "Consider the lilies of the field how thew grow . . ." He was in all likelihood referring to the colorful red and violet anemones which grow so profusely on the Mount of Olives.

We mention this because there is a place in the scheme of things for colorful flowers. Use them in your house of worship, just so they harmonize with the colors of the interior.

Flowers, like people, regardless of color are part of a church.

However, the use of some white in the bouquets is definitely an asset since it gives the appearance of making the bouquet larger and brighter. Light yellows also have this effect. And don't forget the use of the spray paints which we mentioned earlier, a good way to add the white touch if you do not happen to have white flowers.

Evergreen as a backing gives mass and size to your bouquets, so use plenty of it. In the fall, use plenty of autumn foliage. In winter, many of the dried grasses (sprayed with aerosol paints) and everlasting flowers can be used with good effect.

Above all, see that the arrangement is simple and well balanced. If it is not, it will make the members of the congregation uneasy and some will feel like going up to rearrange them during the service.

Plants for Churches: Plants are excellent for decorating churches. Begonias, hydrangeas, mums, cyclamen, poinsettias, ferns, etc. can be used in the same way as vases and be very striking and decorative. They will maintain their original beauty if kept well watered and the church is kept at a uniform temperature of about 60° at night and 72° during the day. Flower committees with limited budgets should consider plants for decorating the church. They provide relief from bouquets and also harmonize well when used with arrangements in containers.

If you do use plants, be sure someone is assigned the job of watering. Usually the church is warm and dry and the plant will take up lots of moisture. Weekdays the temperature should be kept as uniform as possible (between 65° and 75° is ideal.) If the church is kept too warm or too cool, someone should take the plant home and bring it back only for the worship hour.

Incidentally, plants can be made to look larger by using a bow on them and by inserting colored foliage among the stems of the plant. You could use green foliage or spray paint the foliage to match the bloom.

As a final word, keep your arrangements as simple as possible, and see that they are balanced. Avoid fantastic "derangements" which result when an attempt is made to create something unusual.

HOMEMADE CORSAGES ARE FUN

I like to see a homemade corsage. It shows someone loves to work with flowers. Try your hand at making a corsage and see what fun you can have. A corsage is simply a bouquet out of water, fixed in a pleasing pattern.

A corsage is an accessory that accents a lady's charm, whether it be one that comes from the florist's shop or one that is made with flowers from your own garden. It may be worn as costume jewelry, not only on the shoulder or lapel but also on the wrist, in the hair, at the waist or on the pocketbook.

While it is not necessary to have a ribbon on a corsage, it usually does have one. The ribbon should harmonize with the flowers in both texture and color. And both flowers and ribbon should harmonize with the ensemble with which it is to be worn.

Choice of Flowers: In choosing flowers to be used in a corsage, remember they must be the type which will last well, at least 3 hours out of water. For instance, roses or zinnias would last much longer than petunias or cosmos.

Some good corsage flowers are: gladiolus, roses, pompon chrysanthemums, zinnias, carnations, tulips, daffodils, lily of the valley, geraniums, marigolds, grape hyacinths.

Some good greens that can be used for backing your corsages are: euonymous, English ivy, honeysuckle, arborvitae, Japanese yew, dagger fern, mountain laurel, boxwood and gladiolus foliage (looped or cut in pieces) and asparagus fern.

There are other flowers and greens which we have not mentioned that are also good. Practice will tell you which are best. Try them out by hardening off and then keeping them out of water for about 3 hours to test their holding qualities.

Hardening off: First of all, the flowers and greens you choose should be picked at least 2 hours before you're going to use them (preferably the day before) and they must be hardened off. All this means is that they must be put in warm water and let stand in a cool place so they will take up a maximum amount of moisture to carry them over while they are being worn. A good corsage flower which has been treated this way can often be used for several wearings if it is sprinkled with moisture, put in a closed dish or a moisture-proof bag and placed in the refrigerator immediately after wearing. Some flowers are sensitive to water on the petals. A damp piece of cotton underneath the corsage will serve the purpose in this case. The bow should be removed as the moisture will make it floppy and unattractive.

Colors: Remember, choose a color that will harmonize with the dress it is to be worn with. Usually (but not always) it is preferable to make the corsage all of one color and type of blossom. At times, you may want to add a touch of white or blend two harmonizing colors, such as tones of yellow and bronze, or shades of pink and orchid.

Size: If the flower is large enough by itself, you can use it alone with an attractive green backing, perhaps some chenille stems (pipe cleaners) and a bow. If they happen to be medium-sized flowers, quite often 3 are used; if the flowers are small, you may want to use 5 or even 7. It is usually easier to make a corsage with an odd number of flowers, but not always.

Remember to consider the size of the person wearing the corsage and also where it is to be worn on the costume. A shoulder corsage would be larger than one worn on the wrist or in the hair. If you think of the corsage as a piece of costume jewelry you won't be tempted to make it too large or sprawly.

Materials: You will need some fine wire. We find that a #24 wire is about the best all around wire for corsage purposes. If both #24 and #28 is available, it would be well to have both, since the #24 is a trifle heavy for the tender daisy-like blossoms. Remember the higher the number, the finer the wire. Hardware stores should have these different sized wires.

You will also need some kind of tape. The professional floral tape would be ideal, but if you do not have it, there is nothing to worry about. Adhesive tape or Scotch tape (about ½ inch wide) will serve the purpose.

Purpose of Wiring: The wire is used to stiffen the stems (or replace them), hold the heads on and make the flowers bend in the direction you want. The tape holds the wire in place and makes a neater finish.

Now you are ready to wire and tape your flowers. The illustrations will show how to wire different types of blooms. On stiff-stemmed flowers, such as roses, all but about ¾ of an inch of stem can be removed. Insert the wire thru the calyx to the center of the wire

and bend it double. Give it a couple of twists and then tape.

Small daisy-like flowers are wired by putting the wire directly up thru the center of the flower. Then make a small hook and draw the

wire down until the hook is firmly anchored (but not so far as to split the bloom).

Carnations are wired in the same manner as roses, or if the blooms are large, they can be split or "feathered" with a sharp knife. Be careful to cut directly thru the center of the calyx. The halved calyx is

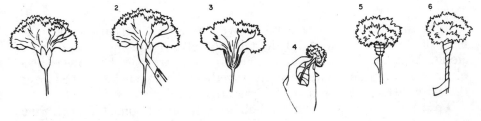

Some florist's carnations are too large and you can make them into smaller ones by "shattering" them, or splitting them into smaller pieces. (1) A whole carnation. (2) Same carnation with sharp knife run down through center. (3) Half of carnation ready for squeezing. (4) Grab base firmly and run small wire through bottom. (5) Wind wire around base 3 or 4 times. (6) Wrap wire and base with floral tape and you have a miniature carnation for your corsage.

then pinched together with thumb and forefinger, covered tightly with moist cotton or florist's tape. Wind with about three twists of wire and bend down to form stem.

Glamelias are made by using three or four glad florets and a bud.

The slightly opened bud is removed from the stem and wired with fine wire. The bottom part of the larger blooms are snipped off just enough to remove the stamens. They are slipped onto the bud stem in sequence from small to large. Then run wire thru florets in opposite directions, bend down and floral-tape carefully; add green backing and a bow.

To wire leaves, form hairpin of wire, insert thru base of leaf and then tape.

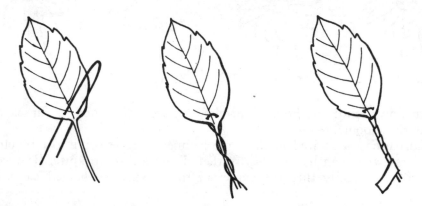

In taping, be sure to tape the flowers snugly. Start just under the head of the flower and wind the tape spirally, tightening it as you go along. After all the wiring and taping is done, arrange the flowers in a pleasing fashion and wire securely together. Tape can be applied over the wire, after the green backing is attached.

To make a bow you will need about 3 ft. of ribbon. This will give you a total of about 12 loops, each about 1½" long. Secure the bow in the center. A piece of floral-taped wire is ideal for fastening the loops together and makes it easier to secure the bow to the corsage. A little practice will make you a professional. Vary the loop size to correspond with the size of the corsage.

(1) Make a half-corsage first. (2) Make another half and put it on other end. Then tie a bow in middle.

(1) Glamellia corsage made from gladiolus florets. (2) Corsage made from "shattered" carnations.

SHOULDER CORSAGE   WRISTLET

Rules for wearing: One-ended corsages (that is a corsage with the bow at the bottom) should be worn with the flowers the way they grow—heads up. Corsages can be worn on either side of the shoulder but if they're worn at a dance, the right side is better since they will be less apt to be crushed.

Care for Your Corsages: Many a recipient of a corsage is irked because the florist gave no instructions for corsage care. Since this has been a common complaint, I'd like to pass along a few tips for keeping your corsages, hoping you'll get better mileage out of yours.

After you've worn a corsage try to remove the ribbon bow, then place a piece of moist cotton underneath it. Lay it in a covered refrigerator dish, a plastic bag or a cellophane bag (be sure the ends of the bag are tightly folded over to seal in the moisture), then place the corsage in the warmest part of the refrigerator. The important thing is to keep it out of the air. If you're traveling and there's no refrigerator available, place moist cotton over the corsage and keep it in the coolest part of the room.

Reviving Corsages: Some startling methods of reviving wilted carnations, roses and gardenias have been passed along to us. Try pouring hot water over wilted carnations or roses in a corsage, wrap in a towel and place them in a refrigerator.

For limp gardenias, trim off the brown edges with scissors and place them face down in a bowl of cold water.

Lasting Qualities of Corsages: Don't expect all corsages to last the same length of time. Some flowers, such as orchids, chrysanthemums, carnations, glads, and callas, naturally last longer than others. Gardenias are tricky and will turn brown quickly. Atomize them with water or hold them under a faucet with water gently dripping on petals. They may also be revived by the above mentioned method of laying them face down in a bowl of water. Then shake off the excess moisture and wrap in tissue, or put them in a corsage bag and place in the warmest part of the refrigerator. Carnations, roses, violets and lily of the valley also like to be atomized or dipped into water. Cold water hardens the petals of these items.

However, water will spot some flowers, such as sweet peas, orchids, camellias and some types of lily blooms, so you shouldn't sprinkle them.

If you get an orchid, keep it in an orchid box in the warmest part of your refrigerator. Most florists put orchids in small plastic tubes which hold water. These keep the blossom fresh for days. If your orchid comes minus the tube, after-care consists of removing the florist's tape from the stem and standing it in water until you're ready to wear it again.

FORCING SHRUBS TO BLOOM IN THE HOME

Homeowners who don't want to wait until spring brings out the blossoms on trees and shrubs can enjoy fresh flowers during the winter without spending a cent simply by cutting twigs of various flowering shrubs. Anyone can make these dry sticks burst into masses of flowers long before their normal blooming time. This is the simplest form of gardening and pays dividends in beauty and enjoyment. All you have to do is put the twigs in a jar of water and place the jar in a sunny window at ordinary room temperature.

Usually, sprays cut a week or two after Christmas will bloom two or three weeks later under proper conditioning. Less time is needed as the season advances. If the entire twigs are soaked in warm water for 15 minutes when first brought into the home, they can be made to bloom in shorter time. Frequent syringing until the buds start to open is helpful. Gardeners should remember that the twigs should not be cut until after a sharp freeze has made them sufficiently dormant. That's why you can't force them in early fall.

For forcing flowers indoors, gardeners select branches from trees and shrubs that need pruning, thus they do two tasks in one. They can cut out twigs which are too thick or detract from the natural beauty of the branches.

Flower buds are formed on the stems of trees and shrubs in the fall after the growing season stops. Young growth with many flower buds is the best to cut when forcing blossoms. Certain plants have separate flower and leaf buds, but it is a simple matter to select branches which have large, flat flower buds that will invariably burst into bloom. Don't cut too many twigs from any one tree or shrub.

Plastic Bags For Forcing Shrubs: To hasten the forcing of dormant twigs into blooms indoors, expose the cut twigs to fumes of ammonia (ordinary household type) or carbon tetrachloride, the solvent used in most cleaning fluids, for ½ hour. You do this by using a tightly closed container, such as one of the thin plastic bags that suits come in from the dry cleaner's.

Soak a cloth with ammonia or carbon "tet" and drop it into the bag. Put in the sprigs (in a bundle) of forsythia, apple, lilac, etc. and close the open ends with rubber bands. After half an hour's exposure to fumes, take the twigs out and place in a container of warm water in filtered sunlight, probably 60° F. or so room temperature. Keep twigs out of direct sunlight. Incidentally, if you don't use the gas treatment to hasten blooming indoors, you can help the branches along by soaking them completely in lukewarm water for 10 minutes before placing ends in a bucket of water.

Here are a few shrubs and trees that might be found in your back-yard which can be forced:

Goldenbells: The forsythias are about the easiest and showiest of flowers to force indoors. Put branches in a deep container and in a warm spot; syringe with water daily. Another method is to wrap the branches in wet burlap; remove wrapping as soon as buds show color. This is hardly necessary for forsythia, but can be done to the following subjects:

Lilacs: Often hard to force. Keep twigs covered with wet burlap, in a warm room. Some varieties force easier than others.

Spireas: The double spireas can be made to bloom out of season. Single types have a great mass of white flowers, but are somewhat less durable.

Apple: Apple blossoms can be brought into flower in February & March. Use pruned trimmings for forcing. Crab apples will bloom well inside, as does the common fruit crab used for jelly.

Pear: Pear blossoms may be forced any time after severe frost until blooming time.

Quince: Flowering quince is one of the best shrubs to force. Blooms last 10 days. Varieties range in color from pink to scarlet.

Redbud: Commonly called Judas tree, forms flowers along main branches and on trunk. Short lengths cut from budded branches will carry flowers.

Dogwood: Dogwood can be forced, but be sure to cut sparingly and only from trees in the garden. Flower buds are enclosed in hard shell which softens and opens only if kept moist through the forcing process.

Peach: Flowering peach, as well as the fruit peach, are suited for home forcing. Most plums, both flowering and fruiting types and the Japanese types, can be forced successfully.

Poplar: Has interesting silky white catkins, which turn red, then yellow. With poplar, sexes are separate, so use twigs from male tree. You can tell a male tree because it has big fat buds.

Rhododendrons: Are usually easily forced. Variety of colors very decorative. Syringe twigs daily, keep in sunny window.

Barberry: Japanese barberry has showy green foliage, followed by tiny yellow flowers.

Magnolia: Wrap branches in wet burlap, keep dampened. Remove wrapping as soon as buds show. Then put cut branches in containers of water.

Honeysuckle: Fragrant and easy to force. All honeysuckles are good.

Hawthorns: Found over countryside in varieties. Wait till March.

There are many others which can be forced: willow, alder, February daphne, shadbush, maples, etc. You can make beautiful Japanese line arrangements by bending the stems of forsythia, Japanese quince, bridal wreath, etc. First soak the stems in warm water for 15 minutes, then bend the stems carefully. You'll be surprised at the fun you can have forcing twigs and at the same time, you'll improve your plant's vigor and vitality.

CHAPTER IX

Plants for

Food and Fun

GROWING HERBS INDOORS

A window garden full of herbs is a sight to behold. By growing several little pots of herbs right on your kitchen window (or any other convenient, well-lighted spot in your home) you can not only provide an interesting display, but supplement the family menu and budget as well. Even a tiny bit of the proper herb can make the simplest dish far more attractive and appealing. Most herbs which grow outdoors can be grown indoors with little effort. Most herbs like a bright window, ample water, feeding once a month and that's about all. Wash off foliage occasionally to keep them fresh looking. Snip off any dead foliage and pinch the tops out so they will be nice and bushy. If insects happen to bother herbs, avoid spraying them with anything but soap and water. In the summer, you can put the potted herbs outdoors and bring them indoors again in fall.

Starting seeds indoors: Most herb seed can be started indoors in a pot of loose, humusy soil, such as a mixture of ⅓ sand, ⅓ peat and ⅓ loam. Do not sow too thickly. After seedlings are about an inch tall, they can be transplanted into small pots or grown together in a 5-inch pot.

Or you can start your herbs outdoors as shown in the chart below, then pot up a clump in the fall and bring indoors for winter use. Trim back extra growth to encourage young shoots.

Herb	Green Thumb Tips	Outdoor Uses	Indoor Uses	Harvesting
Angelica	Start by seeds or plants, grow in light shade. Sow in fall and transplant in spring.	Grows 6 ft. tall, ideal for background plant. Cut flower heads off after blooming for longer life.	Use young leaves with fish, seed for cookies and candies.	Cut seed head before dry and keep in warm airy place.
Anise	Plant seed in May in well-drained soil, full sun. Sow seed direct without transplanting.	2-ft. annual, sprawling and rather slow-growing.	Fresh leaves in salads, soups and stews. Seeds in cake, cookies and fruit pie.	Pick fresh leaves as needed. For seed clip umbels when gray-green; dry in attic.
Basil	Sow seed in well-drained soil after frost. Likes full sun and ample water.	Border plant 2 ft. tall. Attracts bees.	Use fresh or dried leaves in eggs, meat, salads and vegetables.	Cut 6 in. above ground when plants flower; dry. Strip leaves and flower tips; store in opaque jars.
Borage	Seed sown in poor dry soil, full sun. Thin to 12 in. apart.	3-ft. annual, star-shaped blue flowers. Good in rock garden.	Teas and vegetables.	Use fresh. Pick flowers and leaves; dry and store in jars.
English Chamomile	Sow seed in spring or late summer in sunny spot. Thin to 10 in. apart.	Hardy perennial, 12 in. tall. Useful in border or as ground cover.	Herb tea.	Cut flower heads in full bloom and dry in sun. Store in closed containers.
Caraway	Sow seed in spring or fall in dry light soil. Germination is slow.	A biennial 2 ft. tall, white flowers useful in back border.	Seeds in meat, salad, soup, rye bread and cookies.	Cut seed heads before dry and leave on cloth in attic. Store dried seed after separating.

HERB	GREEN THUMB TIPS	OUTDOOR USES	INDOOR USES	HARVESTING
Chervil	Sow seed in spring, grows best in shaded moist spot. Thin to 4 in. apart.	Hardy annual, 2 ft. tall, handsome deep green foliage, ideal in back of border.	Use fresh or dried for aromatic garnish, or use like parsley.	Cut leaves and dry quickly. Keep in glass jars tightly sealed.
Chives	Sow seed in spring or fall, or use divisions. Likes full sun, loamy soil, indoors or outdoors. Divide clumps every 3 or 4 years.	Onion-like perennial, 12 in. clumps with lavender blooms. Good in rock gardens.	Use in omelets, salads, cheese, appetizers and soups.	Cut leaves as needed.
Coriander	Sow seed in late spring, 1 in. deep in well-drained soil; full sun. Thin to a foot apart.	Handsome annual 12 in. tall; do not disturb by cultivating.	Meat, cheese, salads, soups and pickles.	Snip stalks when seeds are ripe, dry in shade, then separate seeds and store in glass jars.
Dill	Sow seed in spring or late fall in full sun. Do not transplant.	4 ft. annual which may need fencing for wind protection.	Cheese, eggs, pickles; seeds in soups, gravies and vegetables.	Pick whole sprays and hang upside down to dry.
Fennel	Sow in rows in May and thin to 6 in. apart. When plants are half grown, draw earth up to them to blanch the bulbous stalk.	Grown as an annual. Common sweet fennel grows similarly.	Valued for its anise-like flavor cooked or in salads.	Plants mature in 60 days and are then dug. Seeds of common fennel used in cookies, cheese and with vegetables.
Horehound	Plant seeds or root divisions in spring. Takes poor soil, full sun.	Coarse perennial, 2 ft. tall, forms bush for background use.	Cakes, cookies, sauces and meats.	Cut stems just before flowering; dry in shade, and store in opaque jars.

Herb	Green Thumb Tips	Outdoor Uses	Indoor Uses	Harvesting
Lemon Balm	Hardy perennial; sow seed in summer, in full sun.	Good border plant, 3 ft. tall. May be a pest if allowed to self-sow.	Valuable in seasoning.	Cut tips 2 or 3 times a season. Store in opaque jars after drying.
Lemon Verbena	Start from cuttings in sand; full sun and ample water.	Fine perennial, also good house plant.	Sachets, perfumes, toilet water. Flavors fruit salads, jellies, beverages.	Pick tender leaves and dry.
Sweet Marjoram	Start early and transplant out in spring; in dry well-drained soil.	Annual, 15 in. high, with gray foliage. white flowers. Front border.	Eggs, sauces, soups, stuffings.	Use fresh, or dry leaves and store in opaque jars.
Parsley	Soak seed in warm water for day, plant outdoors in rich soil. Full sun.	Neat plant 12 in. tall, used in front border or edge. Bring indoors in fall and keep in bright window. Biennial grown as annual.	Use as garnish in egg dishes, meat sauces, salads. High in vitamins.	Cut as needed, or dry in oven and keep in tight jar.
Peppermint	Plant roots or runners in spring. Shade and wet soils are good.	Spreads fast, keep in bounds with metal strips. Set in back border.	Fresh or dried leaves in jellies, desserts, beverages.	Cut stems in bloom, dry and store in tight jars.
Spearmint	Same as for peppermint.			
Rosemary	Start seeds indoors in spring, or root cuttings. Full sun, poor limy soil.	Perennial 4 ft. high, blue flowers. Needs winter protection.	Fresh or dried leaves in poultry, meats or seafoods.	Cut leaves just before blooming period; crush and store in tight container.

Herb	Green Thumb Tips	Outdoor Uses	Indoor Uses	Harvesting
Sage	Seed or cuttings in spring. Full sun and drained soil. Mulch in winter, remove dead wood in spring.	Shrubby perennial 2 ft, light-bluish flowers; fine addition to border.	Chopped, fresh leaves in cheese, pickles or sausage. Powdered leaves in stuffings.	Cut young tips, dry over stove, pulverize leaves and store in tight jar.
Savory	Seed in spring in loamy soil, full sun. Grows fast. Winter savory has same care and uses.	Annual, 18 in. high, bushy, with pinkish flowers.	Fresh leaves in green vegetables. Dried leaves in meats, turnips or cabbage.	Pull up plant and dry; store leaves in sealed jars.
Shallot	Start from new shoots or cloves in spring. Rich moist soil.	Bulbous annual without much ornamental value.	Use in same manner as onion.	Pull up when tops are yellow, dry 2 or 3 days. Cut off tops and store cloves in trays.
Sweet Cicely	Seeds planted in fall or spring, or divide parent plant. Partial shade, any type soil.	Fern-like leaves, fragrant white flowers; 2 ft. to 3 ft. tall.	Seeds have spicy taste, used with other herbs.	Pick seeds when green.
Tarragon	Root cuttings in spring; well-drained soil, full sun or semi-shade. Divide every 2 or 3 years as plants get woody.	Handsome foliage enhances the border.	Flavors sauces, salads, seafoods, stuffings.	Cut any time and hang in loose bundles.

Troubles With Herbs Indoors: Yellowing of foliage due to overwatering, high room temperature or dry soil. Keep soil uniformly moist at all times for most herbs. A bright window helps produce green color.

Woody growth, cut plants back about half to encourage soft tender growth. Also, nipping the tops out will encourage plants to be bushy.

Aphids secrete a "honeydew" which attracts a black fungus on foliage. Wash off leaves in bath tub. It's not a good idea to spray herbs with pesticides.

Brown edges and tips on leaves. Due to hot, dry rooms, or dry soils.

RAISING MUSHROOMS IN THE HOME

Quite often homeowners ask if it is possible to raise mushrooms successfully indoors. My answer is yes, you can, but don't raise them for profit only. Raise them for food and for fun!

One of the easiest ways to start is to buy the so-called mushroom trays, a complete mushroom bed already spawned, ready to grow a crop as soon as the tray is placed in a room of suitable temperature, covered with an inch of garden soil and watered. These trays will make an interesting and worthwhile hobby. The American Mushroom Institute has given me considerable information on mushroom growing and I'm grateful for all their help.

With a bit of luck you can raise your own mushrooms in the basement. Don't expect to get rich on the project, but have a lot of fun.

American Mushroom Institute

GREEN THUMB TIPS

Find a location in the basement as far away as possible from the furnace and where the temperature stays between 55° to 65°. The right place can be found quickly by placing a thermometer in different parts of the basement, until the most desirable location is found. The fruit cellar is usually suitable if the temperature is satisfactory. Avoid placing the trays where there is a draft. After the location is decided upon, remove the wrapping paper and the cardboard cover. Place the trays on blocks, boxes or a bench, so that they are not resting directly on the floor. Place a thermometer near the trays so that the temperature can be checked occasionally.

The compost in the trays should now be covered with just one inch of clay-loam garden soil. It should be crumbled with the hands. In the winter in the northern states, even when the ground is frozen, soil can be secured from the garden by breaking the crust of frozen ground in a protected spot and taking the soil directly under the frozen crust.

In a basement with a heating system, the air is usually drier than it should be for good mushroom growing. This can be easily corrected by keeping a sheet of newspaper over the trays. The paper can be removed to pick mushrooms or to water the soil.

The success of your crop will depend largely on how carefully you watch the moisture of the soil. After the trays have been covered with soil, take a pan or a sprinkling can and pour or sprinkle water over the soil several times so that it is quite wet, unless the soil you placed on the compost was already very wet. After that, check the moisture of the soil every day or two to see if more water is needed. In checking, take a pinch of soil between the fingers. If the soil is dry or crumbly, add more water. If the soil is wet or pasty, wait a day or two before you add water. The top inch of soil is all that needs to be kept damp, as the lower compost has sufficient moisture for the entire crop.

If the temperature and moisture are kept right you should have small mushrooms in about 3 weeks. These tiny pinheads will increase a little in size each day until they mature. Sometimes the formation of small mushrooms is preceded by a moldy looking growth over the surface. This is nothing to be alarmed about and in a couple of days the formation of mushrooms will start.

About one week after the pinheads form, the first mushrooms will be ready to pick. Not all will mature at the same time and it will usually be best to pick the ones that are ready and leave the others to develop. Mushrooms are ready to pick when the veil that connects the lower part of the cap to the stem breaks open. To remove mushrooms from the soil, grip the cap by the hand and twist as you pull so as to break the roots off at the base and not to disturb the soil. The root part of the stem can then be cut off with a knife.

It is characteristic of mushrooms to grow in "flushes" or, in other words, all come up at the same time. Then there will be a period of a few days with nothing more growing. Soon little pinheads will appear and another flush will have started.

Sometimes mushrooms will grow to a large size, and other times they will mature when very small. They must be picked when they become flat even though they are no larger than a dime. Usually when the crop becomes very thick, they mature at a small size.

Mushrooms that are left to mature in the tray will have richer flavor than those that are picked before the veil breaks and the cap is flat. This is one of the advantages of growing your own mushrooms; those that are bought in a store are necessarily picked green. Even if the mushrooms are left growing until the gills turn in color from pink to dark brown, they are still exceedingly delicious.

If conditions and care are favorable, the crop may be harvested for two to four months. At first the flushes will be heavy; after a while the food in the humus will become partly exhausted and fewer mushrooms will appear. The prudent housewife will use the stray ones for flavoring, as many dishes are improved by the addition of mushrooms.

It is not necessary to have a dark room for the trays. Light will not harm them, but the direct rays of the sun should be avoided.

It is suggested that 3 trays be used for the average family. If desired, two can be started together and the third started about a month later.

If mushrooms are growing only around the edges of the trays, this is an indication that you are keeping the soil too wet. Let the soil dry out a little once in a while.

Small mushrooms that turn brown and do not develop can be caused by too high a temperature or an excessively dry or wet condition.

The Rest Cure: When trouble develops with the trays, a rest cure will usually correct the trouble. The rest cure should be used for the following situations: When any of the trays start poorly, when they stop producing after a flush or two, when the mushrooms turn brown and fail to develop, when the trays stop producing after several months of picking, when worms appear or when mushrooms become deformed.

The rest cure simply means to stop watering for at least a month, and allow the trays to become completely dry so that no mushrooms develop. With good luck, you should get two or three crops of mushrooms.

After the crops have finished, the humus in the trays has fertilizing value and can be used in the garden. You may be surprised to find a crop coming up where you dumped the humus.

How to Freeze Mushrooms

To prepare mushrooms for freezing: Wash the mushrooms, drop them whole into boiling water, boil two minutes, take them out and chill in cold water before packaging for the freezer.

Cooking Suggestions

There is no need to peel mushrooms, merely clean them with a vegetable brush. Do not overcook mushrooms or they will lose some of the flavor. Fifteen to twenty minutes of slow cooking should be enough. Mushrooms are best cooked whole or cut in large pieces. Small slices lose their flavor rapidly in cooking.

Here are Several Simple Recipes

French Fried Mushrooms: Dip medium-sized mushrooms in a batter of egg and milk and then into crumbs. Cook in hot fat until crumbs turn brown. They can be served warm or cold. If served cold, they are best served with a dipping sauce.

Fried Mushrooms: Place whole mushrooms in medium-hot pan with melted butter. Add salt and pepper. Cook slowly for ten minutes with lid on the pan, and then ten minutes with the lid off. Turn the mushrooms several times. Don't cook them so long that they turn black.

Cream of Mushroom Soup: Dice the mushrooms and cook as above. Add flour and milk and cook until thick. Add a little butter.

Mushrooms in Roasts: Twenty minutes before the roast is ready to take out of the oven, place whole mushrooms in pan with the meat. Place butter on the top ones, add salt and pepper.

Unusual Mushroom Sauce: Sauté ¼ cup finely minced onion in butter till yellow and clear. Remove to keep warm. Add more butter to skillet and sauté ½ pound fresh mushrooms, thinly sliced or use one 6-oz. can, drained. Season lightly with salt and freshly ground black pepper, a dash of tabasco and a pinch of basil. Stir in 1 tablespoon finely minced chives or parsley. Return onions to skillet. Slowly add 1 cup sour cream, stirring well. Over low heat, simmer just long enough to heat through, not boil. Delicious with fish, cutlets, croquettes and many cold meat servings for summertime.

Dips and Dunks: For cocktail servings, prepare raw mushrooms by simply wiping with damp paper towel and snipping off the end of stem. Cut through the cap and down through the stem, cutting the mushrooms into quarters or bite sized pieces. Run toothpick into each piece and place around bowl of good dip. Nothing is better than the well-tried combination of sour cream and onion soup. It is a nice complement to the delicate flavor of mushrooms.

Quick Dip and Dunk: Stir 2 tablespoons chives, 2 tablespoons lemon juice, a couple dashes of tabasco and 1 teaspoon onion juice into a cup and one-half of sour cream. Chill. To serve, place dip bowl into a bowl of cracked ice. Dunk pieces of raw mushroom into this. Make plenty, it vanishes in crowds.

Mushroom Dip 'N' Dunk Sauce: Drain one 4-oz. can mushrooms, stems and pieces. Chop finely, and add to ¼ cup mayonnaise and ¾ cup sour cream. Stir together. Season with few drops tabasco, or tiny pinch of cayenne pepper; ¼ teaspoon salt, plenty of freshly ground black pepper, 1 teaspoon drained horseradish and 2 teaspoons grated onion. Chill and sprinkle paprika on top. (1 tablespoon brandy or 1 tablespoon dry wine will add flavor to mixture.)

Mushroom and Avocado Dip: A favorite dip. Buy 2 dead-ripe small avocados. Using silver fork, mash pulp. Beat in 1 tablespoon lemon juice, dash salt, few drops tabasco, 1 teaspoon horseradish and 1 teaspoon chives (frozen chives are handy). Now carefully fold in enough sour cream till a smooth thick dunking consistency is reached. Chill at least one hour. A bit of lemon juice on top prevents darkening. To serve: Fill deep glass bowl with this avocado dip. Center in silver plate and surround with cleaned raw mushrooms, cut into halves or quarters thru stem, spear with picks. Note: At the end of market day you'll find bargains in dead-ripe avocados. Select them, not black, but really ripe, and they'll be at peak of flavor. Mushrooms and avocado go nicely together as each is so delicately flavored.

POPCORN

You'd be surprised at the number of home gardeners who grow their own popcorn. If you grow your own, keep in mind that complete maturity is important. However, do not let it remain in the garden until it becomes too dry. Some gardeners feel that their popcorn fails to pop satisfactorily because it wasn't grown properly. It's usually due to the popcorn containing too much or too little moisture. An easy method to bring popcorn to the right moisture content for popping is to hang the popcorn outside for two months during the winter. Another method is to store it in a refrigerator or freezer.

Moisture content can also be raised by adding moisture directly to popcorn. Place the kernels in a fruit jar or coffee can and add one or two tablespoons of water to each quart. The corn should be thoroughly stirred as soon as the water has been added. Close the container tightly and let it stand a few days until the moisture has had time to penetrate the kernels.

Do you know why popcorn pops? It's due to a sudden liberation of steam by pressure. Moisture inside the kernel turns to steam, and when enough steam is generated, the hard kernel walls break. That's what the popping is.

RECIPES FOR THE ADVENTURESOME

ROSES ARE GOOD TO EAT TOO!

The rose is the most popular shrub in America, but not everyone takes advantage of the edible and esthetic qualities of the blossoms! Here are a few novel uses of the rose. We hope you'll take a moment to try them.

Making Rose Water: Rose water is actually a distillate of the fresh petals and can be made at home with everyday items. Gather a pound of fresh, fragrant petals. Wash carefully to remove pesticides. Fill tea-kettle half-full of water, add rose petals and put on low heat. Attach a rubber or plastic hose to spout of kettle with other end draining into a jar on the floor. Submerge middle section of hose in pan of ice water which will cool the stream of water from the kettle and gradually drip your pure rose water into the jar.

Rose Soap: Steep a few drops of rose oil in hot water. Add bits and pieces of hand soap and dissolve over low heat. Pour this hot liquid into a waxed cardboard carton and mold until firm.

Petite Rose Biscuits: Using a packaged mix or your own recipe, make a batch of tiny baking powder biscuits. Serve piping hot with the following:

Rose-Butter: Combine layers of rose petals alternating with sweet butter. Store in a covered crock for several days to let the flavor sink in. Spread on hot biscuits.

Rose Hip Honey: When your rose blossoms fall off, the little hard core that remains on the bush is known as a rose hip. Let these ripen. Then pick about 4 cups. Add water to cover and cook until mushy, adding more water if necessary. Strain and reserve juice. Make apple puree the same way, using 2 or 3 medium apples. Strain apple mixture. Combine apple juice and rose hip juice in a jelly bag. You should have about 2½ cups of juice. Add ½ package of powdered pectin. Stir in and bring to a full boil. Add, all at once, 3 to 3½ cups sugar. Bring to a full rolling boil for one minute. Remove from fire, skim and pour into jars. Seal with paraffin.

Broiled Blushing Grapefruit: Cut grapefruit in half and spread thickly with rose hip honey. Place under broiler until bubbly and slightly browned.

Quick "Fresh Up" Trick: Place a layer of rose petals in the bottom of your compact . . . for milady who likes the unusual.

There are many other rose novelties you can make. My thanks to Howards of Hemet for supplying me with the above items.

Rose Petal Jam: For a good jam made from fresh rose petals, first gather the petals from fresh red roses. Add an equal amount of sugar and a small amount of water ·(just enough to dissolve the sugar). Set the rose-sugar mixture in the sun in a glass covered dish until sugar is well dissolved. Then cook for 20 minutes, stirring frequently. Pour into jam jars and seal tightly. Makes a delicate preserve from your own home-grown garden roses.

Rose Petals in Strawberry Pie: Fill your unbaked pie crust with washed strawberries and the usual flour thickening (1 heaping tablespoonful); add 1 cup of sugar, or more depending on the tartness of the berries. On top of the berries, sprinkle the petals from 3 large roses. Dot with butter. Top crust edges should be well sealed to keep in the juice. Bake at 375°. Eat pie before entirely cold to get the aroma of roses with the flavor of strawberries.

Rose Petal Cakes: Ever make rose petal cakes? Here's the recipe: 1 cup rose petals, 3 cups flour, 1 cup sugar (gran.) ½ cup of margarine or Crisco, 3 eggs, 1 cup milk, 2 tsp. baking powder, 1 lemon, ½ tsp. salt.

Cream shortening and sugar throughly together, then add eggs (well-beaten), flour, baking powder, salt, milk, grated lemon rind, tablespoon of lemon juice and freshly picked rose petals. Pour into greased and floured muffin pans, and bake in 350° oven, 12 to 15 minutes. Makes 35 cakes.

How to Make Rose Hip Tea: Some people love the tea made from rose pods (called hips); others say the tea tastes flat. We've tried it and find it's not bad. There are many recipes available, but not all of them worked out well for us. Vitamin C is an important adjunct to our diet. True, oranges, limes, tomatoes, peppers, and lemons are the main sources of vitamin C, but the richest source so far is in the seed pods of a rose.

Citrus contain 49 milligrams per 100 grams of fruit, but rose pods contain from 1100 to 6900 milligrams of Vitamin C per 100 grams. The best hips are produced by the wild rugosa rose, but such hybrids as Talisman and Herbert Hoover are good sources of Vitamin C. To gather the hips at the right time, usually in the fall when blooming is over, is an essential part of harvesting the rich Vitamin C. They are ripe when a bright scarlet color, overripe when dark maroon, unripe when orange. Pick them when ripe or bright scarlet color.

Trim both ends of the pods with scissors and wash for a few seconds.

For each cup of hips use 1½ cups of water. Bring water to a rolling boil and add the hips. Simmer 20 minutes, drain water and crush through a sieve. Let stand for 24 hours in a pottery vessel in refrigerator. Then strain off liquid puree, and bring to a rolling boil, adding 2 tablespoons of lemon juice for each pint. This rich extract can then be added to fruit juices, jams, soups, salads or eaten straight. To make a honey of this rose "hip" puree, add one pound of raw sugar to two pints of puree, boil together until test sample forms skin when dropped on a cold plate. For soup flavoring add one part puree to three parts of any good vegetable soup. To make rose hip tea, add 2 spoonfuls to cup of hot water.

Recipe No. 2: (Try this one if above doesn't work out). Wash hips, dry, take both ends off, cut in half, put into glass jar and put lid on. For tea, use 1 heaping teaspoon of hips, pour on 1 cup boiling water, steep for 5 minutes, strain, and add a little lemon juice or honey, if you wish.

Rose Hip Soup: Here's a recipe for making soup from rose seed pods (hips), that I think you will like: 1 cup of rose hips with seeds, 7 cups of water, and 2 slices of lemon. Boil in covered enamel pan about 2 hours. Press through a sieve then add ¼ cup of sugar and 1½ tablespoons cornstarch (dissolve in a little cold water). Boil this mixture for a few minutes and set aside to cool. For flavoring, add lemon slices and a few drops of rose water. Soup turns out to be a beautiful dull orange-pink and tastes a bit tart.

Oatmeal and Rose Hip Cookies: To make oatmeal cookies with rose hips, try this: 1 cup brown sugar, ½ cup butter, 1 egg, ½ cup milk, 1¾ cups rolled oats, ½ cup nut meats, 1½ tablespoons rose hip powder, (you can make your own or buy it) plus 1½ cups cake flour; 2 teaspoons baking powder, ½ teaspoon salt, 1 teaspoon of mace, plus ¾ cup chopped raisins. Mix butter and sugar until light, add egg and beat. Sift cake flour with baking powder, salt, mace and rose hip powder. Add in three parts to the butter mixture with a little of the milk each time. Stir in the rolled oats, raisins and nuts. Drop spoonfuls of batter onto a greased baking sheet. Bake in moderate oven, 350°, for 15 to 20 minutes.

How to Make a Rose Jar: The old fashioned rose potpourri, or rose jar is made in several different ways. Here is one method passed along to us that works fine. The purpose of the rose jar is to enable you to fill your house with the delicate scent and delightful aroma of dried, spiced petals. Try this method and tell us what luck you have.

First, gather the rose petals before the sun is high and spread them on a table in the shade until the dew has evaporated. Then arrange in half-inch layers in a covered jar or dish, sprinkling each layer with ordinary table salt.

Add the petals day by day until they measure about two quarts when pressed down solid. Stir thoroughly every morning. Ten days after the last addition has been made, mix together in a separate dish ¼ ounce each of ground mace, cloves and allspice, ½ ounce of ground cinnamon, 2 ounces of powdered orris root, and ¼ pound of dried lavender flowers.

Fill the rose jar with alternate layers of rose petals and the above mixture, and sprinkle each layer of petals with a few drops of any preferred essential oils, such as rose, geranium, bitter almond, or orange flower.

Then over the whole, pour an ounce of any good toilet water or cologne. Various sweet blossoms or fragrant leaves may be added from time to time, such as heliotrope, lemon verbena, rose or lemon geranium, mignonette, etc. Some folks add a few slices of orange or lemon peel, and a few drops of glycerine or alcohol.

Sachet bags to hang among clothes or to lay between linens may be made with rose potpourri. Attar of roses is the oil that gives roses their sweet fragrance. It takes about 100 pounds of petals from 80,000 blooms to produce a single ounce of attar of roses. Little wonder attar of roses is costly!

How to Make Rose Beads: Rose beads are an old fashioned item worth reviving. First you gather rose petals, sprinkle with salt and put them through a meat grinder, letting them fall into an iron kettle, iron frying pan or a bowl in which a chunk of iron is placed. It's the iron that turns them black.

Daily, as more petals are ground up, those collected previously are reground with the new. After a batch of "petal paste" has been collected and darkened, they are worked like putty and molded into small beads. Beads are pierced and strung on a wire and dried with holes for stringing. They can be strung with white or colored beads and the rose fragrance lasts a long time.

EDIBLE FLOWERS—AN INDOOR TREAT!

Our great-grandmothers knew more about cooking with herbs and flowers than do we in our own generation. If you're looking for something to pep up your everyday eating routine, why not take a stroll through your garden and gather some flowers for your table and your menu? However, a note to keep in mind is that not all flowers are edible, so stick to those that are known to be edible. Here are a few items you'll find different and interesting. Many of these were sent to me by readers of our newspaper column. My thanks to them.

Elderberry Blossom Fritters: Select the blossoms at just about the time they are turning into a berry. Leave an inch or two of stem to use as a handle. Dip the blossoms into thin pancake batter and then fry in deep grease until golden brown. Shake off excess grease and sprinkle powdered sugar on top and eat. Taste like waffles; the kids will enjoy them.

French Fried Dandelion Blossoms: Ever try eating dandelion blossoms? They're good french fried, and here's a recipe you'll want to try. First, gather a batch of blossoms, look them over and wash them thoroughly. Roll them in a towel to remove excess moisture. Dip each blossom in flour and fry in deep fat. Sprinkle lightly with salt, you'll find they're delicious.

Dandelion Cordial: A strictly teetotaler's beverage can be made from the blossoms of dandelions. Here's how to make dandelion cordial: Use 1 quart of blooms (pressed down), 2 quarts of boiling water, 3 cups of sugar syrup, 2 oranges, 2 lemons. Pick dandelions close to the blossoms, pour boiling water over them. Set aside to cool, strain and add sugar syrup, oranges and lemons, thinly sliced. Let mixture stand for 2 or 3 days. If kept longer, strain out orange and lemon; bottle and cork tightly. This makes about 2 quarts of a healthy beverage. Not to be construed as dandelion wine.

Clover Blossom Honey: Use 5 cups of white sugar; 1 teaspoon of powdered alum (stirred into the sugar), 1¼ cups water. Stir until dissolved, place over heat to bring to boil, then let boil hard for just 1 minute. Remove from fire. Have ready 15 large red clover blossoms, 40 white clover blossoms and petals from 6 large rose blossoms (any color, as they usually all bloom at same time as clover). Add these to hot syrup, stir and let remain 10-15 minutes. Strain through cheesecloth, press all syrup from strainer. Put in half-pint jars and seal. Will be a nice light-golden color with a delicious clover flavor. Will not granulate.

Candied Blossoms: For this delicacy you can use rose petals, mint leaves, violet blossoms, pansy blossoms. (You can also try others which take your fancy.) Carefully pick, wash and dry the petals or the whole blossom, whichever you are using. Dissolve 1 oz. of gum arabic in ½ cup water in a double boiler. Let it stand until cold. Coat each petal with the gum arabic. Hang the flowers up to dry by running a needle and thread through the center and stringing them so they do not touch.

Mix 1 tablespoon of corn syrup with 1 cup sugar, ½ cup water and bring to a boil. Cook to the soft ball stage. Then let stand until cold. Dip the flowers gently into the syrup, remove and sprinkle with fine granulated sugar. Then lay them on a waxed paper to dry.

Edible Squash Blossoms: Our recipe for pumpkin blossom fritters, here it is:

First pick the false blossoms, the male ones. There are about 20 male blossoms to each female bloom on the vine. These "false" or male blooms can be distinguished from the "true" or female blooms since the female blossoms have a small nub at the base. Male flowers don't.

Pick plenty of male blooms because nature was generous and left plenty for pollination. Soak in salt water to remove any insects, then drain. Mix a batter of 1 egg, 2 tablespoons of flour, add salt, pepper, finely chopped parsley. Dip the blooms in batter, fry in deep fat until brown, drain on absorbent paper. Serve with meat. Makes a fine breakfast dish served with butter and syrup.

Incidentally, if you'd like a try at squash blossom soup, use a good light stock, delicately flavored. Boil the stock and add the blossom petals whole or cut into pieces. Continue to boil for 20 to 30 minutes. The blossoms keep their light yellow color and you'll have a pretty, as well as tasty, dish of soup.

Pumpkin Blossom Salad: Cook a large basket of male blossoms not more than 5 minutes. Then drain. When cool, squeeze out water and chop. Add salt, pepper, chopped onion, parsley and chopped hard boiled egg. Serve with salad dressing or mayonnaise.

If you'd like pumpkin blossoms in a hot dish, here's what you do: Cook up a batch and keep in refrigerator. After frying pork chops, pour off most of the fat. Pile the chops to one side and put some cooked pumpkin or squash blossoms into pan. Season and allow to simmer until warm. Serve with the chops. Pumpkin blossoms go well with cheese, also. Brown some butter, add a little chopped onion. Add some cooked blossoms (with water squeezed out) and fry for about 5 minutes. Serve with grated American or Italian cheese. Some folks add well-beaten eggs to this recipe, for a good omelet.

Edible Squash "Feelers": One of our readers, Mrs. A. Cherry of Clarence Center, passes along a recipe for cooking squash "feelers" or "clingers".

She writes: "We take the runners and a few stems and leaves that are attached to it, and boil them for about half hour. Then drain and put in a frying pan and fry just a little. Then add 2 or 3 scrambled eggs to it. We just love it!"

Rose Geranium Rolls: First, make your favorite rolls. Marinate cube sugar in grated orange rind and chopped rose geranium leaves for several hours. Take a small piece of dough, flatten out, place a cube of sugar in center, pinch dough up around sugar. Let raise until light, bake in a quick oven.

Rose Geranium–Currant Jelly: Pick 5 lbs. of currants, wash, but do not remove the stems. Mash slightly to start juice. Cook slowly until currants are white, drain in jelly bag. Measure juice. For each cup of juice, add ¾ cup of sugar. Boil rapidly to jelly stage. Have ready, well-washed rose geranium leaves which can be placed in the bottom of the jelly glasses. Pour hot into jelly glasses and seal.

Red Bud Blossom Salad: Mrs. C. Barrett of Kent makes a salad of the common redbud tree (commonly called Judas tree). Here's what you do: Gather one cup of the rose-pink blossoms just as they are opening, wash and let them dry. Then add to potato salad or fruit salad. They also make a nice salad by themselves with dressing added.

Bee Balm Tea: The garden flower known as monarda or bee balm was used in place of tea at time of the Boston Tea Party. The leaves and stems are cut up, dried slowly in the shade and then used as tea.

Fiddlehead Fern Salad: Pick ostrich ferns in the fiddlehead stage (still curled). Wash them in salted water. Blanch them, then dip in cold water and use as you would asparagus with your favorite dressing.

Wild Edible Greens: We are often asked what some of the edible greens are which can be found in the woods, fields and swamps. We hesitate to recommend greens that are growing wild because of the possibility of poisoning those who eat them.

Over many generations, rural folks have learned and passed down a knowledge of which wild plants make good eating and are safe to eat.

A few favorites which we know are safe include dandelion greens, fiddleheads (shoots of the ostrich fern), pokeweed, dock and lamb's-quarters, purslane (also called "pusley") and others.

If you're looking for edible greens, you won't find any better than those in your garden. What's any better than lettuce, endive, cress, turnip and beet tops, to name a few? And they're all safe to eat. Avoid rhubarb leaves for greens; they are toxic. The stem is the only part of the rhubarb plant good for eating.

Edible Lilies: Nature was generous with all the edible lilies she gave us—onions, garlic, leeks, shallot and chives. All these pungent lilies have similar flavors and odors that are due to volatile sulphur—and a tossed salad without any one of these lilies is like a wedding without flowers.

The rulers who built the pyramids fed onions to their workmen to give them strength. The Romans made women wear necklaces of garlic to insure vigor.

We don't mean you should make a meal of garlic, leeks, onions, etc., but every garden should have a few plants of each. Garlic, called the atomic bomb of the vegetable world, is a bulbous-rooted perennial, easy to grow. Order a few garlic bulbs and set them out as you would onion sets, about four inches apart in the row, covered two inches deep. When the tops die down, take up the bulbs and dry in a shady place.

If you want to start leeks, sow seed in spring, and they will be ready for fall use. The roots you don't eat by fall may be carried over winter by hilling with earth.

Nasturtium Rolls: Make a tuna relish by mixing 1 can shredded tuna fish, a teaspoon of chopped parsley, 2 or 3 small chopped pickles, some chervil and a few capers chopped into fine pieces. Mix in enough mayonnaise to make a thick paste. Spread the paste on large nasturtium leaves and make a rather thick roll (about as big as a small cigar). Tie the ends tightly with thread, then steep in a hot sauce of vinegar and white wine which has been made by boiling with a bay leaf, a chili pepper, a dash of salt and a sprinkling of thyme. After removing from the hot sauce, pour a few spoons of olive oil over them, garnish with nasturtium flowers and chill. Remove thread and serve.

Broiled Sunflower Buds: Dot sunflower buds with a small piece of butter and grill until a light brown. Remove from grill, add salt and pepper, oil and vinegar, or any good Italian dressing.

Nasturtium Flowers & Seeds: Some folks make a good and attractive sandwich from nasturtium flowers and mayonnaise, or salad dressing. Or you can mix petals of nasturtiums among greens, as one does watercress. Use any green salad for this. Green nasturtium seeds can be bottled in vinegar for a seasoning to be used in salad dressing, or they may be pickled in a syrup, the same as peaches or pears.

Marigolds: Some of my friends tell me that they use marigolds as a kitchen herb for flavoring soups. The petals, fresh or dried, may be used in salads, in scrambled eggs, and in a variety of sandwiches. Flavor, they tell us, is reminiscent of hard-to-get imported saffron.

Violets: Buds provide a luscious lift to salads. The flowers are delicious when pickled in vinegar, and the leaves may be used as a pot herb. They also make a syrup from this flower, to use in flavoring puddings, cakes, frozen desserts or iced drinks.

Peach Tree Leaves: Old-time homemakers used to use these in cookery. They would drop a few of the leaves into milk that was being scalded for a custard. The result was a delicate peach flavor for an old standby dessert. I've never tried this one.

Lazy Petunia Petals: Carnations, petunia petals, heliotrope, narcissi, and tuberoses were used in sandwiches at one time. Dating way back to pre-Civil War days, these floral sandwiches were considered a fashionable, warm weather dainty.

Grape Leaves: Many a homemaker has used grape leaves in pickles. The enzymes from the leaves preserved the pickles. My mother uses grape leaves to make a delectable Syrian dish sounding something like "wart-da-wee-lay." This consists of rice and chopped meat rolled up in grape leaves which have been picked and stored in brine ready for use.

HERB VINEGARS

Many home gardeners are missing out on a good bet by not making their own herb vinegars. You can make your own, starting with pasteurized store vinegar as the basis. Pasteurization stops the mother-forming bacteria. You can use white or red wine vinegars, cider or other fruit vinegars, white or distilled vinegars made by the acetic fermentation of dilute distilled alcohol.

Herb vinegars may be made in many varieties and combinations. The basic vinegar is infused with herbs, seeds, petals of flowers, and seasonings include basil, burnet, borage, tarragon, thymes, marjoram, chives, mints, rose-geranium leaves, rose petals or nasturtium flowers. Time needed for infusion of vinegar varies according to which you use, fresh or dried herbs. If dried herbs are used, boiling vinegar should be poured over them; let stand for ten days. If fresh herbs are used, either place them in cold vinegar, cork and set aside, or put the infusion into a jar, set in a pan of water on the stove till the water boils, then remove, cool and cork. Fresh herb vinegar should stand for from two to four weeks. After it has stood the proper time, strain it through fine muslin, filter papers, and rebottle. These suggestions came from Jane P. Blank writing in a recent issue of the Missouri Botanical Garden Bulletin.

Creole Recipe for Spiced Vinegar: To one quart of cider vinegar add the following: ⅓ oz. dried mint; ⅓ oz. dried parsley; 1 grated clove of garlic or one teaspoon of juice; 2 small onions; 2 whole cloves; 1 teaspoon of coarse pepper; grated corn of nutmeg; salt to taste; 1 tablespoon of sugar; 1 tablespoon of good brandy.

Let stand for three weeks. Strain and bottle. Try a white wine vinegar with sweet basil, lemon thyme, rosemary, crushed celery and lemon peel.

CHAPTER X

Green Thumb Materials
from Your Own Kitchen

NEW USES FOR OLD PLASTIC BAGS

Save those plastic polyethylene bags which laundered shirts, carrots and other items come in. These bags make handy indoor and outdoor gardening aids and are well worth saving. Of course every precaution should be taken to keep from children, just as you would insecticides, drugs and similar items. Here are a few practical uses for them.

Storing Geraniums: When you pull up geraniums from porch or window boxes, place the plants in plastic bags (without soil around roots) and hang them upside down in the cellar. Keep the roots slightly moist during winter. When early spring rolls around, cut the tops back and pot up the remaining plant. You'll be surprised to see how quickly the dead-looking clumps will send forth new shoots which will be in blossom by Memorial Day.

Slipping Houseplants: You can slip houseplants and shrubs, such as roses, by taking cuttings and inserting them in a clay pot of sand, perlite or vermiculite. A plastic bag slipped over the pot acts as a miniature greenhouse, hastening rooting and also eliminating the need for further watering. If watering is needed later on, apply to cuttings by removing the plastic tent, or by merely placing the pot in a dish of water without molesting the plastic bag. Once the cuttings have rooted under the clear plastic film (3 to 5 weeks), you're ready to pot them up in good soil.

Hastening Compost: You can hurry along the process of decay in your compost pile by using the plastic film. Make the compost in the normal manner—alternating layers of leaves, clippings, soil, table scraps, weeds, etc. Then add lime and plant food. I like to use liquid plant foods as the extra water helps the pile to decay faster. Then the plastic sheet is spread over the pile, and wire fence or some rocks are placed on top and on the edges so that the pile is completely enveloped.

The plastic eliminates that chore of "forking the pile". In about 6 or 8 months the pile is in fine shape for use in the garden or flower border. Compost breaks down faster under plastic due to the heat of the sun and the heat from decay being trapped underneath. Flies are no problem with a plastic-covered compost.

Keep Fruit: A friend of mine keeps grapes fresh right up until Christmas by using plastic bags. First, he dips the stem end in melted paraffin Then he trims off any cracked or rotted grape berries. The whole bunch is then placed inside the plastic bag, the kind his carrots come in. A cellar way usually keeps them best because it's the coolest part of the house.

Grafting & Budding: If you like to graft in spring or bud in summer, a plastic bag is a big help. The graft is made in the usual manner, and after some wax has been applied to the union, you wrap the entire graft with a plastic bag and tie with a rubber band. This not only keeps the wax from cracking, but aids the graft in "taking hold," simply by the plastic's ability to prevent moisture loss under the wax. After the graft has started, the plastic tent is removed. Plastic surgery is helpful in budding. Cover the bud with a piece of plastic and see how quickly it takes hold.

Air Layering: The old Chinese method of pot layering items, such as croton, rubber plant, oleander, dracaena, and the tall leggy items such as dieffenbachia (dumb cane), works a lot better with the aid of plastics. To air layer, you simply notch the stem with a knife, wrap a ball of moist sphagnum moss around the wound and place a piece of plastic around the sphagnum ball to trap in the moisture. As soon as roots have developed, the moss is removed, the stem is severed below the new roots, and the young plant is potted up in a good soil mixture. This method is used to shorten tall plants.

Seed Sowing: Home gardeners who start their own seeds in flats or boxes will find plastic bags a real boon. After the seed is sown, water the medium well and slip a plastic bag over the entire box, just as you would a pillow case. The plastic keeps the soil from drying out, hastens germination by maintaining moisture, and prevents fluctuations in temperature. Once the seed has started to germinate, remove the plastic overcoat and place the box in full light.

Plastic Thwarts Japanese Beetles: One gardener I know has spent years fighting Japanese beetles on her roses. She finally licked them by using plastic bags. When the roses start to bud out, she places a plastic bag over the blooms and pins the bottom. The roses will bloom beautifully inside the bags, without molestation from the beetles! She has used bags this way for 3 years and finds it's the only way to thwart the pest.

Protecting Mums From Frost: In some seasons chrysanthemums often do not flower soon enough to avoid freezing. Many gardeners place the plastic tents over the blossoms to protect them on nights when frosts threaten. They can be used over other flowers as well.

Storing Tubers and Bulbs: Tubers of cannas can be stored by placing the entire clumps in the bags and placing them in the coolest part of the cellar. In January or later you should inspect the bags to see if the tubers have rotted or shrivelled. It's also a good idea to add a handful of peat moss to each bag. Dahlia toes, glad corms and dozens of similar items can be successfully stored in plastic bags during the winter months.

Seeding Bare Spots in Lawns: If you have a bare spot in a lawn, or on a bare bank and wish to start grass seed without erosion problems, use plastics. Loosen up the soil, feed and scatter the grass seed. Sprinkle the soil well and cover the patch with plastic. You can place iron rods or stones on the edges to keep the wind from blowing the plastic. As soon as the seed germinates be sure to remove the plastic covering and continue to keep the soil moist. Steep banks can be started with grass by using sheets of plastic. Roll the sheets over the newly seeded area; as soon as the seed has germinated, remove the plastic.

Protecting Tomato Plants: After tomatoes are set out in early spring, some folks take plastic bags and place them over the plants. Four stakes are driven into the soil around the plant, and the plastic tent is slipped over the stakes. When cold nights threaten, the plastic greenhouses keep the plants from freezing. As soon as the plants are large enough to crowd the tent, remove the plastic. In the fall, you can use plastics to protect the tomato plants from early freezes.

Plastic Mulches: Many gardeners use plastic bags to mulch their plants. These can be fastened together or you can buy plastic in rolls, use for mulching evergreens, strawberries, raspberries, and dozens of other items.

Keeping Plants While You Vacation: Plastic bags come in mighty handy for folks who want to take a vacation and still have their plants alive upon returning. First give the pots a good soaking, then place the plastic bags over the plant—pot and all. Tie the opening tight. Two sticks, inserted in the soil before the bag is put on, can serve as tent poles and will prevent the plastic from resting on the plants. The plastic keeps the moisture inside and plants will be kept in good condition for 5 or 6 weeks. Some items, such as African violets, are apt to develop mildew so it's a good idea to have a couple of air holes for air circulation.

Protecting Your Knees: Plastic bags make a good covering to keep your knees from getting grass stains while working in the garden.

Protecting Shovels: Plastic bags placed over the business ends of shovels and other tools will help to keep rust out. They're also good for putting over cans of pesticides to help keep air away. This lengthens the life of the chemicals.

Hotbeds and Cold Frames: Plastic sheets make a good substitute for glass for covering small hotbeds or cold frames. Make your frames of sturdy wood and tack the plastic to the frame.

Cross Pollination: If you're one of those gardeners who like to make your own crosses of seed (such as corn) in the garden, you can use plastic bags over the flower parts to keep the strain pure or to prevent cross pollination.

Protect Strawberries: When frosts seem likely at night, cover your strawberry patch with polyethylene plastic film to save the blossoms. The plastic prevents heat from escaping and may save your entire crop from spring frost, or from frost injury to fruit. Late spring frost injury is usually the cause of nubbin disease (stunted or imperfect fruit). Remove the sheets during hot days.

Plastic Bags for Forcing Shrubs: To hasten the forcing of dormant twigs into bloom indoors, expose the cut twigs to fumes of ammonia (ordinary household type) or carbon tetrachloride, the solvent used in most cleaning fluids, for ½ hour. You do this by using a tightly closed container, such as one of the thin plastic bags that suits come in from the dry cleaners.

Soak a cloth with ammonia or carbon "tet" and drop it into the bag. Put in the sprigs (in a bundle), forsythia, apple, lilac, etc., and close the open ends with rubber bands. After a half an hour exposure to fumes take the twigs out and place in a container of warm water in filtered sunlight, probably 60° F. or so room temperature. Keep twigs out of direct sunlight. Incidentally, if you don't use the gas treatment to hasten blooming indoors, you can help the branches along by soaking them completely in lukewarm water for 10 minutes before placing ends in a bucket of water.

Plastic for Protecting Fruit Trees: I found a new use for old plastic bags. My young fruit trees (planted 2 years ago) were wrapped with wire screen up to the bottom branches. Deep snow during the 1960 winter covered the trunks, the snow line bringing the branches within easy reach of rabbits. These animals, hungered by the snow, started foraging on the branches. To prevent further damage I wrapped plastic sheets (the kind dry-cleaned suits are returned in) around the young trees and so far this has done a fine job to keep rabbits away from the unprotected branches.

Plastic Bag for Keeping Extra Plants: If you start your own seedlings and find you raise more than you need for yourself, instead of discarding the unwanted ones, store them temporarily in plastic bags. Dig up a clump of the seedlings (with soil attached), and set them in the bottom of bag. Then fold the top down and clip or place a rubber band over it. Seedlings keep for days until you've found someone to give them to. Or you can also use the bags for exchanging slips of plants with friends. Just place the plant slips in the bag, close end tight, and it's ideal for carrying with you in the car, bus, etc.

Plastic Bags "Tame" Horseradish: If you love horseradish but hate to make it, try this tip: Place a plastic bag over the end of the grinder and it will confine the fumes of the horseradish. You can grind to your heart's content. Your eyes and nose won't water.

Plastic Protects Peony & Iris: One gardener I know uses large plastic bags to cover his peonies and iris to protect the blossoms from rains and winds. He also finds the plastic bags ideal for mixing potting soil. Top knotted, he tumbles the bag of soil on the table and he can see when the soil is mixed properly.

Plastic Bags Thwart Birds: If birds eat your cherries or blueberries, try this tip. Slip a large plastic garment bag over the end of the limbs, and tie down the end. It allows the cherries to ripen fully and the birds can't get to the ripe fruit. I also use the plastic bags to cover our blueberry bushes at ripening time; it lets the berries ripen, keeps the birds out. Even my grapes are protected in this way when they start to ripen. It keeps birds, bees and hornets out.

Protecting Newly-Planted Shrubs & Trees: Many gardeners use plastic bags for protecting newly-planted nursery stock. After setting the rose bush, fruit tree, or perennial plant in the ground, enclose it with the plastic bags dry cleaners use. The bottom is tied and you get a balloon-like effect. Each plant is enclosed in a plastic greenhouse, protecting it from dry air, hot winds and water loss. When the weather gets real hot, I poke a few holes in the top to let air out. Otherwise, it's not necessary. Plants are watered as usual. When new growth starts it's a good idea to make a few slits or holes for air circulation. I leave the plastic covering on evergreens longer than on shrubs, fruit trees and roses, since evergreens start new growth more slowly. Plants protected with plastic tents seldom ever die.

Plastic Bag Helps Lick Borers: If you have borers in trunks of apple, cherry, mountain ash, lilac or other tree, take an electric drill, drill into the holes you see, then dig a small trench around base of tree. Fill with some calcium cyanide (has trade name of "Cyanogas") cover with soil (2 inches) and wrap a plastic sheet around this, upward, covering soil mound and base of trunk. This forms a gas chamber which gases the borers. Remove after 4 days. If borers are higher up, place some of the powder inside plastic, wrap the sheet around the holes to confine fumes.

Your Kitchen Is a Storehouse of Green Thumb Material

Your kitchen is a storehouse full of good materials which can be used in a horticultural sense by gardeners. The Green Thumb has gathered together many items you can use.

Flour: Certain plants have a waxy surface and when you apply spray materials on this surface, it either rolls off or collects in spots. You can increase the spreading and sticking quality of these fungicides and in-secticides by adding a spreader or sticker and one such material which makes a good spreader or sticker is common flour, having absolutely no chemical reaction with any spray solution. Some gardeners mix flour with lead arsenate or DDT sprays for Japanese beetles, 1½ ounces to a gallon of spray. Another good spreader is skim milk, ideal for bordeaux mixture, lime-sulphur and wettable sulphurs. Two tablespoons of flour, or one cupful of skim milk can be mixed in a gallon of any insecticide or fungicide spray you mix up.

Still another good homemade spreader-sticker is mayonnaise dressing, about a tablespoonful to a gallon of spray material. The mayonnaise dressing helps greatly in making the mixture cover and stick to glossy or waxy leaves on plants such as iris.

Cake Coloring: This material can be used to dye many flowers, and foliages. While not all flowers respond, most of them do to this simple method of dyeing blooms. Simply mix up a solution, a teaspoon of color-ing to a pint of warm water. Place the stems in it and the coloring is automatically absorbed up in the stems and into the blooms. Some take it up faster and better than others, but you can have a lot of fun experi-menting with this.

Epsom Salts: This item makes a fine food for rhododendrons and azaleas. One cup of the crystals to a gallon of water can be applied over the soil surface several times during the summer. This adds magnesium which helps build up chlorophyll and prevents development of chlorosis or yellowing of leaves. Another use for Epsom salts is to sweeten up melons and tomatoes in soils lacking magnesium. University of Mary-land specialists found that flat tasteless melons may be due to a lack of magnesium or boron in the soil. Mix 6½ tablespoons of Epsom salts and 3⅓ tablespoons of borax (household type is OK) to 5 gallons of water. You can mix this with your insecticide and spray your melons or tomatoes. Spray melons when vines start to run, and again when fruits are about 2 inches in diameter.

Common Table Salt: One use for this kitchen cabinet item is to sprinkle it on layers of rose petals when making a rose jar or potpourri. Salt is also a good killer of weeds. One pound to a gallon of water, made into a hot brine, will knock out bad weeds in a jiffy. Salt is helpful in the asparagus patch for keeping weeds down, used at the rate of 1 pound to each 100 sq. ft. Scatter it lightly between rows. Weeds in paths and drives are often destroyed by salt. And salt is handy in the winter for melting ice. If you want to make a good, long-lasting shading compound for your greenhouse glass, add some table salt to the hydrated lime. Salt gives it a more lasting effect than if lime is used alone.

Vinegar: Because it is acid in nature, it helps keep cut flowers longer, by preventing spoilage due to fungi and bacteria. You can use it as an ingredient in a homemade cut flower preservative by mixing 2 table-spoons of white distilled vinegar, 3 teaspoons of cane sugar to a quart of water. The vinegar inhibits the growth of organisms, and the sugar serves as food. Do not use sugar without the vinegar. You can also add 2 tablespoons to a quart of water and water your azaleas with this every few months, since these plants like an acid soil.

Household Soaps: Soaps have been one of the earliest poisons for soft-bodied pests such as aphids, but today we have better insecticides to do the job. However, there's still a place for soaps and detergents. When soap is mixed with an aphid-killer such as nicotine sulfate, it activates the killing power, makes the nicotine sulfate more effective. One tea-spoonful of nicotine sulfate to 2 quarts of soapy water is good for thrips, lice and similar pests. The soap releases the nicotine, also acts as a spreader. If your water is hard, you can use detergents with the same effect as soap. Don't use soap if you live in a hard-water area since the soap is precipitated by lime and rendered useless. You don't get that with detergents. Another good use for soap: It deactivates the tobacco mosaic virus on your hands, so use plenty of it before handling tomatoes, petunias, peppers, eggplants, if you are a tobacco-user.

Ammonia: Ordinary household ammonia is a real friend to the gardener. One of the best uses of ammonia is to clean out sprayers after using weedkillers. Remember many plants are highly susceptible to weed-killers such as 2, 4-D or any in that family, even in tiny amounts. Be sure to flush out the tank with ammonia before you use the sprayer for spraying insects or diseases. This will help remove traces of the weed-killer. We know of nothing better for this purpose. Ordinarily, one quart of ammonia to 25 gallons of water is enough to flush out spray equipment, but on a small-scale basis, gardeners can use about ¼ cup of ammonia to 6 quarts of water. Allow the solution to soak for a day, then rinse with clear water. One of our friends uses ammonia as a dog repellent around shrubs. She soaks cotton in clear ammonia and hangs pieces of it on her harassed evergreens. Also, since ammonia has nitrogen in it, it makes a fine plant booster. One teaspoon to 2 quarts of water helps put pep into sickly houseplants.

Glycerine: This household item is one of the best for putting a gloss on your foliage plants. Put a few drops of glycerine on a cloth and swab the leaves of such vines as philodendrons, snake plants, etc. Glycerine is much better than olive oil since it does not collect dust, as does olive oil. Milk and water makes a fine solution for bathing foliage plants. Both milk and the glycerine impart a glossy sheen to the foliage. Another fine use for glycerine is in preserving dried arrangement materials. To do this you pound the lower ends of leaves or stems with a hammer to split the bark and loosen the wood, then stand the plant stem or leaves in a jar containing a solution of ⅔ water, ⅓ glycerine, so it reaches 3 or 4 inches up the stem. Allow a week or so for the solution to be absorbed. Glycerine changes the colors of some of the materials you may use. Glycerine-treated leaves last for years. Some easy foliages to try include beech, oak, magnolia, laurel, although there are so many more right in your own back yard. Do not discard the glycerine solution after treating the plant materials. Put it in a fruit jar and use it over and over again.

Carbon Tetrachloride: This household item, used as a solvent and cleaning agent for removing spots from clothes, is non-inflammable and is ideal for wasp and hornet control. Find their nests and at nighttime (they are less active and more likely to be in their nests than in daytime) soak a piece of cotton in carbon tetrachloride and plug the nest opening with it. The fumes from the carbon tetrachloride will stupefy the pests enabling you to take the nest down and burn it. Sometimes spraying with DDT or Chlordane will check them if you can concentrate the spray on the nest openings, but this doesn't always get those inside.

$\mathcal{I}$NDEX

Philodendron, 1, 89, 93, 121-124, 130, 131,
    132, 139, 187, 189, 193, 221
Phlox, 195, 220
Phoenix lonreiri, see Pygmy Date Palm
    P. roebelenii, see Palms
Photoperiodism, 2, 19
Physalis franchetti, see Chinese Lantern
Pick-a-Back Plant, 124, 132, 140
Pigtail Plant, *see* Flamingo Flower
Pilea cadierei, see Aluminum Plant
    P. microphylla, see Artillery Plant
Pillbugs, 23
Pinching back, 18, 70, 190, 200
Pine, 223, 225
    Australian, 197
    Austrian, 227
    Japanese black, 198
    Japanese white, 198
    Red, 197, 227
    Scotch, 227
    Swiss mountain (Mugo), 197
    White, 224, 225
Pineapple, 104, 105, 106, 174-175, 178, 179
Pinks, 195
Pinus parviflora, see Japanese white pine
    P. thunbergi, see Japanese black pine
Pittosporum (*P. tobira*), 124-125, 139
Pixie Pie Plate, 177
Plant food, *see* Fertilizers
Plant-Gro lamps, 215
Plant lice, *see* Aphids
Plastic bags, 285-290
    as temporary greenhouses, 4-5
Platycerium, 163
Platycodon, *see* Balloon Flower
Plumeria rubra, see Frangipani
Pocketbook Plant, *see* Calceolaria
Podocarpus (*P. macrophylla*), 139
Poinsettia, 19, 51, 81-83, 131, 133, 242
Pokeweed, 281
Polianthes, 155, 282
Pollination, cross, 30, 32, 288
Polygonum cuspidatum, see Bamboo
Polypodium, 163
Polystichum, 164
Pomegranate, 168, 175-176
Popcorn, 274-275
Poplar, 264
Poppy, 239, 242
    Oriental, 250
Portulaca, 195, 220
Portulacaria afra, see Elephant Bush
Potassium permanganate, 226
Potbound plants, 12, 19, 67, 123, 129, 130
Pothos, 93, 125, 140, 221
    See also Scindapsus
Pots, 4, 7-9, 90, 199-200
    self-watering, 217-218

Prayer Plant, 140, 141
Primrose, 84, 132, 209
Primula, see Primrose
Privet, 14, 218
Propagation:
    budding, 13, 15, 286
    bulbs, 146, 287
    corms, 148, 287
    cuttings, 13-15, 18, 31-87, 97-128, 159,
        206, 211, 285
    division, 13, 36, 50, 53, 63, 64, 66, 72,
        74, 85, 87, 97, 98, 99, 100, 102, 106,
        115, 118, 128
    grafting, 13, 15, 159, 286
    layering, 13, 111, 127, 173, 286
    seed, 12, 15-16, 17, 31-81, 102-120, 159,
        286
    tubers, 40, 147, 148, 287
Pruning, 31, 42, 67, 68, 123, 200
Prunus subhirtella, see Flowering Cherry
Pseudotsuga taxifolia, see Douglas Fir
Pteris, 164
Pumpkin, 279-280
Punica granatum nana, see Pomegranate
Purslane, 281
Pyrethrum, 22
Pythium (Blackleg), 61, 62

Queen Anne's Lace, 249, 251
Quince, Flowering, 198, 264

Rabbit's-foot Fern, *see* Davallia
Radishes, 209
Rain Lily, *see* Habranthus
Ranunculus, 155, 239
Ra-pid-gro, 7, 11, 34, 55, 61, 82, 84, 106,
    123, 147, 170, 183, 190, 197
Raspberries, 287
Rebutia, see Cacti
Red pustules, 221
Red spider mites, 23, 30, 35, 37, 42, 43,
    45, 47, 49, 51, 54, 55, 57, 62, 63,
    66, 67, 70, 71, 74, 80, 81, 85, 96,
    106, 115, 120, 123, 129, 130, 134,
    135, 138, 148, 170, 171, 173, 188,
    197, 206
Redbud, 249, 264, 280
Repotting, 12, 19, 33, 36, 66, 78-79, 97,
    107, 123, 161, 164, 183, 200, 206
Resurrection Plant, 125
Rhizoctonia, 62
Rhizomes, 150, 151
Rhododendrons, 37, 242, 264, 290
Rhoeo, see Moses in the Bullrushes
Rhubarb, 210, 281
Rhus, see Sumac
Rodriguezia, see Orchids
Rooting powders, 14-15